SHIP STYLE

PHILIP DAWSON & BRUCE PETER

# SHIP STYLE

## MODERNISM AND MODERNITY AT SEA IN THE 20TH CENTURY

*With contributions from*
**GILBERT HERBERT**
**PETER KOHLER**
**PAOLO PICCIONE**
**PETER QUARTERMAINE**

CONWAY

A Conway Maritime book

First published in 2010 by Conway,
An imprint of Anova Books Ltd
10 Southcombe Street
London W14 0RA
www.anovabooks.com

10 9 8 7 6 5 4 3 2 1

**Picture Credits**

Images supplied courtesy of: **A. Ernest Glen:** 52 (left). **Alan Irvine:** 206 (left). **Ambrose Greenway:** 11, 20, 23, 24, 48, 49 (left; top right), 50 (left), 87, 88, 89, 91 (top right), 116 (bottom left), 117, 118 (right), 119 (left; top right), 169, 170, 180 (right). **Andrew Kilk:** 196, 215, 217 (right). **Bård Kolltveit:** 184. **Blackpool Pleasure Beach:** 59 (left). **Bruce Peter collection:** 1, 2–3, 30, 33, 40, 41 (bottom left; right), 44–45, 46, 49 (bottom), 50 (right), 52 (right), 53, 54, 56, 60 (top left; bottom left), 62, 63, 64, 65, 66, 67, 73, 74, 75, 76, 77, 80, 81 (right), 90 (bottom left), 91 (left; bottom right), 92, 93, 94 (top left), 96, 97, 98, 99 (bottom), 104 (top left), 107 (left; bottom right), 108, 112 (right), 113, 114, 115, 116 (top left; right), 118 (left), 119 (bottom right), 120, 121, 122 (bottom left; right), 123, 124, 125, 126–127, 128, 129, 130, 131, 132, 133, 134 (top left), 135, 136, 137, 138 (top left), 139 (bottom right), 143, 144 (left), 145, 146, 147, 151, 152, 154 (left), 155, 158, 159, 160 (left), 161, 162, 163, 164, 165 (bottom), 166, 171, 172, 173, 176, 177, 178, 179, 180 (left), 181, 182 (top left; right), 183, 185, 186, 187 (left), 188 (bottom left; right), 189 (left), 190, 191, 193, 194, 195, 197, 198, 199, 201, 203, 204 (bottom), 205, 206 (right), 207, 209, 210, 211, 214 (left), 216, 217 (left), 224, 225, 226, 227, 228, 229, 230, 231. **Conway Image Library:** 6, 18, 25, 27, 41 (top left), 42, 43, 60 (right), 61, 68 (right), 79 (top right; bottom right), 86, 109 (right), 110 (left), 138 (bottom left), 142 (right), 144 (right), 148 (left), 150, 153, 160 (right), 165 (top), 174 (bottom left; right), 175, 188 (top left), 200, 204 (top). **Corbis:** 7, 16, 31 (left), 34, 47, 55 (left), 58, 79 (left), 90 (top left; right), 122 (top left), 142 (left). **Danish Business Archives:** 134 (bottom left), 182 (bottom left). **Getty Images:** 17, 29, 38, 39, 55 (right), 57, 59 (right), 68 (top left), 100, 101, 174 (top left), 218 (right). **Gilbert Herbert:** 154 (right), 156, 157. **John Emery:** 26. **Keld Helmer Petersen:** 134 (right). **Library of Congress:** 19 (right), 21, 22, 28. **National Maritime Museum:** 9 (G10819), 10 (G10843), 31 right (G10800), 32 left (G10883), 32 right (G10831). **Peter Kohler:** 68 (bottom left), 70–71, 81 (left), 82, 83, 104 (bottom left; right), 105, 106, 107 (top right), 109 (left), 111, 112 (left), 138 (right), 139 (top right), 148 (right), 149. **Peter Quartermaine:** 222, 223. **Philip Dawson:** 51, 94 (bottom left; right), 95, 99 (top), 167, 168, 208. **Shawn Drake:** 12. **Shippax Archive:** 218 (left), 219. **STX Europe:** 220, 221. **Susan Fino:** 19 (left). **Tage Wandborg:** 192, 214 (right). **Thomas N. Olesen:** 35, 187 (top right; bottom right), 189 (right). **University of Brighton Design Archives:** 202.

A CIP catalogue record for this book is available from the British Library.

ISBN 978-1-84486-127-9

Page 1: The Tea Bar on British Rail's 1969 Dover Strait car-and-train ferry *Vortigern*, designed by Ward & Austin.
Pages 2–3: The view forward from the base of the *QE2*'s funnel, with slats concealing the air-conditioning plant in the foreground and the mast ahead.

Reproduction by Rival Colour Ltd, London
Printed and bound by 1010 Printing International Ltd, China

# CONTENTS

# INTRODUCTION

A majestic passenger liner at sea – viewed from a low angle and surging towards the picture plane – remains one of the most iconic images of 20th-century design and engineering achievement, symbolising the epitome of luxury and hospitality. Le Corbusier, in particular, was fascinated by ocean liners as exemplars of floating technology. In his iconoclastic *Vers Une Architecture*, published in 1923, he used a Cunard Line publicity montage showing its flagship, the *Aquitania*, to be longer and taller than the most famous triumphal buildings in Paris. The young architect was clearly intrigued by the ability of the ocean liner to be at once technically fit for purpose, yet somehow awe-inspiring. He wrote of 'new architectural forms; elements both vast and intimate, but on man's scale; freedom from the 'styles' that stifle us; good contrast between solids and voids, powerful masses and slender masts…'[1] To the Modernist, liners also demonstrated the potential of highly serviced mega structures to provide ideal living conditions for people.

Le Corbusier was a frequent liner passenger. In 1929, he voyaged to South America, returning to France aboard the *Lutétia* in the company of the Parisian cabaret star, Josephine Baker. As a homage to Baker, on the night of the costume ball, Le Corbusier 'blacked up' and dressed in a costume of bananas and feathers. Later, in 1933, the Congress Internationaux d'Architecture Moderne (CIAM), of which Le Corbusier was a founding member, chartered the steamer *Patris II* to sail from Marseilles to Piraeus en route to their Athens conference. But unlike the glamorous *Lutétia*, the *Patris II* was a rather perfunctory passenger-cargo ship of moderate size and speed, built in 1926 on the Tyne of the London-Greek owned Byron Steamship Company. Powered by reciprocating engines rather than turbines it was, in terms of naval architectural design, even a little old fashioned. Modernist architects who expressed enthusiasm for ships as models for the future of architecture on terra firma, however, seemed to be largely uncomprehending of naval architecture as a distinct discipline with its own heritage, established traditions and modern concerns. To the members of CIAM, a ship was just a ship; it did not matter who designed it and it did not matter how it was propelled, so long as it had a white superstructure with those uninterrupted lines of promenade deck windows and sunny expanses of teak decking with black caulking between the planks.

Two years after chugging along to Piraeus on the *Patris II*, Le Corbusier crossed the Atlantic once again, this time to New York during the maiden season of the magnificent *Normandie*. He travelled First Class and evidently found the liner to be very exhilarating. No wonder: the *Normandie* was unquestionably the most sumptuous passenger ship ever built – a floating modern-day Versailles, containing grand vistas of highly wrought Art Deco to showcase all that was best in the French decorative arts, but finally commissioned ten years after the Paris Exposition des Arts Décoratifs et Industriels Modernes. Le Corbusier's attempts to learn English aboard, with the help of the American surrealist painter Abraham Rattner, capture something of the mood. The list of words and expressions he learned included 'swimming pool', 'sunbathing', 'people who bore me', as well as 'shoulders', 'breast', 'figure', 'drunk', 'cockeye' and 'here's looking at you'.[2]

Costume balls in the ornate grand salons of France's most famous liners seem strangely at odds with our perceived image of mainstream Modernism in general, and of Le Corbusier in particular. Yet, the liner's interiors were simultaneously the antithesis and the perfect fulfilment of his concept of a *machine à habiter*.

*The Compagnie Sud Atlantique liner* Lutétia, *on which Le Corbusier returned from Rio de Janeiro in the company of Josephine Baker.*

Modernism in architecture, design – and naval architecture – can be understood at two levels: philosophical and aesthetic. On the one hand, declaring oneself to be a Modernist signified the adoption of a range of high-minded ideals about the role of the arts and sciences in bringing about radical social reform to achieve egalitarianism. On the other, Modernists sought to develop a futuristic design language which would be universal and, therefore, potentially able to serve with equal conviction any ideological or commercial requirement for a new image.

The Modern Movement had its origins in the latter 19th and early 20th centuries, when a desire arose for a new form of architectural expression that was not solely dependent upon historical styles and which sought 'honesty' in terms of 'function' and in the use of new forms of construction. Its pioneers largely rejected applied ornamentation. Instead, they sought to embrace the machine age and the grace of utility apparent in iron, steel, industrially manufactured glass and reinforced concrete. By the 1860s, iron was used structurally in many large buildings, but its unadorned expression in facades was almost unheard of, and so the realisation of its potential to be beautiful came through the construction of iron bridges. In his *Pioneers of the Modern Movement* (1936), the architectural historian Nikolaus Pevsner argues that the good looks of the Brunel-designed Clifton Suspension Bridge, near Bristol, (1831–64) were the result of its undisguised iron construction. According to him, designs such as this ushered in a new era, a 'daring spirit not witnessed since the building of [the cathedrals at] Amiens, Beauvais or Cologne'.[3] Architecture and engineering were fused together in bridges, railway stations, and in such structures as Joseph Paxton's 1851 Great Exhibition building for Hyde Park, known popularly as the Crystal Palace. Consequently, people came to see these as highly visible examples of a new kind of architecture. Later, that theme was further developed with regard to the machines of travel – trains, cars, aeroplanes and, in particular, ocean liners – which appeared to embody the combined virtues of the age, being supposedly utterly functional and shaped by necessity. From the principle of rationalisation and the reality of machine-based mass production, it was a logical transition to advocate a 'machine aesthetic' of smooth, uncluttered lines that celebrated manufactured objects stripped to their bare (and, therefore, functional) essentials.

The achievement of a technologically charged aesthetic in Modernist architecture was, however, hindered by the limitations of existing building materials. Reinforced concrete came closest to achieving the smooth, sculptural forms desired by progressives – but concrete was actually a rather primitive material, the use of which dated back to classical antiquity. Furthermore, in a polluted urban environment, it weathered badly. In contrast, the immaculate white gloss-painted steelwork and expanses of scrubbed teak decking found on modern passenger liners had far greater aesthetic appeal, the retention of which, unfortunately, required intensive maintenance.

In advertising imagery, white-painted colonial liners were typically depicted grandly aloof at anchor in exotic foreign ports. In the foreground, picturesque natives in vernacular dress posed amid the organised chaos of the dockside – this powerful dialectic affirming the liners' perceived modernity and sophistication (and that of the European nations which brought them into being).

As hermetic worlds unto themselves, liners prefigured the inclination of Modernist architects to design free-standing structures, disconnected from – and, therefore,

*The imposing First-Class Fumoir on the French liner* Normandie *was one of the most opulent shipboard spaces of the inter-war era.*

uncontaminated by – the clutter of the existing cityscape. Such edifices were supposed to be read as fragments of tomorrow's world. (With their free-ranging mobility and sophisticated hidden and visible technologies, liners further extended the concept of physical and temporal detachment from the banalities and compromises of everyday existence.)

Based upon a machine mythology, the Modernist aim was to create a new species of futuristic objects. Aspiring Modernist architects and designers extolled the virtues of 'utilitarian' engineers, but copied them more in aspiration than in practice: appearances proved to be more important, and more influential, than actual construction. A material had to look suitable, a structure logical and a form reasonable. The result may have been close to the Neo-Classical and the use of structure a little more advanced but, even so, architecture took on the clean-cut complexion of the machine and assumed a place alongside the ocean liners and streamlined trains that became enduring symbols of the age – for example, in the well-known posters by the French artist A.M. Cassandre.

These issues were addressed in 1933 by Sir Reginald Blomfield – one of Britain's most reactionary sceptics of the Modern Movement, representing the conservative faction of the architectural establishment – who wrote a strongly worded polemic entitled *Modernismus*. In it, he attacked what he saw as the obsession of certain Modernist architects with speed and technology:

> M. Le Corbusier has much to say about the beauty of liners and motor-cars… But there is a dangerous confusion of ideas in this conversion of efficiency into terms of beauty…The engine of a French express can do its 70 or 80 miles an hour, or whatever is asked of it in the way of traction, but is about as unsightly and squalid an object as it would be possible to find. Efficiency may be perfect and yet the result very far from beautiful; and it seems to me that this most mischievous fallacy, which is based on a very inadequate view of what constitutes efficiency in architecture, lies at the root of the New Architecture and confuses that Art with the applied science of Engineering, the scope of which is wholly utilitarian. The architect is concerned with something more than the plain facts of construction, and whereas the engineer is concerned with construction and little else, the architect starts further back with a plan and ends further on with what he puts on it.[4]

In attempting to prove his point, Blomfield was not entirely correct, however, as engineers designing for public consumption almost invariably focused on aesthetic concerns as well as mere utility. Even Blomfield, however, was not immune to the beauty and majesty of 'a great liner… coming towards one on a sunlit sea, or the fine thin lines of steel construction, such as cranes or electric towers and the like…'[5] Everybody – from Modernism's most convinced advocates to die-hard sceptics, and the public at large – could seemingly agree that ocean liners were magnificent aesthetic and technical achievements. Yet for all their great size and majesty, liners were also among the most ephemeral of structures and usually only existed in service for a maximum of 25 years before being scrapped. This reality was, of course, somewhat at odds with the aims of the Modern Movement in architecture, which aspired to stand the test of time and to outlast stylistic fads by maintaining lofty and eternal 'high cultural' traditions, the origins of which could be traced back to Ancient Greece and Rome.

As with architecture on terra firma, however, naval architecture also traces its origins to the ancient Phoenician and Greek civilisations and the design of the ships they used for their explorations and conquests throughout the known world of their times. There have been sea-going vessels ever since and so the skills of the naval architect have evolved with a healthy respect for the vernacular ship types of the past, each generation of which represented an improvement over its predecessor. With the technical complexities, brought by steam propulsion in the industrial age and capacities of larger iron and steel ships to provide more than the most basic comforts for passengers and crew, came the need for marine engineers and interior architects to become professionally involved as well.

While Edwardian 'four stackers', such as the *Aquitania*, undeniably were externally impressive – and, indeed, were designed specifically to create that impression – their interiors reflected modern hospitality architecture as it had emerged on terra firma during the second half of the 19th century. These years were characterised by conflict between emergent bourgeois culture and the perceived need for rationalisation coming from intellectual circles concerned with the progressive ideals of early Modernism. The former position was linked to a romantic aspiration to emulate the taste of the aristocracy, the latter to technical innovation and social democracy.

During the steam age – with the associated development of railways, connecting urban centres to ports – scheduled liner services effectively put people and commodities in motion as never before. In this context, philosophers, sociologists and cultural commentators have argued that the department stores of Paris – such as the Bon Marché, au Boucheron and the Galleries Lafayette – constructed in the wake of Baron Haussmann's radical re-planning of the city along modern lines – represented the starting point of the modern consumerist society. Their grand and imposing edifices, spectacularly floodlit at night, contained hitherto unimaginable displays of commodities, all seductively presented in theatrical interiors with grand stairways and atria surrounded by open galleries, cutting through many levels. These department stores transformed the shopping experience into an urban spectacle, complete with live music, fine dining and electric lighting used on a larger scale than anywhere else. Most significantly – as with latter day phenomena such as the casino resorts of Las Vegas and indeed liners, ferries and cruise ships – the department stores were hermetic and, once inside, consumers were entirely subsumed in totally designed and synthetic environments of colour, light, movement and commodities wherever they looked.

Paris was, of course, a great administrative centre not only for France, but also for the wider French empire. Although its new stores, restaurants and entertainments attracted wide cross-sections of society, they relied largely on the growing wealth of the expanding middle classes – the bourgeoisie. Ever since, this section of society has increased as a relative proportion of the overall population throughout the Western World. It is the bourgeoisie who travel most frequently and who buy the most consumer goods; these are people who work hard and have relatively high expectations from life – particularly in terms of receiving what they believe to be 'good value for money'.

In terms of their responses to modernity, however, the bourgeoisie have demonstrated a paradox. On the one hand, they are the most rapacious consumers of the latest popular design trends, but on the other hand, they demonstrate an innate conservatism and a suspicion of anything too avant-garde. This situation can be explained by the concept of 'conservative modernity' – which, Janus-like, is simultaneously forward and backward looking, combining an interest in the latest design trends with nostalgia for the past. The Modern Movement had great difficulty in understanding and accommodating the inevitable stylistic inconsistencies which often resulted from attempts simultaneously to represent the past, present and future – but the commercial need to fulfil such desires bears directly upon passenger ship design as it developed throughout the 20th century.

Since the latter 19th century, hospitality architecture has sold itself on the promise of luxury and escapism in exchange for money. So, logically, the favoured design styles for variety theatres, ballrooms, department stores, hotels – and the interiors of passenger liners – were those of the French court at Versailles, the Baroque and the Rococo. In terms of debates surrounding 'good' design and Modernism, however, these florid aesthetics have been challenged as problematic. Why? The reason is they were once associated with decadence and with a corrupt regime whose end was brought about by popular revolution. Thus, throughout much of the 20th century,

*The First-Class Palladian Lounge on Cunard's 1914 trans-Atlantic liner* Aquitania *shows the grandeur in which the wealthiest passengers quickly became used to travelling overseas.*

there was a clear binary opposition between, on the one hand, the ideal of aesthetic restraint associated with much of the design debates surrounding Modernism and, on the other, by the need of the commercial sector to lure consumers through the promise of outstanding hospitality and grand luxury.

For business entrepreneurs, civil servants, diplomats and senior military officers – as well as entertainers and celebrities – the hotels of César Ritz were among the most desirable places to stay when travelling in Europe. To attract such wealthy travellers, hospitality architecture required to be impressive, but not overwhelming, and it also needed to exude comfort and a kind of universality of design language so that visitors from far afield would not feel alienated. Ritz's architect, Charles Mewès, became an expert at creating an atmosphere of collective bon vivant in his hotel and restaurant interiors. Apart from warm-toned marble, a variety of rich Empire hardwoods, expanses of sumptuous carpeting, grand electroliers and wall sconces for lighting, the usage of upholstery fabrics and drapery was crucial to the overall effect of the architecture of hospitality, both on terra firma and at sea. Mewès, and his protégé Arthur J. Davis, became the favoured interior architects of steamship lines in the Edwardian era. Davis's work on the *Aquitania*, for example, was a free mix of Baroque and Palladian elements which won great acclaim from First-Class trans-Atlantic passengers, to whom the liner became known as 'the ship beautiful'. Emigrants seeking a new life in the United States and travelling in Third Class, would, in contrast, have had a very spartan impression of liner travel, with dormitory accommodation and dining rooms arranged more like school or workhouse canteens than the lofty frescoed heights of the First-Class saloons. In that sense, these vessels were close reflections of the society they served.

The aftermath of World War I brought a widespread desire for social and political change and, across Europe, many progressive thinkers and commentators hoped for an end to the feudalism that had brought about so much unnecessary death and destruction. In architectural debates, it was argued that the modern imperial city represented jingoism and conflict in its heroic Neo-Classical edifices and hierarchical planning. Moreover, to function, it required an underclass to serve those with wealth and power. Technology – of the kind embodied in modern passenger ships – it was argued, could surely be harnessed in more imaginative ways to benefit the many, rather than the few (even though ships too were serviced by a large – and literal – 'underclass', most of whom worked and resided below decks, out of sight of fare-paying passengers).

Modernism came with a social and political mandate to build anew. It was hoped by some that new functional and egalitarian architecture would, in theory at least, replace feudal styles and established distinctions, and so contribute to the creation of a new and cohesive society, most likely based upon Marxist principles. For the generation who survived the war, cosmopolitanism was understandably preferable to conflict. Thus, avant-garde movements of the 1920s, such as De Stijl in the Netherlands, placed emphasis on universality through the use of primary colours and forms – squares, rectangles, cubes and cylinders. The aim was to create a design language understandable to all peoples, which could cut across national, political and religious boundaries. Henry Russell Hitchcock and Philip Johnson, who curated an exhibition at the Museum of Modern Art in New York in 1931 entitled The International Style, further developed this theme. Consequently, much discourse relating to the Modern Movement has stressed its supposed universality, rather than any regional characteristics (though such 'universality' was rather narrowly based, excluding as it did any consideration of whether non-Western cultures might have different – yet, equally valid – principles).

To an extent, trans-Atlantic passenger ships of the latter 1920s offered a more egalitarian experience than their Edwardian predecessors – particularly with regard to the comfort of their least expensive accommodations. As migration to the United States declined, liner operators aimed to attract a growing market of American tourists visiting Europe and so 'steerage' was replaced by a relatively comfortable

*Opposite: The cover of a Norddeutscher Lloyd brochure, advertising express trans-Atlantic travel on the* Bremen *– but also promoting the liner's operating companions, the* Europa *and the smaller, older* Columbus. *The striking graphic design emphasises the speed and modernity of these record-breaking liners.*

*Below: Third-Class (Steerage) passengers had a very different experience of ocean travel, as shown by this dining saloon on the* Aquitania, *with its long benches, fixed seating, exposed pipes and ducts in the deck head. The atmosphere is more akin to a works canteen, or mess room on a large naval battleship.*

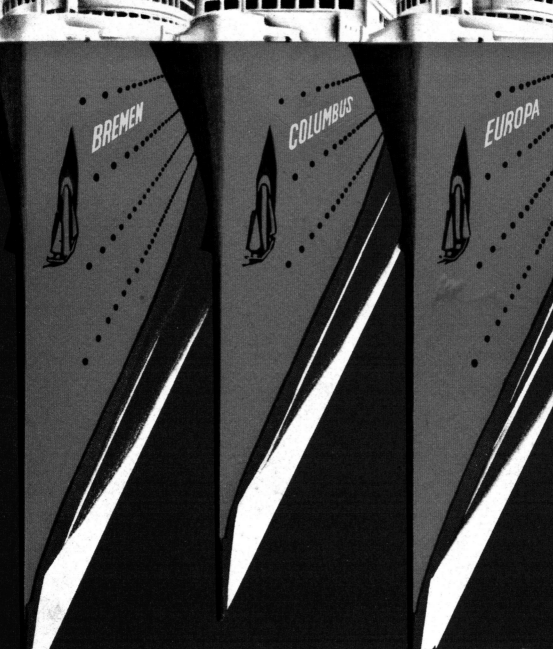

Viewed from the quay, liners appeared aloof yet alluring 'other worlds', the best accommodations of which were the preserve of the wealthy. Here, the upper superstructure and funnel of Norwegian America's 1965 Sagafjord are illuminated at night.

(and lucrative) Tourist Class. Large new ships, such as the French *Ile de France*, the Swedish *Kungsholm* and the German *Bremen* and *Europa*, constructed in the wake of the 1925 Exposition des Arts Décoratifs, combined hotel-like comfort with modern romanticism to give passengers a taste of the cultural sophistication and technological advancement of their owning nations from the moment they stepped aboard. Increasing mechanical complexity brought about the increase in comfort of passenger liners of the latter 1920s and 30s. Edwardian vessels had been coal-fired and often powered by steam-reciprocating machinery, whereas many of the new generation used oil-fired boilers to power steam turbines. Moreover, beneath the wall and ceiling panelling of the corridors, cabins and saloons, there were increasingly intricate systems of plumbing, wiring and ventilation ducts. To progressive design commentators, ships of this kind represented a glimpse of the shape of things to come – even though strict class segregations and social hierarchies remained.

At the point of design, however, the functions and aesthetics of a passenger ship were necessarily related to less tangible criteria than pure functionalism (whatever that might have meant in practice) – such as visual appeal, fashionability and national or regional identities. Consequently, ships posed several fundamental problems as inspirations for the Modern Movement. For a start, several of the greatest trans-Atlantic passenger liners were actually state-sponsored floating ambassadors, meaning that they were anything but internationalist in conception. Prestigious operators such as the Italian Line, the French Line and the United States Line were Government-controlled companies and so the external appearance and interior outfitting of their ships, as well as the service, cuisine and entertainment provided onboard, were intended to reflect the 'better image' of their nations of origin. The majority of smaller liners, however, belonged to businesses seeking to profit their shareholders and so their interior designs were expressions of commercial pride, as much as anything else. In fact, successful passenger liner décor typically fused national identity with commercialism. Consequently, the inspirations for modern ship interiors lay in the more ornamental strains of design discourse in the early 20th century, namely Art Nouveau and its successor, Art Deco. In using the new industrial processes for decorative ends, these styles ran counter to mainstream Modernism – after all, complex shapes and forms could be produced all the more easily thanks to mechanisation.[6] From the intellectualised perspective of design critics at the time and since, this situation was seriously problematic because mechanically produced naturalism was surely a visual lie. Nature was God-given and, therefore, successfully imitating His creation was the highest aspiration for any skilled artist or craftsman. To produce Baroque- or Rococo-derived imagery by using industrial processes was a sleight of hand which threatened to undermine the entire European high cultural tradition, dating back to classical antiquity. Instead, it was argued that, in the industrial age, new abstract and non-naturalistic forms of representation would be required to reflect contemporary culture, encompassing the distinct qualities of engineering and technology.

This notwithstanding, many liners of the inter-war era epitomised Art Deco in their interior design, whilst their exteriors exemplified the aims of mainstream Modernism perhaps more convincingly than any land-based structure. Of course, to the true Modernist, Art Deco was an unfortunate – even dangerous – aberration. This may have been because its vocabulary played upon those very areas that Puritanism (and, by extension, the mainstream of Modernist architecture) mistrusts: colour, femininity, ornamentation and extravagance. On the other hand, mainstream Modernism, with its technological obsession, was rather masculine in character. Art Deco, in contrast, directly provoked and celebrated desire.

The ideological and functional tension between envelope and interior lies at the heart of design debates pertaining to the modern passenger ship. From the latter half of the 19th century, the better standards of accommodation on liners and passenger-cargo vessels plying a wide variety of routes world-wide sought to impress potential passengers with luxury, often in styles that some progressive commentators felt to be inappropriate. A ship, the Modernists argued, should be honestly 'ship-like' in its design, and not pretend to be a floating hotel with false half-timbered walls and marble fireplaces. This point of view retains its intellectual appeal, but passengers like to feel at home (and to forget those rough seas outside), a state of mind arguably best achieved either through familiar – or else exaggerated and escapist – décor, however nautically inappropriate design critics might consider these. After all, passenger ships *are* also floating hotels. Writing in the 1930s, George Orwell observed that the 'modern civilised man's… idea of pleasure is already partly attained in the more magnificent dance halls, movie palaces, hotels, restaurants and luxury liners.' He felt that on 'a pleasure cruise… one already gets something more than a glimpse of this future paradise'.[7]

Modernism frequently aspired to achieve the external qualities of passenger liners in architecture on terra firma, but the complex problems of ship design – and of reconciling these with the aspirations of nations, owners and passengers – is an intriguing and usually overlooked area of design history. Designing a ship involves co-ordinating a wide variety of skilled professionals, all with their own emphases and, sometimes, conflicting interests – naval architects, a variety of engineers, financiers, the shipyard's directors and skilled workers, the classification societies and the ship owner. Shipbuilding has always been an expensive, labour-intensive and time-consuming process, and there are substantial risks for all involved. This situation can make the roles of architects and designers particularly challenging. Furthermore, successful ship interiors may have to solve conflicting requirements. On the one hand, they need to reflect the technology and modernity of the vessels themselves – animated structures which shift and flex – and on the other, they have to combine passenger comfort with a sense of security and solidity – and yet capture the glamour and adventure of a sea voyage.

# 001: TOWARDS A FLOATING CITY

The notion of ships as ocean-going hotels is largely a product of 19th-century industrialisation and urbanisation. As railway lines converged on the cities, there arose a need to provide large numbers of travellers with food and lodgings. The railway companies themselves were among the first to introduce this sort of hospitality in the grand hotels built as part of their mainline station terminals. Ships – both mercantile and military – extended the reach of the European industrial nations overseas. Indeed, these liners were vital parts of a globalised and highly integrated transportation system, all powered by steam. In line with Enlightenment thinking, steam ships and trains put people, commodities and finance in motion, as never before and, in doing so, made the modern world possible. The modern passenger ship, in turn, came to be influenced by retail and hospitality architecture on terra firma.

Baron Georges-Eugène Haussmann's reconstruction of Paris shaped the standards of modern urban society and culture throughout the Western World and, arguably, provided the quintessential model for urban design in the modern era. Indeed, the ocean-going 'hotel' arguably found its vestigial origins in the Parisian shopping arcades of the mid-19th century.

By then, Paris, like many other European cities, had grown exponentially through a vast influx of population needed to meet industrialisation's insatiable appetite for labour. Without long-term planning and direction, the ganglia of disease- and crime-ridden narrow streets, with perfunctory sanitary facilities, could no longer sustain the population's everyday welfare.[1] With a chronic shortage of fresh drinking water and woefully inadequate sewage and waste disposal facilities, the city was prone to frequent cholera epidemics that killed tens of thousands of people at a time.

Haussmann was appointed by Emperor Napoleon III in 1853 as *Prefét de la Seine*, and given the responsibility for modernising and *regularising* Paris. This was to involve extensive re-mapping and rebuilding of the city as a modern commercial and industrial metropolis with activity centred upon its railway stations, industrial buildings, department stores and large hotels. Wide new boulevards were cut in straight lines through the city's existing fabric and building stock. From the new railway terminals,

*Right: Joseph Paxton's vast iron-framed glazed structure housing the 1851 Great Exhibition demonstrated the possibilities of using iron and steel girders to span large enclosed spaces – as subsequently shown in grand department stores and onboard liners.*

*Opposite: The lofty internal atrium of the Galleries Lafayette department store in Paris, opened in 1912, combined structural expression with Baroque ornamentation to make a striking modern retail environment.*

The French CGT 'four stacker' France of 1912 brought Parisian modernity to the trans-Atlantic service from Le Havre to New York.

train services fanned out across the nation – with principal routes connecting the capital with the port cities of Le Harve, Cherbourg and Marseilles.

The nouveau riche, consisting of the emerging merchant and business classes, were able to indulge in the enjoyment of their leisure time and so a vibrant café culture emerged, together with a heightened interest in the visual and performing arts. People had time to stroll along the wide *trotoires* of the tree-lined boulevards, dine and dance at the fashionable hotels and attend performances at the new Opéra de Paris, opened in 1875. The pleasures of these pastimes were, in effect, on public display, where persons of lesser standing could at least participate as spectators, with the added inspiration to aspire to better things in their own lives.

Among the many fine public and commercial building types to be constructed during these years, the iron-framed, glass-roofed indoor arcade or *passage* needed large amounts of well-lighted and accessible space to display luxury merchandise of various types for sale to the upwardly mobile public. In terms of structure, the arcade's example lent itself ideally to the construction of larger clear-span buildings – such as stations, department stores and factories – due to their repeated 'modular' iron, steel and glass components. The Crystal Palace, built in London for the Great Exhibition of 1851, was one of the most notable followers of the arcade principle – and its open-plan design, with large multi-tiered internal atria, continues to influence modern commercial space – including ship interiors – even today.

Le Bon Marché opened in 1852 as one the first department stores in Europe, before moving to its present location on Boulevard Haussmann in 1869, where Alexandre Gustave Eiffel (1823–1932) assisted the architect Louis Charles Boileau in designing a steel-framed structure that would provide the largest possible expanses of plate-glass window area within the building's outer walls. By that time, the opulent Second Empire Renaissance style of rival store au Printemps, with its vast glass-domed atrium-plan interior, had already been open for four years, while the nearby premises of Les Galleries Lafayette opened in 1912. Buildings of this kind made their mark as cathedrals of commerce, purpose-built to entrance their consumer congregations with the wares of modern industrialised society.

As important as it was for the store owners to encourage their customers to spend money, the shopping experience itself had to be viewed for its social significance. Just as the boulevards and the colonnaded buildings along their sides encouraged promenading and spectatorship – or *flanêurie* – shopping in a department store was as much a social outing, often with lunch being enjoyed in the establishment's restaurant. Apart from the choices of goods on display, one could also observe how other shoppers were dressed and turned out, what appeared to be their tastes and interests and, for those who dared, there was an opportunity to make a bold public statement of one's own tastes and means by dressing up in the latest fashions.

As a thriving modern urban metropolis well adapted to the domestic, commercial and cultural exigencies of the latter 19th century, Paris was regarded as one of the world's most progressive cities and an imperial capital par excellence. Similar standards of planning were adopted in other major French conurbations – including Bordeaux, Lille, Lyon, Marseilles, Rouen and Toulouse – and, overseas, in the development of cities such as Barcelona, Buenos Aires and Detroit.

Such modern planning, constructional and aesthetic principles were a central influence upon the design of ever-larger iron- and steel-hulled passenger liners of the same era. As the extent of passenger facilities aboard these increased, a distinctly modern shipboard architecture began to emerge. While ships' superstructures became larger, the narrow open-access deck spaces along their sides were progressively widened – and, later, glassed in – to serve as passenger promenades with similar functions to those in modern cities on terra firma. Yet, in its shipboard adaptation, the promenade was always less democratic as class barriers continued to be imposed and strictly enforced at sea, with these spaces being the exclusive preserve of First Class, while passengers of lesser standing remained relegated to the ends of the decks beneath.

The mass-produced steel structural elements being used ashore in place of traditional masonry were readily adaptable to the inherently smaller scale of shipboard public spaces, as were the principles of 'arcade planning'. By this means, glazed clerestories and domes served to illuminate wide, low-ceilinged public rooms on the uppermost decks and to bring daylight into the stairwells and dining rooms by way of vertical atria, extending through multiple deck heights. Some of the most spectacular marine interiors of this genre were to be found aboard the large Mississippi River and Great Lakes passenger steamers, built during the latter decades of the 19th century.

Axial planning of the public spaces aboard deep-sea ocean liners would be introduced in the early 20th century, replicating the arcade concept more fully along the ship's centreline, with the funnel uptakes, staircases and other vertical cores divided along either side of a central internal promenade space.

Beyond the practicality of the 'arcade' idiom for the sequences of public rooms needed for ships' passengers to pass days at sea, some of the more sophisticated Parisian arcades ashore offered wide diversities of cafés, restaurants, and even intimate hotels, such as the example of Hôtel Chopin within the Passage Jouffroy, opened in 1847.[2] The ornate Baroque decoration was 'scenography' for the enjoyment of elegant and orderly urban living within remarkably compact dimensions and this approach also suited the image being sought by Europe's leading steamship lines.

Apart from the uniqueness of their national identity, and of the special attention

*Below (left): The* France *and the* Paris *berthed together at the French Line pier in New York in the mid-1920s.*

*Below (right): Part of a First-Class cabin on the* France, *showing not only the luxurious finishes but also the cosy domesticity and well-resolved details of this compact environment.*

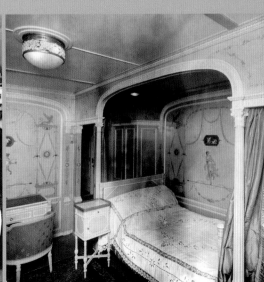

*The 1905 Hamburg-Amerika liner
Kaiserin Auguste Victoria had First-
Class interiors by the French hotel
architect Charles Mewès, intended to
appeal to an international clientele –
rather than only to Germans.*

to service and exceptional cuisine this entailed, French passenger ships of La Belle
Époque tended to be distinguished by their relatively open planning, along with the
added touches of a Gallic sense of chic *grande gesture* and *joie de vivre*.

The French maintained an especially strong sense of this social atmosphere in
their ocean-going adaptations of these developments. Aboard the 23,666-ton trans-
Atlantic liner *France*, delivered to Compagnie Générale Transatlantique (CGT) in
1912 for express service between Le Havre and New York, the public room plan
made the pastimes of promenading and people-watching the centre of onboard
activity. The interior design was entrusted to the firms of Nelson and Remon et Fils –
two leading Parisian decorators of the era. An extensive suite of public spaces with a
total length of 500ft (152m) occupied virtually the full length of the boat deck (which
was designated 'promenade deck' on passenger accommodation plans). The boat
deck also served as an open veranda, surrounding the public rooms.

The drawing room, main lounge and smoking room were arranged in a fairly
conventional manner as rectangular saloons between the four funnel uptakes,
though with the areas to either side of the uptakes treated as separate galleries
and circulating spaces, rather than as part of the rooms themselves. Central among
these was the domed lobby, housing the First-Class main stairway, arranged on an
H-shaped plan with galleries on either beam. As a whole, this layout created an
impression of spaciousness and diversity. The internal galleries, which were amply
furnished with chairs, tables and settees, formed a processional route, circulating
among the various rooms. The French language designations of the main lounge as
Salon Mixte showed a more open disposition towards ladies and gentlemen spending
much of the day in company together, as opposed to the greater segregation aboard
American and British ships of that era, where the smoking room was strictly a male
preserve, and a small drawing room might be offered exclusively as a ladies' lounge.

Below on decks C and D, the mezzanine-plan dining salon was arranged to offer
the spectacle of the *grande descente*, as First-Class passengers entered the room
at its upper level and descended to the main floor by way of wide processional
staircases, arranged beneath a proscenium arch. At nearly double the size of its
immediate predecessors, the *France* was CGT's first ship large enough to make an
impression in a manner reminiscent of the staircase at the au Printemps department

store. Indeed, this remained a hallmark feature of French ocean liners until the third *France* was completed in 1961.

The *France*'s interiors reflected the revivalist styles of the era, with the main dining room being an adaptation from the Hôtel du Comte de Toulouse.[3] The cupola above the boat-deck main lobby clearly appeared to have been inspired by the much larger iron and glass dome at au Printemps in Paris.

While the French Line continued to combine essentially modern layouts with revivalist décor, rooted in Baroque and the Rococo – and likely to appeal to a bourgeois, conservative clientele – in Germany, France's great continental design rival, vigorous ideological debates took place as to how best to reflect modernity in terms of aesthetics, as well as in plan.

German liners simultaneously made significant advances so far as passenger comfort and onboard servicing were concerned. The period between 1870 and 1914 saw the birth and expansion of German capitalism and commercial rivals elsewhere closely observed the country's technical and industrial development. The issues for debate were how Germany's existing national identity and craft traditions might be reconciled with modern industrial processes.

The division of labour to serve industry had created a displaced working class, whose role was that of the means of production and who, in a factory setting, repetitively carried out the same tasks according to decisions made and instructions given by others. Design and social reformers felt that this situation was demeaning to human dignity and that a re-orientation back towards craft traditions would give manual workers higher skills and greater self-respect, as well as improving the quality of manufactured output. Moreover, national identity had been threatened by the industrial revolution and the parallel emergence of a manufactured 'mass culture' of consumer goods and imagery. In pre-industrial societies, the traditional idealised view of culture and identity resulted from a balance between the 'vernacular' culture of the rural peasantry and the 'high' culture of the educated upper classes. The advent of mechanised production appeared seriously to threaten vernacular culture

*The First-Class winter garden on the Kaiserin Auguste Victoria features rattan furniture and potted palms beneath a glazed cupola – a world away from the Atlantic swells outboard.*

*Above (left): A hand-tinted photograph showing the opulent First-Class smoking saloon on the* Kaiser Wilhelm der Grosse.

*Above (right): The Baroque enrichments of a corner of the ladies' lounge on the* Kaiser Wilhelm der Grosse: *as can be seen, this card room is located on one side of a top-lit open balcony.*

in Germany, as elsewhere, and so the German Arts and Crafts Movement sought to address this problem. In the ensuing debates, opinion varied, however, between those who advocated the abandonment of industrial manufacture altogether – notwithstanding its very obvious benefits – and those who sought to embrace modern industrial processes, but to improve the quality and attractiveness of factory output. A great deal was at stake as Germany and Britain were then in tough competition to be regarded as leading economic and cultural powers – and 'culture wars' of this kind were as important in reinforcing identity as military conflicts.

Initially, the discussion of design reform was centred upon the design of modern buildings, interiors and consumer goods and it stimulated the foundation of several German associations – for example the Vereinigte Werkstätten für Kunst im Handwerk (United Workshop for Arts and Crafts), established in Munich in April 1898. Among its founders were significant figures in progressive German architectural and artistic culture – Peter Behrens, Theodor Fischer, Hermann Obrist, Bruno Paul, Berhard Pankok, Richard Riemerschmid and Paul Shulze-Naumburg. The aim of the group, under the leadership of the painter Franz August Otto Kruger, was to promote and rejuvenate applied art through a rationalisation of production. In its own workshops, the Vereinigte Werkstätten made a wide range of furnishing items, designed mostly by members of the group, and took part in key international exhibitions of the decorative arts. Similar co-operatives also sprang up in different parts of the German empire. Among these were the Dresdener Werkstätten für Handwerkskunst, founded in 1899 by the master carpenter Karl Schmidt while, in Austria, Josef Hoffmannn and Koloman Moser founded the Wiener Werkstätten in 1903. This latter group, in particular, played a fundamental role in applying the English Arts and Crafts principles of Ruskin and Morris, creating a style which became known as the 'Vienna Secession'.

Throughout Europe, such Arts and Crafts-orientated groupings aimed to develop high quality modern vernacular design forms with the intention of providing an attractive alternative to purely commercial factory production, which was sometimes of a low quality and frequently in arguably dubious taste. Quality craftsmanship always had been an expensive luxury, however, afforded only by a wealthy few. While the aim was high-minded and sought to make 'good' design available to broad cross-sections of society, in reality, throughout Europe, highly wrought modern craft items for the home were most easily afforded by the *haute bourgeoisie*. This prosperous social class – consisting of civil servants, business tycoons, bankers and merchants – also happened to form the majority of ocean liner passengers. Besides, notwithstanding their usage and representation of leading edge technology, ships were highly crafted objects, built largely by hand and involving the employment of vast amounts of skilled labour. Thus, arguably, the design of liner passenger accommodation lent itself to an Arts and Crafts-inspired design approach as it would all need to be made and installed by craftsmen.

In this context of progressive crafted design and social prosperity, German shipping companies and their vessels came to occupy a key role in the story of modern hospitality architecture at sea. While developments in shipbuilding techniques and naval technology took place mostly in Britain, Germany arguably led the way in up-to-date research on interior design for passenger vessels.

The Norddeutscher Lloyd (NDL) and the Hamburg-Amerika Line (Hamburg-Amerikanische Packetfhart Aktien Gesellschaft, or HAPAG) were based in the Hanseatic free cities of Bremen and Hamburg and were the main shipping companies of the German Empire. NDL had been founded in 1858 and it operated direct services worldwide, while Hamburg-Amerika, founded in 1856, ran liner services to North America and, through subsidiaries, to other parts of the world. These two companies soon became the chief competitors of British lines on the Atlantic, and the efforts of German designers, naval architects and outfitters concentrated, above all, on enhancing passenger comfort as a means of distinguishing Teutonic liners from all others.

As in France, German liners of the latter 19th century initially echoed grand designs for commerce and hospitality ashore. In 1877, Johann Georg Lohmann, a notable figure in Hanseatic maritime affairs, became chairman of NDL and he gave the Bremen architect Johann George Poppe (1837–1915) responsibility for designing interiors for all of the company's new vessels. Poppe, then the leading interpreter of the opulent bourgeois taste of Bremen's prosperous merchant families, never departed from his academic roots. In Bremen, he completed many significant buildings, including the Public Library, the Stock Exchange and NDL's own administrative headquarters, not to mention numerous villas for wealthy citizens.

Towards the 1890s, NDL embarked on a large fleet expansion with significant support from the Imperial Government which, as part of its protectionism policy, introduced construction grants for fast steamships built in national yards. The ships built by NDL carried the names of famous members of the German imperial family; the first of these was the *Kaiser Wilhelm der Grosse*, built in Stettin in 1897, and, at that time, the largest and fastest ship in the world. The *Kaiser Friedrich* followed the same year, the *Kronprinz Wilhelm* in 1901 and the *Kaiser Wilhelm II* in 1903. These ships, while technically sophisticated for their time, were severely criticised in progressive architectural circles for the anachronistic décor and furnishings designed by Poppe which were intended to disguise or even hide altogether the

*The* Kaiser Wilhelm der Grosse *of 1897 was, at the time of its completion, the largest and fastest ship in the world, giving her owners, the Norddeutscher Lloyd, a prime position in the trans-Atlantic passenger trade.*

structures of the vessels. Indeed, Poppe's Baroque style was diametrically opposed to those new formal and stylistic innovations that were then spreading throughout Continental Europe.

At the start of the 20th century, Hamburg-Amerika, the passenger department of which was headed by Albert Ballin, built two large trans-Atlantic liners, which he intended to name the *Amerika* and *Europa*, with the clear aim of challenging NDL. The *Amerika* was ordered from Harland & Wolff of Belfast, and the second came from the Vulcan shipyard in Stettin. Kaiser Wilhelm II requested that this be renamed *Kaiserin Auguste Victoria* in homage to the Empress.

Albert Ballin was alert to the emerging Arts and Crafts-inspired movements in decorative culture, and so he assigned the project for the interior décor of the new ships to the forward-looking Belgian architect Henry Van de Velde. The commission was not carried out, however, because the direct intervention of the Kaiser blocked it. He expressed to Ballin his distaste for Arts and Crafts approaches, as opposed to the grand Prussian Baroque with which he was more familiar, commenting that he had no wish to suffer 'sea sickness'.[4] This decision was also unquestionably political, however, since the Belgian government had expressed socialist and pacifist ideals that were anathema to the conservative politics of imperial Germany. Moreover, Van de Velde proved openly hostile to the established Prussian philosophy that subordinated the individual expression of a particular 'celebrity' designer to the collective discipline of academicised German practitioners of 'high Baroque'. (It was probably in order to make amends for this injustice that, in 1908, Ballin offered Van de Velde a voyage to the Orient aboard a Hamburg-Amerika steamer.) Only after World War I did Van de Velde have the possibility of designing the interiors of two much smaller and less prestigious vessels, the *Batavier II* and *Batavier V*, built in 1921 for the Rotterdam–London service of Wm. Muller & Co., owned by a Dutch family that had already given him several architectural commissions on terra firma.[5] (Later, in the early 1930s, Van de Velde also drew up interiors for the fast Belgian cross-Channel motor ship *Prince Baudouin*, introduced in 1934 on the Oostende–Dover route.[6])

In 1900, Albert Ballin visited London's fashionable new Ritz Hotel. The building's interiors were the work of Charles Mewès (1860–1914), an architect from Alsace

*The* Kronprinzessin Cecilie, *completed in 1907 for the Norddeutscher Lloyd, was somewhat more progressive with regard to interior design than its trans-Atlantic fleetmates. Externally, she was typical of the great German liners of her era, with four lofty funnels split into forward and aft groupings.*

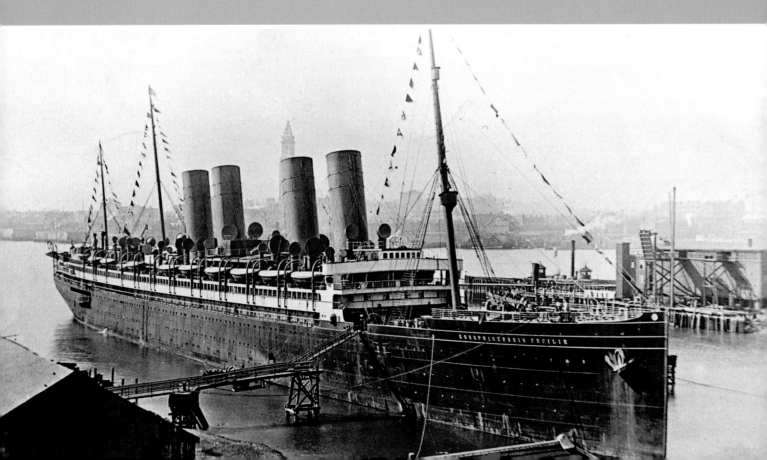

in France whose greatest triumph at the time had been the new Paris Ritz Hotel at Place Vendôme, completed two years previously. In his approach to designing for the emerging luxury hospitality industry, Mewès understood the underlying need to create an atmosphere of universal bon vivant in elegant surroundings that could be enjoyed and experienced within the guests' own terms of reference. Hospitality architecture had to appeal to a broad cross-section of humanity to make a stimulating background for social occasion without trying to assert itself as an overbearing focus of attention. While these values perhaps only influenced Albert Ballin subliminally, he immediately saw in the London Ritz interiors a design aesthetic that was eminently appropriate to be adapted aboard ship, and so the *Amerika* and *Kaiserin Auguste Victoria* were both entrusted to Mewès, who opened a branch office in Cologne to handle this work. Better onboard customer service was Ballin's strategy for seeing off competition, and the Ritz group was, in fact, given responsibility for First-Class hospitality on the two ships. Nevertheless, the resulting interiors, on which Mewès' British partner, Arthur J. Davis, also collaborated, were characterised by traditional and historical styles, mostly of French origin, with no hint whatsoever of contemporary design styles, German or otherwise. In manifesting the *haute bourgeois* Frenchified aesthetic of the expanding European hospitality industry, however, the ships were certainly cosmopolitan in design and atmosphere – and, thanks to the involvement of the Ritz group, they also represented the last word in terms of staff training and servicing.

There was, however, a growing gulf between this emerging 'hotelier' aesthetic, based upon arguably lightweight and inconsequential free mixes of historic European styles, and more serious theoretical discussions in Germany about the future role of the applied arts and design. These revolved around the relationships between the arts, craftsmanship and the manufacturing industry and, at the beginning of the 20th century, they also extended to naval architecture and modern shipboard design. Emphasis was placed on the passenger vessel as a standard bearer of national culture, and this was the field in which research was concentrated. In 1907, the architect Hermann Muthesius (1876–1950), who was Professor of Applied Arts at the Berlin Handelshochschule, voiced harsh criticism of shipowners by arguing forcefully that the development of design aesthetics representing the best of contemporary Germany should become a priority:

> Most to blame are our great shipping companies, who constantly ignore the fact that here in Germany we have recently developed an art of interior decoration

*A Norddeutscher Lloyd official postcard showing both the liner Kronprinzessin Cecilie and the Crown Princess. The card's design reflects the elegance and sophistication of the image created by liner companies in the pre-World War I era. For Steerage passengers and crew members, however, life onboard ship was often harsh.*

*The First-Class dining saloon on the Kaiserin Auguste Victoria was a double-height space with further seating and a musicians' gallery above the main seating area. By arranging the furniture around individual tables, rather than installing long trestles, a hotel-like atmosphere was achieved, rather than that of an officers' wardroom on a large naval vessel.*

whose artistic value and essential purity has gradually been recognised throughout the world. These shipping companies could not only diffuse this worldwide, but would be the first to benefit from this new development. Instead, in the décor of their vessels the shipping companies cling to old and pretentious styles of imitation, only seeking approval from those who are uncultured and have bad taste, who feel at ease in Louis XIV-style surroundings, a style born, like its successors, to glorify the absolute figure of an absolute monarch, but antithetical to the simplicity of bourgeois sentiment and thought of our time.[7]

Such pleas were widely commented upon within the shipbuilding circles of the Hanseatic cities. Heinrich Wiegand, who replaced Lohmann in 1893 as chairman of NDL, accepted the challenge, and made the first important, albeit cautious, change of direction in the interior design of German passenger vessels. He understood the cultural significance of the emerging continental Arts and Crafts Movement, on the one hand, and of Jugendstil, on the other, and was keen to apply these new architectural languages to ships. His opportunity came with the *Kronprinzessin Cecilie*, a large vessel launched in December 1906 at Stettin, and for this ship, NDL held a competition in which progressive young architects were welcomed. Wiegand also signed an agreement with the Munich Vereinigte Werkstätten für Kunst im Handwerk to open a Bremen branch for ship outfitting. Not only did several architectural studios in Bremen take part in the competition – Carl Eeg & Edgard Runge, Runge & Scotland, Abbehusen & Blendermann, Wellerman & Frolich – but, importantly, the younger generation of architects secured commissions: Bruno Paul, Joseph Maria Olbrich and Richard Riemerschmid. The competition was limited to the design of 30 cabins and suites for passengers and officers, while public rooms and the First-Class saloons remained strictly under Poppe's direction to retain a more conservative sense of grandeur.

Different blocks of cabins were allotted to Olbrich, Paula and Riemerschmid. The first, an exponent of the Viennese Secession, was also the principal inspiration behind the construction of the Mathildenhöhe at Darmstadt; the second, who had already taken part in many exhibitions and was director of the Kunstgewerbeschule, became director of the Berlin Kunstgewerbemuseum in 1907; and the third was a leading interior designer in Bavaria. In addition, all three were members of the Munich Vereinigte Werkstätten. Thus, their shipboard design was shaped by research into the interaction between the structures of ships and their appropriate decoration. They attempted to use materials which could be justified as being technically, or aesthetically, appropriate for such usage. Thus, for the first time, design styles of the industrial age made their presence felt at sea on a large and prestigious German liner.

Gustav Pauli, director of the Kunsthalle of Bremen, described a suite furnished by Olbrich comprising a sitting room, a bedroom and a bathroom as follows:

> The bedroom has white walls and doors bordered with white roundels decorated with green leaves. The curtains and bedspreads are of white linen edged with blue and green silk. In the sitting room the walls and sofas are covered with pressed leather, matt silver grey in colour. Everything harmonises perfectly with the warm brown of the matt varnished wooden panels and of the furniture edged with gilded borders. The arrangement of some fittings is especially thoughtful, in particular the wardrobes, which are lit internally and have a large mirror on the reverse of the door.[8]

A few months after the maiden voyage of the *Kronprinzessin Cecilie,* the Deutscher Werkbund (German Union of Work) was founded in Munich on 5 October 1907. The Werkbund sought to encourage German industrialists and government agencies to collaborate with progressive architects, designers and artists with the aim of raising the aesthetic and functional qualities of German manufactured goods. An important objective was achieved when the two most important shipping companies, NDL and Hamburg-Amerika, joined the Werkbund.

The cabins designed by Paul, Riemerschmid and Olbrich aboard the *Kronprinzessin Cecilie* were praised by critics and the travelling public alike and this convinced Wiegand to appoint Paul as artistic consultant for the décor of subsequent NDL ships. However, commitments at the Berlin Kunstgewerbemuseum prevented him from accepting this position, which went instead to Poppe. Nevertheless, Paul's collaboration with NDL bore significant fruit with the design of the smoking room of the small steamer *Derfflinger* and the First-Class dining saloon of the larger *Prinz Friedrich Wilhelm*, both carried out in 1908 by the Vereinigte Werkstätten.

*The Hamburg Sudamerikanische Dampfschiffahrts Geselschaft's 1911* Cap Finisterre *brought a less ostentatious approach to the interior design of German liners. Generally, vessels operating on services other than the North Atlantic routes to New York were more progressive in design because the means by which national identity was represented was less high a priority. Here, the liner steams up the Elbe towards Hamburg, crossing the new pedestrian tunnel.*

Cap Finisterre über dem Elbtunnel.

*The Imperator was the first of three giant flagship liners for the German trans-Atlantic fleet, completed just prior to the outbreak of World War I. When first completed, the liner's bow was ornamented with an imperial eagle – but this subsequently washed overboard in an Atlantic storm.*

Hermann Muthesius was, at that time, Counsellor with the Industry Federal Office in Berlin, and stressed the innovative significance of the Werkbund in passenger ship décor, aware that his earlier critical comments had borne fruit:

In this change of intentions, one sees not only a positive sign of the new arts triumphing, but also a victory of incalculable significance. In fact, those people in international trade can accomplish a cultural worldwide mission for German production: the great German shipping companies carry international passengers who live during the voyage in enforced leisure and are easily influenced by the prevailing taste on board. We can observe how, compared with the pretentious and often deplorable taste exhibited until now on German ships, the new interior design created by the best artistic forces of German craftsmanship delights passengers and will undoubtedly contribute towards the recognition of German art.[9]

In 1908, NDL commissioned Paul to design the prestigious trans-Atlantic liner *George Washington* – a ship of almost 23,000 tons, built at Stettin – which entered service on the Bremen–Southampton–New York route in 1909. The interior design was specifically planned to embody a contemporary nautical quality. By using only geometric lines and a variety of wood inlays, Paul devised comfortable spaces of austere elegance, and all without any applied historicist ornamentation whatsoever. This commission was shared with the Bremen architect Rudolf Alexander Schroder, who designed a luxury suite and the First-Class dining saloon, and with the painter Franz August Otto Kruger.

The interior areas entrusted to Paul – the social hall, the reading and writing room, the smoking room, the foyer and adjacent grand staircase – were distinguished by their formal coherence. Schroder, by contrast, arranged the Second-Class dining room using the kind of spatial approach favoured by Poppe in his existing shipboard output, with a large cupola and a gallery, but without any of the latter's applied Baroque enrichments. Thus, in terms of internal design, the *George Washington* can justifiably be considered the first entirely modern ship, in the sense that all of the spaces, fixtures and fittings were planned in accordance with contemporary principles and without any reference to historical styles pre-dating the industrial age.

Thereafter, contracts continued to be awarded to artistic firms connected with the Werkbund, and these were required not only to undertake the execution of interior outfitting but, occasionally, also to participate in its planning. This was the case with the 1909 steamer *Berlin*, designed by August Bembe of Mainz and by Heinrich

Pallemberg of Cologne. Among interior spaces in the fashionable Jugendstil aesthetic, the First-Class lounge – with its large geometric skylight and walls decorated with stylised floral motifs in the manner of Otto Wagner – was one of the finest examples of the aesthetic at sea.

Jugendstil – or Art Nouveau, as it was better known in France and Britain – may have been stylistically similar to the output of practitioners loyal to the aims of the Arts and Crafts Movement, but it was very different in terms of theoretical approach. Whereas Arts and Crafts thinkers were suspicious of the human and cultural consequences of modern manufacturing techniques, Jugendstil embraced industry. After all, fashionable naturalistic ornamentation could be made all the more easily through industrial processes. While such extreme differences of aim were only too apparent in the manufactured quality and relative cost of consumer goods, in the context of ship design and construction, the two were so closely related as to be nearly indistinguishable. Modern passenger ships, after all, were simultaneously products of industrial processes and unique examples of extraordinarily high design skill, individual and collective expertise.

The Hamburg Südamerikanische Dampfschiffahrts Gesellschaft, more popularly known as Hamburg-Sud, had been founded in 1871 using German and British capital to operate German services to Latin America. In August 1911, this company launched at its home port the first great liner of its fleet: the 14,500-ton *Cap Finisterre*, with interior design by Emil Rudolf Janda (1855–1915), then one of the city's most distinguished architects. Born in Bohemia, Janda had moved to Hamburg in the 1880s, working initially with the architect Haller and, later, with Puttfarcken. His projects were mostly villas for the city's merchant class in the upmarket residential areas of Eppendorf, Rotherbaum and Winterhude, and the preferred aesthetic to please such prosperous and fashionable clients was, of course, Jugendstil, tempered by the inclusion of geometric forms and patterning, inspired by the Werkbund architects.

The interior design work on the *Cap Finisterre*, however, was characterised both by simplicity of general arrangement and restrained decoration. The dining saloon, which spanned the entire width of the vessel and extended two decks high in the forward part of the superstructure, was the most impressive space. The same formal coherence was applied to the winter garden and to the First-Class drawing room, the former being enclosed by a large glass and iron skylight and the latter lined with inlaid hardwood panelling that made decorative references to the Vienna Secession.

*Below (left): The Imperator's interiors were lavish; here we see bathers posing amid the splendour of the First-Class Pompeian Baths. This facility was modelled on the swimming pool in the Royal Automobile Club in London.*

*Below (right): Looking down the oval-shaped void in the middle of the Imperator's First-Class stairway gives a sense of the increased open planning found in the most progressive liners of the era.*

A lofty First-Class lounge on Cunard's *Mauretania of 1906, designed by Harold A. Peto in a Neo-Classical idiom; the style is rather more sedate than the high Baroque found on the grandest German liners of the era.*

Janda designed two subsequent vessels for the same company, the *Cap Trafalgar* and *Cap Polonio*, but their interiors lacked the geometrical clarity of the *Cap Finisterre* and reflected a more traditional approach, with Neo-Classical references and restrained Baroque details – but no excessive decoration.

Among those architects belonging to the Deutscher Werkbund, Bruno Paul and, particularly, Paul Ludwig Troost (1878–1934) were employed most frequently by NDL for their interior design work. Troost had trained with Ludwig Hoffmann at the Damstardt Technische Hochschule, commencing his career thereafter with Martin Dulfer in Munich. From the outset, he showed a propensity towards German Neo-Classicism, with Biedermeier references, rather than adopting the Jugendstil of Riemerschmid and Paul, whose training had been at the Munich school. Troost had been a founder member of the Vereinigte Werkstätten, and his office and workshop in Munich was in direct contact with the group. In 1912, he took over from Paul as the favoured interior architect of NDL liners. In the latter pre-World War I era, Troost's shipboard style was more conservative and rigidly academic than had been typical of forward-looking German liners, completed earlier in the decade.

The Werkbund had little influence on the business of interior décor for ships owned by Hamburg-Amerika, which favoured the period styles of upmarket commercial hospitality design, also successfully adopted on British liners. Albert Ballin, it would appear, lacked the same openness to experimentation as Wiegand had shown in running the rival NDL. Indeed, a heated discussion in the press between Ballin and Professor Schumacher – who was the Head of Architecture at the Dresden Technische Hochschule, Architect for the Municipality of Hamburg and a leading exponent of the Werkbund's principles – caused a considerable stir, but Ballin remained unmoved in his existing position with regard to what worked best onboard ships.

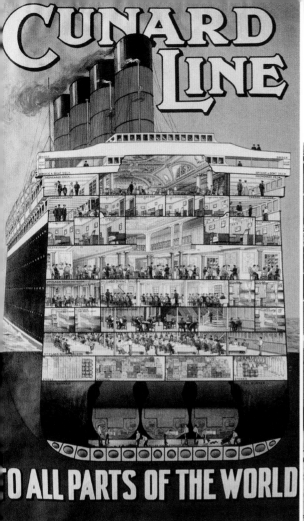

The German passenger fleet reached its zenith in early 1910 when generous support from the government in Berlin enabled Hamburg-Amerika to order three large trans-Atlantic liners from the Blohm & Voss shipyards in Hamburg. The 52,000-ton *Imperator* entered service in 1913; the 54,000-ton *Vaterland* in 1914, while the 56,500-ton *Bismark* was still under construction at the outbreak of World War I. No British ship of that time equalled these giant German vessels. Indeed, it was not until the 1930s that a larger vessel was launched.

Ballin once again placed Charles Mewès in charge of designing the interiors for these ships and this commission was the highest point of his professional career (he died in 1914). The *Imperator* class marked the definitive shift towards 'grand hotel' design with regard to internal arrangements. In commercial terms, this was arguably the logical response to the expectations of a powerful plutocracy and to the aspirations of the *haute bourgeois* travelling public. Furthermore, these vessels featured many areas dedicated to leisure and to the new rituals of the upper-middle class: restaurants with private rooms, a winter garden, a theatre, thermal and Turkish baths and a Pompeian-style heated indoor swimming pool. Subsequent European liners would also be modelled on these three remarkable ships, and the terms 'floating cities' and 'moving hotels' became superlatives fixed in the collective imagination to describe such outstanding passenger liners. (Ironically, Hamburg-Amerika continued to earn the bulk of their profits from emigrant traffic and, ever attentive to market needs, Albert Ballin ensures that this was of a superior standard to 'the steerage' of earlier liners.)

More fundamentally, the second and third vessels of the class – the *Vaterland* and *Bismark* – set a precedent for the future of liner design by utilising spectacular axial interior layouts with divided funnel uptakes, meaning that there were no intrusive vertical casings to break up the flow of spaces. In that sense, they were designed

*Above (left): The liner as floating city: a Cunard publicity poster for the* Aquitania *(1914) showing a cross-section through the forward superstructure with Steerage accommodation in the lowest decks, above the boilers, and the grand First-Class saloons on the upper decks, bounded by semi-enclosed promenades.*

*Above (right): The slender lines of the* Aquitania's *counter stern and four propellers are shown in this view of the liner in drydock.*

from the inside out and the starting point of the design process clearly had been the intention to create hotel environments with ships wrapped around, rather than designing ships and only later working out how to fit hotels inside them.

This was an important distinction but, nevertheless, the interiors of the *Imperator* and its sisters were strongly criticised by architects belonging to the Deutscher Werkbund and, perhaps, in response to this (and in the light of Mewès' death in 1914) Ballin sought advice from Hermann Muthesius on the interior design of three new vessels ordered for service to South America, which also featured divided uptakes and axial open planning. Muthesius had, in the meantime, designed Hamburg-Amerika's pavilion for the major 1914 Werkbund exhibition in Cologne and his suggestions resulted in the Hellerau Deutsche Werkstätten being given the commission for the new ships. Richard Riemerschmid, together with Karl Bertsch and Adalbert Niemayer, undertook the planning of the *Johann Heinrich Burchard* and her sister ships *William O'Swald* and *Admiral Von Tirpitz*. These three vessels, each measuring 20,000 tons, were effectively smaller versions of the three colossal ships of the *Imperator* class, and had a similar profile, featuring three tall funnels. Due to the outbreak of World War I, however, they were prevented from entering service. In terms of design, they proved to be a compromise, dictated by the company's desire to maintain its established image. However, their First-Class drawing rooms, positioned on their upper decks and covered by large skylights, had clear lines and references to the Deutsche Werkstätten's output, as shown at the Cologne Exhibition.

Germany's great industrial rival, Britain, was understandably anxious to emulate Teutonic success on the prestigious North Atlantic route to New York and so lines in Britain were eager to engage the services of experienced hotel architects. The interior design of Cunard Line's *Lusitania* and *Mauretania* had been carried by the British commercial architects James Miller and Harold A. Peto respectively. Charles Mewès himself was initially prevented from working for other shipping lines by the exclusive agreement he had signed with the Hamburg-Amerika Line. This problem was soon overcome by an arrangement whereby work for Cunard was handled through the architect's London office, headed by Arthur J. Davis, who had been a protégé of Mewès in Paris during his architectural studies and had previously assisted him in designing the London Ritz Hotel and liner interiors for Hamburg-Amerika.

The First-Class interiors of Cunard Line's 1914-delivered *Aquitania* were a

*Below (left): The* Aquitania's *First-Class Carolean Smoking Room has something of the atmosphere of a London gentlemen's club.*

*Below (right): The bedroom of a First-Class suite on the* Aquitania's *bridge deck. Cabins of this type were equipped with private baths and toilets.*

significant accomplishment for the Mewès and Davis partnership. In his approach to the *Aquitania*'s design, Davis was particularly concerned about the natural lighting conditions of the ship's interiors. In a paper, published by the *Architectural Review* in 1914, he explained that 'In a room where comfort is above all things desirable it is generally advisable to avoid the exaggerated use of skylights, glass domes, etc. With the exception of vestibules, galleries and staircases, all reception rooms wherever possible should be lighted laterally.'[10]

Following on from the modern hotelier standard of the First-Class cabin accommodation onboard the rival White Star liner *Olympic*, the *Aquitania*'s designers arranged the highest possible proportion of large rectangular rooms with full-size bedsteads and their own en-suite toilet facilities. These followed the American 'compact bathroom' model, then bringing about new sanitation standards throughout the world's hospitality industry.

While en-suite bathrooms were already a standard feature of luxury establishments in Britain and continental Europe – such as the London and Paris Ritz hotels and New York's Waldorf Astoria – by 1908, Ellsworth M. Statler had introduced the modern modular-type bathroom throughout his new standard-class Statler Hotel in Buffalo, New York. Offering 'a room and a bath for a dollar and a half', the hotel became an immediate trend-setter. En-suite accommodations aboard both the *Olympic* and *Aquitania* generally followed the Statler plan, which, by its compact nature, was of great interest to the shipbuilding industry.

As European shipping lines began to adopt various loosely 'modern' architectural interior styles aboard their new liners built during the 1920s, British ship owners remained confident with the status quo of traditional 'grand hotel' design at sea. Cunard, White Star, P&O, Royal Mail and Union Castle were among the world's largest and most successful steamship companies. They served routes reaching around the globe from their homeports of Liverpool, Southampton and London, from which nearby Continental harbours offered the opportunities to also pick up a large share of the European trade to and from Africa, The Americas, Australia and New Zealand, Asia and the Far East.

All of the liners described so far were coal-fired steamships, the majority of which used reciprocating machinery. Vessels of this kind needed to be loaded with vast tonnages of coal before the commencement of each voyage – and this was a costly,

*The pioneering commercial steam turbine-driven vessel was the Glasgow-based Clyde steamer* King Edward, *delivered in 1901. Turbine propulsion transformed the speed and payload potential of liners in the decades thereafter.*

time-consuming and dirty process. In Liverpool, for example, where the Cunard liners began their voyages to America, there were extensive railway sidings for coal wagons. The liners loaded and unloaded passengers and cargo at a deep-water landing stage in the River Mersey, but were coaled from floating barges, fitted with elevators, in the middle of the river, as this lessened the amount of dust blown ashore. Between the end of one voyage and the commencement of the next, a liner would have to move numerous times between the landing stage and the coaling barges, a process lasting several days. Having disembarked its passengers, it would then be pulled by tug into the middle of the river to take on its first supply of coal, then shift back to the landing stage to be cleaned and to embark Third Class – or 'steerage' – passengers while the coaling barges themselves were replenished. Then, it would be moved again for more coal and back to embark Second-Class passengers. A further coaling would take place before, finally, First-Class passengers were embarked and mail was loaded. Only then was it ready to put to sea. For the Mersey Docks and Harbour Company, which earned money by charging fixed-rate harbour dues, berthing and supplying a large Cunarder with coal was a loss-making exercise and so the company was not too disappointed when Cunard subsequently re-located its biggest liners to Southampton. For passengers, especially those in Third Class, it was possible to be required to board the ship several days before it was due actually to sail and to have to endure the coaling process from close quarters. During the voyage itself, armies of stokers were employed to feed the furnaces with coal and this too was labour-intensive, dirty and possibly dangerous, due to the potential of coal dust exploding if it accidently came in contact with a spark.

Clearly, the coal-fired steamer did not represent the best way forward for passenger ships, in particular, although countries with extensive coalfields, such as Britain and Poland, continued to build coal-burning freighters until well into the 1950s. Two innovations made around the turn of the century, however, transformed ship propulsion. Firstly, the Newcastle engineer, Charles Parsons (1854–1931) developed his turbine electric generator into a geared propulsion system for ships. This was supplied with steam from a watertube boiler and consisted of sets of angled rotating blades, which, through a system of gears, could turn a propeller shaft. The process was relatively clean, efficient, near silent and gave a high-power output without vibration. In 1894, an experimental vessel called the *Turbinia* was completed to demonstrate Parsons' invention, which attracted considerable interest. Although only small in size, the *Turbinia* was the fastest ship in the world and it caused a sensation when it was demonstrated at the 1897 Diamond Jubilee Naval Review off Spithead.

Fundamental technological advances of this kind would be unlikely to be instituted on a trans-Atlantic or colonial passenger liner, however, but, instead, on a smaller and less prestigious ship, where failure would not risk bringing about international ridicule and embarrassment, or a substantial financial loss. Such was the case with the introduction of the steam turbine to the British merchant fleet.

The first commercial turbine steamer was ordered by a Glasgow-based firm called the Turbine Steamer Syndicate, established specifically to finance and operate the pioneering *King Edward*. Ordered from William Denny & Bros of Dumbarton and delivered in 1901, this revolutionary vessel became the prototype in terms of propulsion for practically every major British ship thereafter – from the grandest of ocean liners, to warships, express cargo vessels and ferries. Indeed, the Parsons steam turbine remained the favoured mode of propulsion for British ships until the mid-1960s. The pioneering turbine-powered trans-Atlantic liners of the Edwardian era included the Blue Riband-winning Cunard vessels *Lusitania* and *Mauretania*, whose great speed and size clearly demonstrated the potential of turbine propulsion. (Being awarded the Blue Riband for the fastest Atlantic crossing was an eagerly sought accolade for liner companies during the first half of the 20th century.)

In Denmark, the development of Rudolf Diesel's internal combustion engine by the Burmeister and Wain (B&W) shipyard and engine works in Copenhagen led

*New York skyscrapers and the funnels of trans-Atlantic liners were both powerful symbols of modernity and here feature side-by-side in this early 1920s Cunard poster.*

The Danish East Asiatic Company's 1912 passenger cargo liner Selandia was the world's first ocean-going motor ship. As was typical of early diesel vessels, there was no funnel and instead slender exhaust pipes were attached to the centre mast.

to the manufacture there of the world's first effective marine diesel for an ocean-going ship. This was installed in the passenger-cargo liner *Selandia*, delivered to the East Asiatic Company in 1912. Later, in the 1920s, B&W developed an uprated diesel which, after further development, eventually became the most widely used marine power plant in the world. Diesels were more economical than steam turbines and took up less space, leaving more for profitable passengers or cargo. Besides, unlike Britain, none of the Scandinavian countries had significant coalfields, and this fuel was bulky and expensive to import. Compared with steam turbines, however, diesels were noisy and early designs were also slow, meaning that they were a better choice for freighters, rather than passenger ships, in which speed and silence were expected.

The use of motor propulsion also had implications for the appearance of ships. The *Selandia* and its later sisters for the East Asiatic Company remarkably had no funnels, and the exhaust instead went up pipes attached to one of their masts, giving them external profiles more closely resembling large sailing ships. By the early 20th century, however, the funnel had been established symbolically as a sign of modernity and seaworthiness. So, even though motor ships did not necessarily require funnels, naval architects, shipowners, freight customers and passengers all agreed that a modern ship without a funnel appeared less fit to survive the stormy oceans. Only the East Asiatic Company continued to build cargo vessels without funnels until the 1940s, but nearly all other motor ships were given suitably impressive smoke stacks, just like their steam-powered cousins. Later on, in the 1920s, fashionable motor passenger liners were distinguished by having shorter, wider funnels than steamers as these could also house generators, ventilators and other unsightly machinery to give these vessels a more modern uncluttered profile. Le Corbusier failed to acknowledge that the shapes and formal relationships of the principal design features of modern ships were indeed highly symbolic and, as with architecture on terra firma, naval architecture also had its own aesthetic conventions.

Despite the technical advancement of their diesel machinery and contemporary motor ship appearance of their exteriors, vessels of the 1920s – such as White Star Line's *Britannic* and *Georgic*, Royal Mail's *Asturias* and *Alcantara* and Union Castle's *Carnarvon Castle*, *Winchester Castle* and *Warwick Castle*, all of which were built by Harland & Wolff in Belfast – still featured the same sort of Edwardian-style interior design as the pre-war *Imperator*, *Olympic* or *Aquitania*. The owners of these ships and their builder were unshakably confident that the existing 'grand hotel' idiom was the best aesthetic bromide against *mal de mer* or any sense of trepidation passengers may have had about making a trans-oceanic voyage.

# 002: IN THE WAKE OF THE PARIS EXHIBITION

The mechanised death and destruction brought about by World War I brought in its wake a profound desire for political and economic change right across Europe. For many, Internationalism was infinitely preferable to jingoism and conflict – and this, in turn, gave modernising tendencies in European design debates renewed impetus. That Modernism became the design aesthetic favoured in the post-revolutionary Soviet Union caused widespread admiration amongst forward-looking and left-leaning artists, architects and designers from across the Continent. After the turbulence of the Revolution, however, the Soviet economy was negatively affected and so Constructivism, as the new technologically charged Soviet Cubist aesthetic became known, appeared more in poster art and domestic tableware design, rather than in large and expensive constructions, such as ships.

More widely, the loss or injury of the greater part of a generation of young men from across Europe created a social and economic malaise, which meant that few new passenger ships were ordered until the mid-1920s, by which time a new world order was emerging with America as the economic driving force for the first time. Also, the decline in emigration to the United States meant that trans-Atlantic liners also had to change with 'the steerage' being replaced by a more comfortable Tourist Class to attract newly prosperous Americans, often the descendents of migrants, to visit Europe. Old rivalries continued, however – particularly those between Britain, France and Germany. The situation was made more fraught by the harsh conditions imposed upon Germany in the post-war settlement, which demilitarised much of the country and demanded swingeing war reparation payments.

The fleets of European trans-Atlantic companies emerged from the war severely reduced, with heavy British and German losses from submarine attack. German companies were forced to transfer their prestigious liners to the victors: Hamburg-

*The pavilion of the Galleries Lafayette department store at the Exposition des Arts Décoratifs reflects the eclectic modern decorative styles and colonial influences which typified the event's overall design aesthetic.*

Amerika relinquished the great *Imperator, Vaterland* and *Bismark*, which became respectively Cunard's *Berengaria*, the United States Line's *Leviathan* and White Star Line's *Majestic*. The Norddeutscher Lloyd, too, saw itself compelled to give up highly prestigious vessels in its fleet, including the *Kronprinzessin Cecilie, Kaiser Wilhelm II* and *George Washington*.

Germany was now a republic, following the drafting of a new constitution in Weimar in 1917. At the same time, a young and newly demobbed architect called Walter Gropius approached the authorities in Weimar to set up a design school in order to boost German output and to help the economy to recover. Gropius was a progressive by instinct, but, through his training, he had also gained a broadly based understanding of the various competing strands of German design history and theory. Thus, the Bauhaus school, which he established, initially embraced a range of forward-looking approaches to art, design and social reform. On the one hand, the Arts and Crafts desire for *gesamtkunstwerk* (synthesis of the arts) was acknowledged through such early successes as the Sommerfeld House, a villa constructed in a Berlin suburb in 1920–21. Its design and construction employed numerous Bauhaus students and professors and it literally fulfilled the school's name, which was an inversion of 'haus bau', German for building a house.[1]

Another increasingly powerful faction within the Bauhaus school rejected craft altogether in favour of mechanised mass production and, as the 1920s progressed, this position became Bauhaus orthodoxy. The school moved to a new building, designed by Gropius, in the industrial city of Dessau and, from then onwards, its output was associated with a highly refined and rationalist approach to architecture, industrial design and graphics – exemplified by the school building itself, with its flat roofs, white rendered elevations and curtain wall glazing.

During the 1920s, German industry enjoyed substantial investment from America,

*The peripherally located Pavillion de l'Esprit Nouveau by Le Corbusier was starkly unadorned in comparison with most other exhibits. It promoted an ideology for the future direction of society, rather than merely displaying luxury goods – and this caught the imagination of critics and commentators. As with the other exhibits, the pavilion was demolished following the exhibition's closure, but a replica was subsequently built in Boulogne, shown here.*

resulting in a growing trans-Atlantic trade of both passengers and cargo. Many Germans, ranging from factory workers to leftist academics, however, looked east with envy, hoping that the Marxist revolution would also come their way. Others in the establishment – and, indeed, throughout the social spectrum – neither liked the idea of American nor Soviet interference and dreamed instead that, one day, Germany might become a great imperial power, just like France and Britain.

Consequently, architectural and design debates were, if anything, more fractious than in the pre-war era, as each of these opposing positions had its own favoured aesthetic – from the German vernacular and Prussian Baroque, on the one hand, to Bauhaus minimalism, on the other. In designing new liners, somehow, these wildly diverse visions of Germany would require to be reconciled if the ships were to be truly representative as floating ambassadors for the nation and if they were to attract sufficiently broad ranges of passengers. Just as in the pre-war era, compromise would be required.

In 1923, Hamburg-Amerika introduced the new medium-sized steamers *Albert Ballin* and *Deutschland* on its Hamburg–New York route, and these were followed in 1925 by the *New York* and *Hamburg*. The Dusseldorf architect Karl Wach (1878–1942) was involved in their interior design: he had begun a distinguished career by graduating from Hannover's Technical University in 1905, later becoming a professor at Dusseldorf's Academy of Art. His architectural style evolved progressively from that of late Jugendstil to Expressionism by the 1920s, as seen in his Phonix A.G. headquarters in Dusseldorf. Working in collaboration with the architect Heinrich Rosskotten, he later completed buildings exemplifying Bauhaus Modernism, such as the elegant Allianz-Konzern headquarters in Cologne. As an architect of interiors, he had wide experience in the design of furniture, and was involved in the interior design of both naval and railway projects. His designs for Hamburg-Amerika, on which the architect Paul Griesser also worked, illustrate the transition from a decorative and essentially historical vocabulary to a more geometric one, closer in spirit to Expressionism.

Partially in response to German progressive developments in architecture, technology and the decorative arts, in 1925, France attempted to re-assert its authority as the pre-eminent international style leader for haute couture and luxury goods design and production by staging a showcase international exhibition in the heart of Paris, around the Eiffel Tower. The Exposition des Arts Décoratifs et Industriels Modernes has passed into legend as the progenitor of what is today known as the Art Deco style. The exhibition, however, was heavily politicised and Germany, France's main rival in the manufacture of all that was modern and desirable, pointedly was not invited to attend. As Britain had staged its own Empire Exhibition at Wembley in London the previous year, its exhibit was only perfunctory. America, on the other hand, claimed that, as it copied all of its 'high end' design output from European precedents, it would have nothing original to contribute – an ironic situation indeed, given that increasing numbers of European architects were, at that very moment, trooping to America in droves to marvel at Manhattan skyscrapers and the chaser lights and billboard advertisements of Times Square. It was even more ironic that the French émigré designer Raymond Loewy was to become arguably the highest profile American industrial designer during the ensuing decade by marrying efficient Fordist manufacturing principles and planned obsolescence to the aesthetics of Modernism.[2]

For the most part, the Paris Exhibition showcased lavish and highly crafted French couture design, with an emphasis upon interiors and fashion, all of which utilised very expensive and highly crafted materials and aesthetics rooted in the Rococo, mixed with elements of Art Nouveau and an eclectic mix of French colonial styles from North and West Africa, French Indo-China and Central America. French Art Deco, as it emerged during the 1920s, was very luxurious and it became highly desirable amongst the fashionable set on both sides of the Atlantic – and elsewhere.

Squeezed into peripheral sites on the fringes of the exhibition, however, were two smaller pavilions which demonstrated an alternative set of principles. If Art Deco was all about style, then the Pavillion de l'Esprit Nouveau, designed by Le Corbusier, and the Soviet Pavillion, by Konstantin Melnikov, each represented a revolutionary social ideology with profound effects for the direction of design debates and practices in the period thereafter.

*Below (left, top and bottom): The CGT's* Paris *of 1921 perhaps marked the beginning in ship interior design of what much later became known as the Art Deco style. Structurally and in terms of layout, the liner was very much a development of the* France *of 1912.*

*Below (right): Geometrically patterned upholstery, glossy veneers and concealed lighting are features of the sitting area in this First-Class suite deluxe onboard the 1927* Ile de France.

Le Corbusier's work from the 1920s belonged to the broader theoretical framework of rationalism, functionalism and constructivism, then shaping the international Modern Movement in architecture and design for industry in the hope of bringing about a fundamental social and cultural re-ordering and entirely new ways of living. Thus, at the Paris Exhibition, a binary opposition emerged between the populist luxury of the most prominent exhibits and pavilions and the *success de scandale* of Le Corbusier's audacious Modernist Pavillion de l'Esprit Nouveau.

Two years later, however, full-blown Art Deco, at its most chic and sumptuous, took to the high seas in the form of CGT's sensational *Ile de France* and, in so doing, brought the spirit of the 1925 Paris Exhibition to the New World upon its maiden arrival in New York. The French Line's first large post-war new building, the *Paris* of 1921, had already brought late Art Nouveau styling to the North Atlantic run, inserted into a shell not very different from the 1912 *France*. The commercial architect Richard Bouwens de Boijen who coordinated the interiors of the *Paris*, was Dutch-born. Previously, he had designed the mighty Parisian headquarters of Crédit Lyonnais (completed in 1880), the grand Baroque edifice of which fronted a series of glazed iron-framed galleries, filling the courtyard behind. As on the earlier *France*, Remon et Fils was retained to decorate the astonishing Art Nouveau-style dining room, while René Lalique decorated the Grand Salon with fountains of glass. Other spaces mixed Art Nouveau with Moorish and other colonial styles – unconsciously offering a foretaste of the Paris Exhibition and, arguably, heralding the Art Deco age.

Only three years later, in 1924, a building contract for the 43,153-ton *Ile de France* was signed and construction was already well underway by the time the Paris Exhibition opened the following spring. Although the new liner's structural envelope was essentially a larger and somewhat evolved version of the *Paris*, the CGT president John Dal Piaz wanted the interior design to present a worthy impression of contemporary French design, fashion and living. He is widely quoted on his questioning, 'Why Mesdames, would you, with your short skirts and bobbed hair, want to sit down on Louis XVI bergères?'[3]

The *Ile de France* also featured a number of significant technical and structural advances. It was among the first liners to be fitted with modern overhead gravity davits for the lifeboats, with the deck space below being given sufficient headroom for passenger usage and, consequently, the outlook from deck house windows was unobstructed. Of the obligatory three funnels, required to assert an imposing silhouette, only the forward two served as working boiler uptakes, thanks to advances in ship propulsion technology. This, in turn, allowed for a greater degree of openness in the First-Class public spaces beneath the dummy aft funnel.

There were no domes above the First-Class public rooms, and, thanks to advances in the technology of structural steelwork, the largest of these spaces were constructed as entirely clear spans, without the need for supporting columns, as

*Below (left): The* Ile de France, *completed in 1927, was in terms of construction a development of the* Paris, *but the interiors – influenced by the 1925 Paris Exhibition – caused a sensation on both sides of the Atlantic.*

*Below (right): The grand First-Class dining saloon on the* Ile de France *by Pierre Patou rose through three decks. Clad in marble slabs and with concealed lighting, the atmosphere was very different from equivalent spaces on the liner's highly-ornamented rivals.*

there had been in earlier liners. Most notably, the principal deck lobby and *grande descente* became an integral part of the adjacent Salon de Thé, supporting its role as the ship's main lounge. The open space at the lobby's centre effectively formed an atrium, extending down two levels to the ship's entrance foyer on B deck. In a general move towards greater informality of social life at sea, the smoking room and its entire boat-deck mezzanine were designated as the Grand Café, further diminishing the segregation of social activity for ladies and gentlemen in First Class.

The interior design, decoration and furnishing of the *Ile de France*'s First-Class spaces were carried out by a cadre of prominent French designers and artisans, largely in the style and character of Jacques-Emile Ruhlmann (1879–1933), whose work featured prominently at the 1925 Exhibition. Ruhlmann is himself widely credited as being a leading proponent of Moderne, indeed, his speciality was the design and manufacture of high-quality furniture.

Influenced, in part, by the Arts and Crafts Movement and by the Weiner Werkstätte, Ruhlmann followed an elitist view of his art, believing that high-quality furnishings had to be individually hand crafted by skilled artisans as unique one-of-a-kind pieces, made to order for each client. Many of his contemporaries, however, held the opposite view that modern furnishings could – and, indeed, should – be manufactured so as to be affordable to greater numbers of people. Ruhlmann was consulted on the choice of architects and designers for *Ile de France*'s First-Class interiors – Richard Bouwens de Boijen, André Mare, Henri Pacon, Pierre Patout and Louis Süe – and even developed concepts for a number of the spaces himself.

Among these, Henri Pacon (1884–1946) and Pierre Patout (1879–1965) were also practising architects, who had both designed private houses in Paris and some of the pavilions for the Paris Exhibition. Pacon's later work also included commissions for the French national railways, SNCF, including locomotives and passenger coaches, as well as stations and other structures. Among the more notable of these was the Gare Maritime at Le Havre, designed as an appropriately modern combined rail and ship terminal to serve the subsequent CGT liner *Normandie* when delivered in 1935. The partnership of Süe et Mare specialised in a broad range of decorative arts work, ranging from furniture and cabinet making to wallpaper design. In particular,

*The First-Class grand saloon by Süe et Mare used high-gloss veneered wall panelling and sculptures set in back-lit niches. The coffered ceiling used indirect lighting and the windows spanned two deck heights.*

they produced hand-crafted frameless cabinetry with inlaid veneer designs and decorative Bakelite accessories with rounded horizontal edges, known as 'waterfall furniture' because of this feature.[4]

While the internal spaces aboard the *Ile de France* were, for the most part, already defined by the naval architects, the vibrancy of the ship's First-Class public interiors, and many of the higher grade cabins and suites, was noteworthy. This was achieved through the use of vivid saturated colours and in the textures and patterns of the carpets, furnishings and artworks, rather than through historicist decoration. Gone were the elaborate leaded-glass domes, cornices, beadings, dados and other decorative curlicues of the *France* and its contemporaries, along with the Art Nouveau flourishes of *Paris,* in favour of a far less embellished approach which seemed brilliantly to capture the spirit of the era. In short, the *Ile de France* was the most modern and stylish ship yet seen and immediately rendered its competitors hopelessly unfashionable.

Henri Pacon's smoking room, with its light ash walls, where the panels were divided vertically by protruding bright metallic strips, provided a grand, yet elegantly understated, backdrop against which to socialise, while Pierre Patou's treatment of the dining room in cool marble, with uniform rows of square recessed light fixtures ascending the walls and crossing the ceiling, three decks above, in perfect formation, was a veritable tour de force of ocean-going Moderne. The *grande descente*, by Bouwens de Boijen, was finished in grey Lanel stone and yellow marble, enlivened with metal banisters and railings cast in geometrical patterns. The Grand Salon, designed by the partnership of Süe et Mare, featured clustered pilasters in deep burgundy, decorated only with simple gilded capitals, and set against unadorned high-gloss dark veneer wall panelling, enlivened with sculptures set into back-lit niches. In between, full-height plate-glass windows spanned the height of the surrounding promenade and boat decks. A deeply coffered ceiling in white contained an indirect lighting scheme that cast a warm, even glow over the room and its boldly geometric carpeting and soft furnishings. In his concept for the adjacent Salon de Thé Jacques-Emile Ruhlmann used a flat-panelled white ceiling, evenly lit from large urns located around the room. Indeed, the *Ile de France* was among the first ships to make significant use of indirect architectural lighting at sea. This produced a sufficiently high level of ambient illumination in large rooms with a minimal load of the limited auxiliary generating capacity, typical of most merchant ships at that time. Then, before the advent of cold-cathode fluorescent lighting and the widespread

use of air-conditioning, reducing the number of tungsten lamps also helped to keep these spaces cooler through the summer months and on tropical cruises.

From the time of its maiden voyage to New York in 1927, the *Ile de France* proved so popular that, for the first few years of its career, it was said to have carried more First-Class passengers than any other ship on the North Atlantic.[5] Yet, the majority of those who sailed aboard the liner did so in its Cabin and Tourist-Third accommodations, attracted, like many Americans, to visit Paris and to get there on the most glamorous ship, even if not in its best accommodation.

As the United States emerged into an era of prosperity, at least until the 1929 Wall Street stock market crash, greater numbers of people found themselves with the money and available free time to travel overseas. Among the noted American authors who lived and wrote in Paris during the 1920s and 30s were T.S. Eliot, F. Scott Fitzgerald, Ernest Hemingway, Ezra Pound and Gertrude Stein. The great attraction that Paris held for these people was succinctly expressed by Stein while living in an apartment on the Rue de Fleurus, 'It's not so much what France gives you… It's what it doesn't take away.'[6] The *Ile de France* quickly became the ship of choice for those Americans who had read about France in books such as Hemingway's *The Sun Also Rises* and Fitzgerald's *Tender is the Night*. Later, in his history of the North Atlantic ferry, *The Only Way to Cross*, John Maxtone-Graham wrote of the *Ile de France*, explaining its standing in the eyes of Middle America as, 'the original whoopee ship symbolising an abandonment that was unthinkable in the pompous authenticity of the *France*. The absence of traditional frills and the relentless modernity, coupled with the seductive Parisian dream, guaranteed her success.'[7]

In Scandinavia, meanwhile, 'second wave' industrialisation grew apace during the 1920s and Sweden, in particular, became recognised as an emerging design leader in Northern Europe – and one whose output perhaps most successfully reconciled modern requirements of efficiency with inherited traditions. Significantly, Sweden was not debilitated by World War I in the way that Britain, France and Germany had been – meaning that the country's growth had continued unbroken throughout the early 20th century. Until the mid-1920s, migrant traffic to the United States had been an important source of revenue for Danish, Norwegian and Swedish trans-Atlantic lines alike – but tougher immigrant quotas necessitated a new direction and so, instead, the focus switched to tourist traffic. Thus, the idea was to give Americans, many of whom would have been descended from Scandinavian émigrés, a taste of 'the old country' from the moment they stepped aboard.

*The Ile de France enjoyed a lengthy career with the CGT. Following distinguished war service, the liner was refurbished and the First-Class dining saloon was updated, as shown here. Throughout the 1950s, the liner retained its élan and popularity.*

Swedish American Line's British-built *Gripsholm* of 1925 took its decorative cues from Swedish royal architecture and so, as an ornate 'floating palace', the vessel had a great deal in common with liners of the preceding era. With the prospect of expanding tourist traffic, however, Swedish American Line ordered another ship, the 21,250-ton *Kungsholm*, which was built by Blohm & Voss in Hamburg and introduced in 1928.

As with numerous Scandinavian vessels of its era, including the recent *Gripsholm*, the new Swedish American flagship was a motor liner. Many such ships of the period, such as the Italian Cosulich liners *Saturnia* and *Vulcania* and the White Star *Britannic* and *Georgic*, were rather tubby in appearance, with short, squat flat-topped funnels. The *Kungsholm*, in contrast, had two tall, well-raked steamship-type stacks and, after being repainted in Swedish American's new all-white livery in 1933, the liner became the epitome of elegance. All subsequent Swedish American liners were turned out in this manner and they became known collectively as 'The White Viking Fleet'.[8]

Decoratively, the new liner was radically different from previous Scandinavian ships. During the 1920s, Swedish architecture, art and design earned a solid international reputation for craftsmanship and innovation. Carl Bergsten, the architect of the highly regarded Swedish Pavillion at the 1925 Exposition des Arts Décoratifs in Paris, designed the new ship's interiors. The richly coloured modern romantic décor was highly distinctive stylistically, but shared a similar palette of exotic and colourful finishes as the French Art Deco on the *Ile de France*. Sailing opposite the *Gripsholm*, the new *Kungsholm* became very popular both as an Atlantic liner and, occasionally, as a cruise ship, with trips to the Norwegian fjords, the Mediterranean and from New York to the Caribbean.

Between 1929 and 1930, Germany's Norddeutscher Lloyd responded to the challenge of the *Ile de France* and *Kungsholm* with no less than two revolutionary *schnelldamfer* (fast steamships), the *Bremen* and *Europa*. These approximately 51,000-ton liners introduced significant breakthroughs in the design of structural framing and underwater hull lines but, above all, in the shaping of their superstructures, which were aerodynamically formed to lessen resistance while under way. The fronts of all decks were rounded and there were two low, elliptical funnels, giving the aggressive, futuristic appearance of true Atlantic greyhounds. All subsequent large trans-Atlantic liners were strongly influenced by their design, especially the Italian *Conte di Savoia* and the Dutch *Niew Amsterdam*.

*Opposite: An advertising poster for Swedish American Line's trans-Atlantic services featuring the* Gripsholm *and the* Kungsholm *in their original black-hulled guise. The liners have been considerably vertically elongated and their funnels are much larger than they were in reality. Indeed, the* Gripsholm *was roundly criticised for her small motor ship smokestacks.*

*Below (top): The 1928 Swedish American liner* Kungsholm *departs Gothenburg for New York in the latter 1930s. In common with many liner companies which sent their vessels on winter cruises during the 1930s, Swedish American adopted a white hull livery and thereafter marketed themselves as 'The White Viking Fleet'.*

*Below (bottom): The First-Class lounge on the* Kungsholm, *designed by Carl Bergsten, was decorated in the Swedish Modern-Romantic idiom with restrained Neo-Classical details, as this rare colour image from the early 1930s shows.*

*Below (right): The First-Class smoking saloon on the* Kungsholm *was decorated in black and red with inlaid polished-metal details. Of course, practically every piece of furniture was specially designed and made for the ship.*

*Above (left): Although the* Bremen *and the* Europa *were outwardly very similar, the latter was rather more conservative in terms of interior design than its sister. Here we see the First-Class lounge on the* Europa *by Paul Ludwig Troost.*

*Above (right): The* Europa's *First-Class social hall, also by Troost, was one of the liner's more progressive interiors, yet retaining a formal Teutonic Neo-Classicism.*

NDL's relationship with the Deutscher Werkbund dated from the latter's foundation in 1907, and for the interior design of both the *Bremen* and the *Europa*, the company turned to firms associated with that organisation. The result, however, on two almost identical vessels, revealed the opposing tendencies of the Deutscher Werkbund and of German culture more widely. Onboard, the *Bremen* exemplified the progressive architects of the Werkbund, devoted to the promotion of the most up-to-date image for Germany and its applied arts products, while the *Europa* reflected a growing reactionary conservatism, shaped by historical legacies and by the decorative tradition of the German bourgeoisie.

The *Bremen*'s interiors were coordinated by the splendidly named Dusseldorf architect and academic Professor Fritz August Breuhaus de Groot (1883–1960), who was assisted by Rudolf Alexander Schoder, Paul Hoffmann and Karl Rotermund from Bremen, and by Karl Wach and Bruno Paul.[9] Breuhaus himself designed most of the First-Class spaces, including the dining saloon, the library and the writing room, the ballroom, the grand staircases, gallery of shops, and children's playrooms. Schroder, meanwhile, drew up the First-Class smoking saloon and the general layout of Second-Class accommodation, while the covered swimming pool, the gymnasium, a number of luxury cabins and all Third-Class cabins were designed by Karl Wach. Rotermund and Paul were responsible for the luxury suites and the First-Class cabins.

Breuhaus was, at the time, one of the most successful German interior architects. He had studied at the Dusseldorf Kunstgewerbeschule as a student of Peter Behrens and, subsequently, at the Stuttgart and Darmstadt Technische Hochschule. He was an example par excellence of those German architects who, while attentive to the technical and aesthetic developments of the Bauhaus, actually had closer links with commercial culture and whose architectural vocabulary lay somewhere between the more advanced aspects of Modernist theory and the capitalist pragmatism of his regular clients. His output, apart from public buildings, included many upper-middle-class apartments and villas, especially notable being the villa for Alexander Koch,

the editor of the journals *Moderne Bauformen* and *Innen Dekoration,* and the castle of the Dukes of Arenberg. His first shipping commission had been to design First-Class accommodation on the little 1927 NDL passenger-cargo steamer *Orotava,* which ran to the Canary Islands. Later on, after his important work on the *Bremen,* he designed the Pullman and sleeping cars for Mitropa and passenger accommodation on the LZ 128 airship *Hindenberg.* This latter project used open planning, aluminium wall and ceiling panels and tubular metal furniture to save weight, but it was also adorned with *gemütlich* little wall paintings of traditional German villages, better to reflect the National Socialist ideology of the mid-1930s. Breuhaus was evidently a highly skilled and technically competent designer – but certainly not an ideologue as, with only superficial changes, his designs could be used in any context requiring a modern image. Perhaps this apparent lack of political conviction made him an effective hospitality and transport design expert as he ensured that his work had a broadly based popular appeal, while studiously avoiding the possibility of offending any strongly held viewpoints. Breuhaus outlined his aims as follows:

> The ostentatious luxury of the past, that has no interest for the modern individual, has been avoided in the interior design, while stress has been placed upon purity of form, on the beauty of line and the superior quality of materials. The *Bremen*'s architecture breaks free of a period no longer relevant and embraces the grandeur of the present, in which we wish to breathe, not suffocate… The skeleton of the ship itself, in harmony with the highly efficient technical system, is a work of art in every detail, a technical creation brought alive by the human spirit, constructed with the most noble materials, and shaped by a human will that unites the continents.[10]

Breuhaus fully understood the aesthetic potential of technical structure, and sought to adjust his designs to express it, rather than conceal it. The *Bremen*'s First-Class Gesellschafts Halle was the largest space he drew up and was divided by two

*Above (left): The* Bremen*'s heated indoor swimming pool was one of a number of health facilities onboard. Other liners of the latter 1920s had similar facilities, reflecting both advances in shipboard technology and servicing as well as increasing fashion and political agendas to emphasise fitness and 'the body beautiful'.*

*Above (top): Surrounded by tugs and other small craft, the* Europa *leaves Hamburg at the commencement of the maiden trans-Atlantic crossing. The liner's short, broad funnels and curved forward superstructure were suggestive of great power and speed and reflected emerging trends in passenger-ship aesthetics.*

*Above (bottom): One of the spacious enclosed promenade decks on the* Bremen*; such spaces appealed to the sensibility of would-be Modernist architects, due to their pristine white paintwork, caulked teak decking and partially exposed structure in the deck head. For trans-Atlantic passengers, fresh air, shelter and bouillon served at one's steamer chair were the attractions.*

*Above (left): A First-Class luxury cabin on the* Bremen, *designed by Bruno Paul and featuring armchairs upholstered in modern striped fabric.*

*Above (right): With its clean lines and indirect lighting, the First-Class ballroom on the* Bremen, *designed by Fritz August Breuhaus de Groot, perhaps resembled equivalent spaces in modern hotels in Berlin.*

rows of columns into three parallel volumes with rosewood panelling on the walls. Among the more progressively designed areas was his gallery of shops, the outfitting of which made extensive use of steel and glass in the Bauhaus manner.

Karl Wach designed the First-Class smoking room and the swimming pool, for which he specified marble and onyx finishes. (Incidentally, the onyx initially reserved for the ship was requisitioned instead to complete Ludwig Mies van der Rohe's iconic pavilion at the 1929 International Exhibition in Barcelona.) Wach additionally produced all of the Third-Class areas, which often were superior in sheer practicality, architectural rigour and harmonious décor to the First Class. Bruno Paul contributed some very refined First-Class suites, characterised by the attention paid to colour palettes and the textural contrasts of precious wood veneers and other sumptuous materials. Thus, the interiors of the *Bremen* represented a significant break with widespread decorative practice and received great critical acclaim. Many architectural journals reviewed – or dedicated whole issues to – the ship, among them the German *Moderne Bauformen* and *Innen Dekoration*, the Italian *Domus* and *Casabella*, as well as *The Architectural Review* and *American Architect*.

In contrast, the interiors of the *Europa* were entirely entrusted to Paul Ludwig Troost and occasioned far less interest. Troost employed his favoured German Neo-Classicism and as a result, the atmosphere onboard the ship was distinctly different from the 'swinging' modernity of the *Bremen*. Both ships were briefly successful, each firing the public imagination on both sides of the Atlantic by capturing the Blue Riband for record-breaking crossings. In addition, catapults were fitted between the funnels to launch light aircraft whilst at sea, enabling the Imperial German Mail to be delivered to New York hours before the liners got there. This innovation was, however, probably more successful as a talking point to generate excitement and publicity, than a truly practical measure to speed postal distribution. Most unfortunately, the 1929 Wall Street Crash, the ensuing Great Depression and consequent German political instability undermined the liners' reputations.

The advent of National Socialism in Germany brought opposition to almost any form of progressive architectural and artistic experimentation or research – unless wholly linked to new technology, for example, cars, aircraft or trains. Passenger ships, apparently, were categorised with items required to demonstrate German tradition, rather than modernity, no matter how up-to-date they actually were in terms of technology. It was not by chance that the traditionalist Troost was selected as Hitler's chief artistic adviser and architect of the Third Reich, to be replaced upon his death in 1934 by the young Albert Speer. Troost had been a National Socialist since 1924, and had transformed the Barlow Palace in Munich into the Brown House in 1931. Later, he completed the Munich Haus der Deutschen Kunst and the 'Temples of Honour' which celebrated those who had died in the failed *putsch* of 1923. These structures were to become the symbols of Nazi architecture and their inauguration, after Troost's death, was a propaganda event for the regime.

In Britain, meanwhile, Canadian Pacific's 42,350-ton British-built and registered *Empress of Britain* was completed during 1931 as one of the world's then largest and most lavishly appointed ocean liners. The rationale for *Empress of Britain*'s size and luxury was that her owners, the Canadian Pacific Railway Company, were keen to compete directly with the new German *Bremen* and *Europa* on the basis of being able to offer direct rail connections between their Quebec City terminus and Chicago, reducing the overall travel time to and from the American Midwest with its large populations of expatriate European peoples. The ship's building expenses were also justified on the basis of its being able to make world cruises during the winter season, which ultimately turned out to be the greatest success.

The *Empress of Britain*'s planning drew from the hotel experience of the Canadian Pacific Railway's large urban and resort hotels across Canada. While the First-Class Mayfair Lounge, designed essentially as a period piece by Sir Charles Allom, set a fairly traditional theme for the ship as a whole, a number of other spaces were quite advanced for their time. Of these, the smoking room, named Cathay Lounge in an effort to make it more appealing to lady passengers, was created by Edmond Dulac,

*Below (left): The* Empress of Britain*'s Knickerbocker Bar was a cocktail lounge, taking its name from a New York hotel. The walls and ceiling niches were decorated with whimsical murals by the British cartoonist W. Heath Robinson. While the chromed metal bar stools seem appropriate, the remaining furniture appears to have been brought in from elsewhere.*

*Below (top): The Cathay Lounge, decorated in an oriental Art Deco idiom, was the* Empress of Britain*'s First-Class smoking saloon. Perhaps Edmond Dulac's stylistic choice reflected a desire to attract both ladies and gentlemen to use the space equally through the avoidance of the traditionally masculine character of a gentleman's club. Furthermore, although the liner was employed exclusively on trans-Atlantic service, the owner, Canadian Pacific, also operated cross-Pacific routes to the Far East.*

*Below (bottom): The main First-Class hallway and surrounding circulation spaces on the* Empress of Britain *were bright and understated with the spacious and relaxing atmosphere of a modern hotel.*

hitherto best known for his book illustrations. The Knickerbocker Bar, a small cocktail lounge on the lounge deck port side, was decorated by the humourous cartoonist W. Heath Robinson. His work featured a series of wall and ceiling murals depicting a whimsical history of the cocktail, using complicated contraptions for which his illustrations were well-known throughout the English-speaking world.

Four decks lower down, Frank Brangwyn, then at the height of his distinguished painting career and a Royal Academy member, created the Salle Jacques Cartier First-Class dining room's decorative theme. With its light oak panelling, indirect lighting scheme and vivid murals, depicting the French explorer's discovery of the St. Lawrence River, this space and its two adjacent private dining rooms were arguably the most forward-looking in design terms of any British ship interior at that time.[11]

In France, a new flagship liner for service to South American ports, named *l'Atlantique* represented a clear turning point in modern Gallic naval architecture. Its precursors from the Chantier et Ateliers de Saint-Nazaire (Penhoët) shipyard – the second *France*, *Paris* and *Ile de France* – had all followed an evolutionary continuum, with each ship introducing new refinements to a well tried and proven overall design strategy. In the main, the *Ile de France*'s immense popularity was primarily a triumph of the decorative arts, rather than any quantum innovation in her structure or engineering.

The 40,905-ton *l'Atlantique*, delivered in 1931 to Compagnie de Navigation Sud-Atlantique, was both the largest ship then to be delivered by a European yard and the biggest built for South Atlantic service. The designers were also required to minimise the hull's draft for navigation in the Gironde estuary at Bordeaux and the Rio de la Plata estuary between Montevideo and Buenos Aires, while also maintaining adequate sea-keeping qualities and stability for the long deep-sea passage between Europe and South America. While her beam was the same as that of the larger *Ile de France*, the slightly reduced height of *l'Atlantique* allowed for public rooms of exceptional size to be located on the upper decks, as well as for a more creative arrangement of open spaces for passengers' enjoyment of the long trans-equatorial tropical voyage. *l'Atlantique* was, furthermore, structurally modern in that her decks were flat from bow to stern, with none of the traditional curvature of fore-and-aft sheer and beam-wise camber.

At the time *l'Atlantique* was built, before air-conditioning came into widespread use at sea, it was customary for the public rooms to be surrounded by deep, covered shade decks. There was also a preference for the dining rooms, at least in First Class, to be located on the superstructure decks, with large openable windows, rather than for these to be situated as low in the hull as possible to minimise the effects of

*Below:* l'Atlantique's *open planning may have enabled grand internal vistas, but it also allowed fire to spread. After a very short career, the ruined vessel was sold for scrap on the Clyde, as this 1936 photograph shows.*

*Below (right): The uncluttered expanse of* l'Atlantique's *topmost deck, between the funnels. By grouping the liner's vertical services into cores, the clutter of fans, ventilators and other pipework which had characterised similar spaces on previous liners was avoided.*

rolling motion in North Atlantic waters. With these factors borne in mind, and with the added interior layout advantages of the funnel casings, stairways and other vertical accesses being divided to either side of the ship's centreline, as on the pre-war German *Vaterland* and *Bismarck*, *l'Atlantique*'s designers came up with a highly original and practical axial plan throughout the public areas and accommodation decks in First Class.

The main public rooms, located forward on *l'Atlantique*'s promenade deck, were designed as an integral series of double-height spaces, with the forward and midship deck vestibules widely divided at either side of the ship's centreline, so that the individual spaces directly adjoined one another. Furthest aft of these, the main dining room was arranged with its floor one deck lower down so as to include a single-flight *grande descente*, via a wide processional stairway between the divided centre funnel casings.

André Nizery, marine superintendent of the associated company Chargeurs Réunis which managed Sudatlantique's operations, assumed a leading role in *l'Atlantique*'s design and construction. The Moderne-style interior architecture and decoration was coordinated by the prominent painter and graphic artist Albert Besnard, with much of the design work itself carried out by Patout, Raguenet et Maillard and Ateliers Marc Simon.[12]

The Grand Salon and Salle à Manger, both of which were rectangular in plan and in section, differed in that the Grand Salon showed a predominantly light palette, its walls clad in white marble, with inset black marble pilasters and a freestanding sculpture by Raymond Rivoire, depicting a young woman tending a dog on a leash. The Salle à Manger was decorated with mural panels, painted by Jouve and Schmied, depicting scenes from Rudyard Kipling's *Jungle Book*, set against dark lacquered wall sections along the room's outer sides.

The intimate grill restaurant, with its sycamore panelling and luxuriant patterned carpeting, was designed by the Chechnyan-born, London-based interior designer Serge Chermayeff, who, at that time, worked for Waring and Gillow's Modern Art

*The three-deck-high First-Class entrance hall on l'Atlantique, showing the liner's central 'rues' stretching into the distance: spaces of this kind continue to be built on modern cruise ships and ferries – albeit benefiting from great advances in fire safety management.*

Studio in London. This firm was a well-established British interior decorator, which carried out upscale domestic and commercial commissions, mainly for London-based aristocratic families and captains of industry. Following the success of the Paris Exhibition, Lord Waring, the chairman, had decided to create a special department to produce Moderne interiors for wealthy clients in London and Paris and so Chermayeff was employed to assist in carrying out this work.[13] In being commissioned to design and outfit part of *l'Atlantique*, however, Waring and Gillow was, effectively, selling Art Deco back to the French – but this situation was merely a reflection of the same specialisation and internationalisation in European design that had earlier seen Charles Mewès and Arthur J. Davis producing interiors for the German Hamburg-Amerika company and for Cunard.

Subsequently, Chermayeff found international fame as an architect when he established a practice in London with the German émigré Eric Mendelsohn. Their design work for the celebrated De La Warr Pavilion at Bexhill in England shows a distinct nautical influence that could well have been partially derived from Chermayeff's previous involvement with *l'Atlantique*.

Quite apart from the axial plan of her public rooms, *l'Atlantique* was perhaps most notable for her remarkable ocean-going *rues* (streets), which ran through a triple-height atrium space, facilitating a very workable single centreline corridor cabin plan for so large a ship. With the greater emphasis on modern hotel-grade accommodation with en-suite bathrooms in post-World War I ship design, *l'Atlantique*'s designers had better opportunities for creatively using space inboard of the bedrooms. Apart from merely providing a simplified cabin plan, *l'Atlantique*'s central *rues* also offered something of a pedestrian street life of their own, with the E-deck *rue* widening into the embarkation hall's various shops and other communal services and its D-deck counterpart emerging into a gallery around the atrium's mid-level.

Unfortunately, *l'Atlantique* suffered the grave injustice of being a little-known masterpiece. The liner never attained the public attention of North Atlantic service, and the opportunity to show off in the United States, where the modern design and supreme luxury would undoubtedly have attracted great interest. *l'Atlantique* also suffered the misfortune of a tragically short service life when, only 15 months after the September 1931 maiden voyage to Rio de Janeiro, Santos, Montevideo and Buenos Aires, fire broke out in January 1933 while sailing from Bordeaux for a routine drydocking at Le Havre with only a skeleton crew onboard. The ship lay adrift for days in the English Channel while the flames completely consumed its innards, leaving only a charred hulk to be written off eventually as a constructive total loss and finally scrapped at Port Glasgow in May 1936.

The conceptualising, planning, building and outfitting of the *Normandie*, a vast new North Atlantic express liner nearly double the size of *l'Atlantique* and about a third larger than Norddeutscher Lloyd's record-breakers *Bremen* and *Europa*, was an oeuvre of unprecedented magnitude and scale. The new superliner would call for new approaches in naval architecture and structural design. As with the successful German sisters, the superstructure and funnels would need an aerodynamic form to minimise air drag while being propelled along at high speed above the waves. The internal volumes of so large and spacious a liner would also offer new possibilities for exploiting the greater spaciousness and modern open planning first seen on *l'Atlantique*.

The *Normandie* was, at the time of its conception, one of three '1,000-foot' liners being planned to meet what was then seen as an insatiable need for sustained passenger capacity on the North Atlantic, competitively driven by the quest for ever shorter voyage times and higher levels of onboard luxury and service. Undoubtedly the greatest technical achievement of *Normandie*'s design and construction was the remarkable hull, intended to achieve optimum performance from the propulsion plant by virtue of its underwater form, designed to minimise the amount of wake along its sides and the drag this creates. Known later as the Yourkevitch hull form, this was the brainchild of Russian-born-and-educated shipbuilding engineer, Vladimir Ivanovich Yourkevitch (1885–1964). During his studies at the St Petersburg Polytechnic Institute, Yourkevitch developed his hypothesis for perfecting an underwater hull form for large, fast ships. After graduating, he worked at the Baltic Shipyards, attaining his membership in the Russian Corps of Naval Constructors by the age of 25, and securing a senior position on the design team for Russia's Dreadnaught-class *Sevastopol* and the later Borodino-class battleships, due to be commissioned by 1920. Following the Bolshevik Revolution, however, Yourkevitch left Russia as a

*Below (left): The magnificent* Normandie *makes its maiden arrival in New York. Ideas first tried on* Ile de France *and* l'Atlantique *were combined on this, arguably the most magnificent ocean liner ever built.*

*Below: The* Normandie *is launched from the Penhoët shipyard on 29 October 1932. The liner's whaleback bow and fine hull lines are evident in this photograph. The subsequent livery application, with a false sheer line, further enhanced the impression of speed and power.*

The Normandie's First-Class interiors were spectacularly ostentatious. The Grand Salon, where passengers sat on ornately embroidered chairs, was illuminated by Lalique glass fountains. The staircase to the rear was a replica of the one designed by Charles Letrosne in the Grand Palais at the 1925 Paris Exhibition.

refugee, going first to Constantinople and, eventually, ending up in France, where, among other things, he worked as a machinist at a Renault car factory, before finally securing a position in ship design at Chantiers et Ateliers de Saint-Nazaire.

While working elsewhere in the shipyard's technical department, Yourkevitch managed to gain some insight into the preliminary design progress being made for *Normandie* and, in his own free time, prepared counter proposals for the ship, based on his studies in St Petersburg and his experience at the Baltic Shipyards. He put his heart and soul into these proposals, lobbying furtively for the support of his French colleagues designing *Normandie*. Eventually, his concepts were adopted for trial on one of 25 different hull models tested at the Hamburg Model Experiment Establishment. Yourkevitch's model was shown to yield the best performance, earning him praise for his contribution to the science of shipbuilding in the unbiased opinion of the test basin's director, Dr Kemper.[14] Yourkevitch otherwise received no special recognition for his achievement, either on the part of CGT or of the shipyard, where his significant input was seen as merely contributing to the overall team effort that went into *Normandie*'s design and building. This project was, of course, officially to be understood by all as a wholly French national achievement.

Yourkevitch's remarkable hull had a refined form at the waterline, with the bow lines following a slightly concave arc as they diverged outwards towards the midbody, causing the natural flow of the bow wave to follow the sides of the ship as closely as possible and, thereby, creating less turbulence. Aft, the waterline form converged gradually in a long continuation of the curved lines around the midbody, allowing the water's surface to close astern of the ship with a minimum of wake being caused by the hull itself. To compensate for the fineness of its waterline profile – and to provide the needed margins of buoyancy and vertical stability – the underwater shape was

fuller, giving the hull an almost pear-shaped midships cross section, with a noticeable tumblehome of the ship's sides above the waterline. The *Normandie*'s bow was also given a bulbous forefoot below the waterline as a means of further stabilising the ship's forward movement below the surface. This also slightly altered the amplitude of the waves hitting the bow, creating less resistance for the remainder of the hull.

Above the waterline, there was a marked widening of the forebody and stern quarters to provide the needed internal space for grand passenger accommodations. In terms of speed and power, the performance of Yourkevitch's *Normandie* hull form, propulsion machinery and propellers could only be matched with an additional 20 per cent of propulsion power needed to force the British rival *Queen Mary*'s more conventional hull to pound along at the same speeds.

The *Normandie*'s unprecedented size, and adoption of *l'Atlantique*'s divided uptakes and axial layout, provided an opportunity to create a radically different sensation of shipboard living on the North Atlantic. Moreover, the sheer scale of the ship presented new possibilities.

Built with government loan guarantees, the *Normandie* was also expected to fulfil a public obligation of service in an ambassadorial role for France, showcasing engineering and technical accomplishment as well as the art and culture of the Republic and its people. This, in itself, ensured that the ship's interiors would be lavishly decorated – indeed, the *Normandie* was to be a latterday Art Deco version of the Palace at Versailles, with all that entailed in terms of eye-popping ostentation. To achieve the necessary overwhelming effect, the liner's extensive First-Class public domain comprised two triple-height strata of magnificent open spaces arranged, on an axial centreline plan. Their architecture and decoration was divided between two separate design groups, with Henri Pacon and Pierre Patout responsible for

*Each of the First-Class staterooms on the* Normandie *was unique in terms of decoration and furnishing. In all three classes, the liner offered a higher level of service than any other yet constructed. Indeed, the Tourist accommodation was more than the equal of First Class on many trans-Atlantic rivals.*

the main dining room, lower embarkation hall and chapel, together with the indoor swimming pool and bar on D deck. The team of Richard Bouwens de Boijen and Roger-Henri Expert was commissioned to design the main suite of the promenade deck public rooms and the Café-Grill, aft on the boat deck. Works of art were specially commissioned from numerous other artists, painters, sculptors and graphic designers to complete the decoration of the public areas, suites and cabins.

The main suite of the promenade deck public rooms – with its 700ft (210m) axial vista along the ship's centreline, contained the Grand Salon and Fumoir and their adjoining spaces – extended up through the deck above, with tall windows on either side. The grand staircase ascending from the Fumoir to the Café-Grill offered a ceremonial focus. Those familiar with the 1925 Exhibition, its pavilions and other structures, would readily recognise the Fumoir staircase and its surrounding architectural features as being a scaled-down rendition of architect Charles Letrosne's great hall of honour from his Grand Palais, designed as one of the Exhibition's most prominent venues.

The Grand Salon's walls – adorned with glass reliefs by Jean Dupas showing ancient mythological scenes from the Chariot of Poseidon and the Rape of Europa, the Chariot of Thetis and the Birth of Aphrodite – and the Fumoir's lacquered panels, in ancient Egyptian-style, were the creations of Jean Dunand. At the head of the

*A corner of the Normandie's Grand Salon, showing the liner's elaborately crafted decorations. In terms of scale and opulence, the First-Class spaces represented a modern equivalent of Versailles. The mural to the left by Dupas is entitled 'The Birth of Aphrodite', while the lacquered metalwork composition surrounding the lift doors depicts 'The Chariot of Poseidon'.*

Café-Grill stairway was a larger-than-life statue of a young woman in a long Greek robe by Léon Baudry called 'La Normandie'. The *Normandie*'s suite of public rooms also offered the diversity of several smaller spaces of more intimate character. Among these were the Café-Grill, with its panoramic views over the ship's stern, and a further suite of rooms forward on the promenade deck including a winter garden overlooking the bow, together with the library and writing room.

The First-Class Salle à Manger was arguably the *Normandie*'s greatest design triumph, both structurally and architecturally. This open space was designed entirely without internal supporting columns, extended 330ft (100m) along the ship's centreline for the full height of three decks and was 46ft (14m) wide. With a deeply coffered ceiling, walls clad in Labouret decorative hammered glass tile, bas-relief panels depicting sport and competition, maritime heritage and arts of the Normandy region, and illuminated by 38 tall linear glass sconces and 10 free-standing Lalique lumiere obelisks, the room was also a veritable cathedral in which to enjoy the pleasures of the culinary arts. All 700 First-Class passengers were accommodated at a single sitting, with the service facilities arranged to suit the protocols of formal à-la-carte dining in its highest and purest form, making the presentation of each meal, including breakfast, a special occasion. Publicity material boasted that the space was not only larger than the Hall of Mirrors at Versailles, but also contained more mirrors.

The *Normandie*'s Tourist- and Third-Class accommodations were less ostentatious – but more than equal to First Class on many lesser liners. The Tourist-Class Salle à Manger aft on C deck, for instance, was designed around an elegant double-height central domed space in dark lacquered woods with indirect lighting on a white ceiling. The majority of seating was actually provided in two spacious pale-ash-panelled dining annexes at the ship's sides, their outer walls lined with large portholes. This room's Third-Class counterpart, two levels below on E deck aft, was again an inside space, though nonetheless featuring a large square double-height central space with diffused lighting and its walls, which were panelled in blonde veneers, giving it a light and deftly modern atmosphere.

From stem to stern, keel to masts, the *Normandie* was a great technological triumph and a masterpiece of the decorative arts. It was also a very intimidating ship, however, in which there were few spaces in which to relax without being viewed against an expansive backdrop of the grandest and most sumptuous design. In First Class, in particular, the open-plan interiors demanded dressing up and behaving with decorous sophistication at all times. Perhaps as a result, the liner was never a great financial success. When World War II was declared, the *Normandie* was in New York, where it was impounded by the Americans and, eventually, converted to a troop transporter. During this work, the liner caught fire and, like *l'Atlantique* around a decade previously, the open-plan interior layout ensured that the fire swept from stem

*Above (left): Ashore in Britain, several prominent Modernist architects designed new leisure attractions – and these both provoked controversy and fired the public's imagination for new design thinking. The Fun House at Blackpool Pleasure Beach, completed in 1934 to a Joseph Emberton design, was a commercial development to provide indoor entertainment in inclement weather.*

*Above: Much more controversial was the publicly funded De La Warr Pavilion at Bexhill-on-Sea, completed in 1935 to a design by Eric Mendelsohn and Serge Chermayeff – both of whom were émigré architects. Popular with visitors, the pavilion was initially disliked by many locals. Its overtly nautical aesthetic and coastal location allowed visitors to fantasise about being aboard a liner – but with no risk of seasickness.*

*Above (top): The* Queen Mary's *interior design was glamorous without being nearly so ostentatious as the* Normandie. *The Tourist-Class smoking room, with its polished veneer and metal inlays, typifies the aesthetic.*

*Above: (bottom): The Tourist-Class cocktail bar was among the* Queen Mary's *more fashionable spaces. The colour scheme was bright red with horizontal inlaid metal banding and matching chromed steel furniture.*

*Above (right): The* Queen Mary *in drydock at Southampton. Construction was delayed due to the Great Depression, meaning that the latest developments in hydrodynamic design were not incorporated.*

to stern. The *Normandie* capsized at the quay in Manhattan and was subsequently consigned for scrap. The loss was a psychological blow for France – and also a clear demonstration that Le Corbusier's demand for *plan libre* (a free plan) as a necessary prerequisite for modern architecture had serious safety consequences in the context of passenger-ship design.

As the *Normandie* was being built, consternation was expressed in British design circles that Cunard's new superliner, the *Queen Mary*, would emerge with a far less modern appearance than this and other recent European ships. Predictably, Cunard's response was that they best knew what the travelling public expected of their ships. Cunard's steady progression to larger and more modern liners was curtailed following the *Aquitania*'s completion as the status quo of world shipping was upset by World War I and the circumstances of its aftermath. While Norddeutscher Lloyd and the companies that were brought together under state auspices to form the Italian Line progressed to prestigious new record-breaking Atlantic liners in the early 1930s, the ultimate dream of building the 1,000-ft liner became more attainable as the inevitable next step in asserting supremacy in the continuing spiral of North Atlantic competition. At the end of December 1930, the keel was laid at John Brown & Co., Clydebank for Cunard's 1,000-ft flagship, then known merely as yard number 534.

Meanwhile, there were a number of significant examples of Modernist architecture appearing on terra firma in Britain. Eric Mendelsohn and Serge Chermayeff's De La Warr Pavilion at Bexhill-on-Sea, Oliver Hill's Midland Hotel at Morecambe, Joseph Emberton's Fun House at Blackpool Pleasure Beach, and Berthold Lubetkin's Penguin Pool at London Zoo generated much excitement about the idea of Modernism, which appeared to be slick, glamorous and daring. In addition, the refurbished Savoy Hotel by Basil Ionides, the Strand Hotel, decorated by Oliver Bernard, and the BBC Broadcasting House, with interiors by Serge Chermayeff, Wells Coates, Raymond McGrath and others, had shown that contemporary design was indeed compatible both with the best of British hospitality and forward-looking national institutions.

A critical essay published in the *Architects' Journal*'s 25 January 1934 issue pointed out that new ships flying the French, German and Swedish flags could offer accommodation and service of the highest standards in well-bred modern surroundings that were unpretentious and straightforward, though tasteful and entirely comfortable. The recent redecorating of a 597ft (182m) Tourist-Class gallery aboard *Berengaria* in ersatz Tudor style with half-timbered walls and wrought-iron work was fiercely derided as an example of what seemed to be chronically wrong with the nation's shipboard architecture. The essay's author, Baird Dennison, went on to implore that, 'Even if the new Cunarder *must* have an outlandish name ending in 'ia' (and how wearisome those obscure Roman provinces are becoming) let it be something nearer *Contemporania*… Fly the pennant of our brave new world from her mizzen, not the pseudo antique's.'[15]

Although Cunard distanced itself from the Modern Movement per se, Sir Percy Bates, then the line's chairman, was also keen to ensure that the new express liner should reflect the tastes of the great numbers of Americans who would inevitably patronise it in service. Sir Percy first appointed the New York architect Benjamin Wistar Morris to advise him on the decoration of the interiors. Morris came from a similar Beaux Arts background to Charles Mewès and Arthur J. Davis, and had already designed Cunard's Renaissance-style office building in Lower Manhattan. After assessing the project's great scale and scope, Morris suggested that Davis should be commissioned to work with him as his London counterpart to overcome the great difficulty of fully executing his responsibilities from the opposite side of the Atlantic.

*Below (left): An early 1950s view of the* Queen Elizabeth *berthed at the then-new Ocean Terminal in Southampton: technically this was a much more modern ship than the* Queen Mary, *but somehow it never gained such a loyal following.*

*Below (right): Cunard's Queens each boasted two indoor swimming pools – one for First- and the other for Tourist-Class passengers. This is the* Queen Elizabeth's *First-Class swimming pool.*

Once the spaces to be decorated were determined with the naval architects and shipbuilders early in the ship's planning, the architects' role was largely to select artists who would create the decorative schemes for each space and to coordinate their work as a whole throughout the ship. Among those selected were the landscape painter Bertram Nicholls, who painted the murals of Sussex's pastoral countryside for the Long Gallery; the theatrical costume designer Doris Zinkeisen, commissioned for the canvas murals and other decorative elements of the Verandah Grill, and her sister, Anna, who painted panels depicting the four seasons for the ballroom. A.R. Thomson painted the mural 'Royal Jubilee Week' above the Observation Lounge bar. Bas-reliefs for the main lounge were produced by Maurice Lambert, and the dining room decorative wall map with its clock and animated models of the *Queen Mary* on the trans-Atlantic route, was the work of Macdonald Gill.

When delivered in May 1936, the *Queen Mary* emerged as the evolutionary logical progression from *Aquitania*, with an extended and enlarged arrangement of the familiar pattern of smoking room aft, main lounge amidships and other special-purpose rooms forward.

The *Queen Mary*'s architectural design was, for the most part, essentially modernistic in that it applied contemporary 'streamlined' finishes to an otherwise conventional structure and layout. Cove lighting and indirect illumination of unadorned white coffered ceilings were widely used throughout the *Queen Mary*'s public rooms. Extensive – possibly excessive – use was also made of exotic veneers seeming to represent every known arboreal species throughout the British Empire. The aspiring Modernists were naturally disappointed, with the ship's interior décor being criticised as having too much the look of a Leicester Square movie palace.[16]

The *Architect and Building News*'s critic, however, wrote positively of the romance of the ship lying in the contrast between the frightening inhumanity of the steel hull cutting its way through inhospitable seas and the cozy intimate interior warmth, within which all facets of everyday human life are lived to the strains of the ship's orchestra and against the background of animated colour and cocktail-hour conversation. While the craftsmanship and finish, the soft lighting and luxuriant furnishings were praised, he concluded, nonetheless, that the great variety of decoration and artwork created

*The First-Class lounge on the* Queen Elizabeth *and a grandly formal space – rather similar in manner to the architect George Grey Wornum's earlier RIBA Headquarters in London's Portland Place. Brown and beige fabrics with powder blue accents harmonised with polished veneered wall finishes and indirect lighting.*

an overall effect of 'mild and expensive vulgarity.'[17] Be that as it may, Cunard and their passengers were obviously satisfied as the ship retained much of the original interior design until withdrawal from service in 1967.

Originally to have been completed five years later, but finally entering commercial service after World War II was over following heroic service as a troop transport, the *Queen Elizabeth* was in many respects a considerably more modern ship. Externally, the liner had two, rather than three funnels, and these were entirely freestanding without need of the supporting guy wires. The two files of large rectangular ventilator cowals atop the *Queen Mary*'s deckhouse were replaced by the altogether more modern arrangement of consolidated fan houses at the base of the funnels. The forward well deck was also eliminated in favour of a continuous plating of the main deck from the bow to the superstructure front – and this also contributed to the ship's rather more sleek outer appearance. Indeed, the exterior forms of these two great Cunarders arguably established the most iconic and enduring impression of the inter-war ocean liner.

The *Queen Elizabeth*'s interior design was coordinated by George Grey Wornum, hitherto best known for his 1932 competition-winning design for the Royal Incorporation of British Architects (RIBA) Headquarters in Portland Place, and by Benjamin Morris, who had been retained by Sir Percy Bates as a personal advisor since being commissioned for the *Queen Mary*'s design. The overall impression of the *Queen Elizabeth*'s interiors was that they were rather less streamlined, but more architecturally correct than those of its older sister ship – indeed, they closely resembled the spaces in Wornum's RIBA building.[18]

The design of Britain's flagship liners for the North Atlantic reflected the fact that they were subjected to scrutiny from a broad range of both progressive and conservative vested interests – including the Royal Family. Yet, despite – or, maybe, because of this – they were undeniably successful from a commercial standpoint, unlike all of the other 1,000-ft express liners. Perhaps this was also because their less open-plan layouts, fitted around centreline funnel uptakes, made them relatively cosy, comfortable and relaxed, with neither the intimidating grandeur of the *Normandie*, nor the Fascist political associations of the German and Italian liners.

*Several of the First-Class hallways on the* Queen Elizabeth *were lofty double-height spaces. In this Cunard publicity photograph, models pose in the fashionable evening dress of the early-1950s. At this point, Cunard's Queens were entering their post-war prime.*

British liners on the less prestigious colonial routes, in contrast, were regarded as being workaday ships, designed to carry out a transport function as effectively as possible. Thus, although British colonial liners frequently were much as conservative in design as their trans-Atlantic cousins, the opportunity was nonetheless there to design innovative ships, if only progressive shipowners would seize it.

Orient Line's 23,371-ton *Orion* was completed in 1935 as a colonial liner of essentially the same type as P&O's progressive turbo-electric *Strathnaver* and *Strathaird* of 1931–32, the cool and light appearance of whose dominant all-white superstructures and hulls, along with the solid buff colour of their triple steamer funnels, made an enduring impression of the modern British tropical liner.[19] These set the standard for P&O's later *Strathmore*, *Stratheden*, and *Strathallan* of 1936–37, as well as for Orient Line's fleet-building programme. The *Orion*'s design introduced a characteristic Orient Line profile, emphasising a single midships funnel and an evenly balanced profile of the superstructure elements forward and aft of it.[20]

The informal onboard atmosphere reflected an extensively open-plan environment in which the functions of various spaces were more diffused than on typical colonial or trans-Atlantic vessels of the period. For example, the smoking room became the lido café during the daytime hours, the ballroom bar in the evening or the crush bar in the intermission of a film show. There was also the possibility to serve light meals in the lounge, or to use it as a card room for bridge tournaments and whist drives, and for space to be cleared in the dining room for dinner-hour dancing.[21]

The *Orion*'s contemporary informality was achieved on the initiative of Colin

*Orient Line's* Orion *on the UK–Australia service was arguably a more fundamentally modern liner than most trans-Atlantic contemporaries. Light colours and open-plan design reflected an emerging Modernist sensibility – and were appropriate for operation in tropical conditions.*

Anderson, then a young and upcoming director in Orient Line's owning body of Anderson Greene and Company, who was keen to modernise the line's image. Anderson was also a prominent member of the Design and Industries Association, or DIA for short. This lobby group, comprising both designers and industrialists, sought to influence government policy towards modernisation in a manner similar to the Deutscher Werkbund in Germany. Indeed, the DIA was cosmopolitan in outlook and very much pro-Modernist in its aesthetic preferences.

The Orient Line senior directors were supportive of Anderson's keenness to seek new directions in the shipping industry, and gave him the opportunity to entrust the design of the Orion's passenger accommodations to a like-minded designer. Appropriately, the commission was granted to Brian O'Rorke, a young New Zealand-born architect working in London with a variety of successful projects already to his credit. He was involved early enough in the Orion's planning to have at least some influence on defining the layout of the ship's public areas and he also had the experience and ability to handle the commission completely from the architecture of the spaces themselves to designing the furnishings and fittings to go into them. Thus, the ship's interiors were designed as a completely cohesive entity, with variety enough to satisfy passengers who would be aboard for a number of weeks, rather than days, without resorting to an eclectic mix of decorative influences.

On the promenade deck, the First-Class public rooms were arranged as a series of open-plan spaces, flowing one into the other without the usual emphasis on connecting elements of lobbies, vestibules and galleries. The plan was wrapped around the single funnel casing amidships, with the main lounge and library forward, an indoor/outdoor ballroom directly aft and a café, furthest astern. With the limited use of air-conditioning in those days, shade and natural ventilation were still important aspects of passenger comfort on long tropical voyages. O'Rorke recognised the need for plenty of large windows and other openings to the shaded deck veranda surrounding the public rooms and for the ease of air circulation throughout the vessel. Depending on the climate, the ballroom could either be used as a space flowing out to the surrounding promenade or, with its glass side walls swung down and closed,

*The* Nieuw Amsterdam*'s First-Class dining room had light brown buttoned-leather ceiling panelling and Murano-glass light fittings. Note the orchestra gallery above the doorway in this colourful promotional brochure image.*

as a bright inside room for various daytime or evening functions. Likewise, the café, aft, and tavern, on the deck below, with its own retractable glazed wall, offered both flexibility and modern informality.

In his treatment of the interior decoration, O'Rorke took a pragmatic middle-of-the-road approach – neither ornate nor going overboard in the opposite direction of extreme 'functional' severity. Instead of using exotic polished veneers, as found on the *Queen Mary*, he chose durable high-quality varnished plywoods and even to bring the white-painted metal of the superstructure itself into interior spaces, such as the indoor/outdoor ballroom. Matt wall and ceiling coverings were used wherever possible to diffuse and soften the glare of the tropical seas beyond the deck rails. His schemes, nonetheless, provided an abundance of colour and visual interest through the carpeting, soft furnishings and indirect lighting.[22]

The cabin decks were also innovatively arranged. The majority of the First-Class sleeping accommodation was designed as mirrored pairs of L-shaped double-berth cabins fitted around smaller single rooms, arranged so that each had an outside exposure with its own windows or portholes. These, and other cabins and suites, made extensive use of built-in furnishings and fitments, including wardrobes, chests of drawers, writing and dressing tables, all carefully dimensioned to hold the clothing and other personal belongings passengers were most likely to bring aboard for a lengthy voyage to Australia. Wall mirrors above the dressing tables were designed with opening wing panels, concealing built-in storage for cosmetics and toiletries. These compact and functional furnishings, flat white wall and ceiling surfaces and the careful choice of soft furnishings and carpeting in light and bright colours created a remarkable sense of spaciousness and coolness.

The largest new liners of the 1930s, the *Normandie* and the *Queen Mary*, set very high standards of expectation in the public eye for anything that was to follow them. In the latter 1930s, plans were even being made for a slightly larger 85,000-ton consort for the *Normandie*, expected to be of similar design, though incorporating

minor improvements of engineering, layout and outfitting. To have been named *Bretagne*, this ship's keel was to have been laid in early 1940, with the delivery expected in time for the 1944 summer season. A counter proposal for the *Bretagne*, however, was offered by Vladimir Yourkevitch from his New York office, based on a far more progressive approach for a ship of around 100,000 tons, with a service speed of 34 knots and luxury accommodation for 5,000 passengers to be carried in a single class – completely in line with Modernist egalitarianism, but unheard of on an existing 'ship of state'.[23] Norddeutscher Lloyd, meanwhile, was planning an 80,000-ton contender of its own with a remarkably high speed of 37 knots and space for 2,000 passengers in three classes, originally to have been named *Amerika* and later changed to *Viktoria* in anticipation of a German victory in World War II. None of these proposals ultimately proceeded beyond their formative planning stages.

Other national shipping lines, unprepared to invest in such large tonnage, would have to compete by introducing smaller ships incorporating similar design features and service as attracted passengers to the big 1,000-ft express liners. Holland America Line's *Nieuw Amsterdam*, Swedish American Line's *Stockholm*, Norwegian America's *Oslofjord* and United States Line's *America* were all delivered in the late 1930s, each incorporating some of the modern design advances and greater living comforts of the *Normandie* and the *Queen Mary*, albeit on an altogether smaller scale. Likewise, Cunard's second *Mauretania*, completed in 1939, and the *Caronia*, delivered a decade later, were ships of intermediate size and speed, outfitted to essentially the same style and standards of passenger comfort and service as the *Queens*. These ships belonged to a prestigious generation, created partly under the continuing spell of the 1925 Paris Exhibition and partly influenced by various facets of the Modern Movement in architecture, industrial design and the decorative arts.

Holland America's 36,287-ton *Nieuw Amsterdam*, built by the Rotterdam Drydock Company and delivered in 1938, represented just such an intriguing mixture of Art Deco and Dutch Modernist De Stijl design elements.[24]

*Above (left): The Tourist-Class cocktail bar on the* Nieuw Amsterdam, *designed by the Rotterdam architect J.J.P. Oud, featured De Stijl's primary colour palette and an abstract decorative panel suggestive of enjoying drinking cocktails on the bar front. Generally, the most radically modern liner interiors, such as this, were given over to Tourist- and Cabin-Class passengers, while those in First Class enjoyed lavish Art Deco styling.*

*Above (right): Models in evening dress glide down the grand staircase in the* Nieuw Amsterdam*'s First-Class hallway. This striking space was the work of Hendrik Wijdeveld.*

De Stijl had emerged in the wake of World War I as a radical grouping of artists, designers and architects who sought to create a universal design language of primary forms and colours – as seen, for example, in Piet Mondrian's flat canvases, or in Gerrit Rietvald's houses and furniture. One theory was that the symbolism of the past, with its inherited cultural associations, had brought about the war by dividing humanity into opposing cultural, religious and political groups – and so De Stijl sought to do no less than replace all historical visual culture with supposedly 'universal' squares, circles, cubes and spheres in primary white, black, red, yellow and blue.

When applied to ships, such as the *Nieuw Amsterdam*, however, De Stijl became merely a bright and fresh aesthetic, suitable for the decoration of Tourist-Class cabins and some public rooms. First-Class passengers, however, got glamorous Art Deco of the kind found on the *Normandie*. The *Nieuw Amsterdam*, likewise, featured a series of double-height public rooms to be arranged along a central axis. So, in the context of a class-divided luxury liner, supposedly egalitarian Modernist approaches, such as De Stijl, apparently, were perceived to be decidedly second class.

The space between the grand hall and smoking room formed a wide central foyer at the head of the midships staircase, with the card room and library to either side and a centreline staircase to the Ritz Carlton Café above. Aft of the smoking room, and beyond doors that would remain closed while in North Atlantic liner service, a second deck lobby gave access to the Cabin-Class café and lido lounge, allowing these – and other spaces on the decks below – to be integrated for use while cruising. Three decks below, the *Nieuw Amsterdam*'s First- and Cabin-Class dining rooms had doors that could be opened to join the First- and Second-Class saloons into a single connected space while cruising. Service was by way of escalators concealed within narrow casings on either side. This arrangement set the standard for the Rotterdam Lloyd liner *Willem Ruys*, laid down in 1939 and only delivered two years after the War's end in 1947, and Holland America's fifth *Rotterdam*, completed in 1959.

A progressive grouping of 16 Dutch architects, industrial designers and artists was assembled to handle the architectural design and decoration of *Nieuw Amsterdam*. Sailing regularly from Rotterdam – a cosmopolitan port city at the mouth of the Rhine – the overall impression of the *Nieuw Amsterdam* was European, rather than Dutch per se. Among the liner's more notable interiors were the grand hall, the First-Class dining room and the Tourist-Class cocktail bar. The former was designed by Hendrik

*Below (top): Spectators gaze at the burned out hulk of the* Morro Castle, *beached by Asbury Park, New Jersey, following a disastrous fire in September 1934.*

*Below (bottom): The* America's *streamlined interiors emphasised comfort and modernity – as shown by this circular lounge space.*

*Below (right): The* America *had two distinctive funnels with winged 'sampan' tops, located well forward. Here, the liner is seen berthed at night at Southampton's Ocean Terminal in the mid-1950s.*

Wijdeveld (1885–1987), a visionary architect who believed that the conditions of modernity could best be reflected and celebrated through theatricality, rather than mainstream Modernism's more 'scientific' approaches to design and urban planning. Wijdeveld was not a De Stijl man, but was instead closely involved with the rival Amsterdam School – which sought to marry futurist and expressionist streamlined aesthetics with traditional Dutch brick construction techniques. Indeed, while his manifesto 'De Nieuwe Richting' ('The New Order') used a similar language of violent renewal to Italian futurism, his life was complex and contradictory, his positions straddling distinctly right- and left-wing agendas. In 1918 he visited Berlin, where he befriended the Expressionist architect Erich Mendelsohn and met the critic Alfred Behne. Thereafter, in 1925 he was responsible for designing the Dutch section of the Paris Exhibition.[25] His unbuilt projects on terra firma included a landscaped community for Amsterdam's Vondelpark, with a large People's Theatre as its central focus, surrounded by a ring of high towers. The theatre was controversial for the apparent resemblance of its entrance portal to a woman's vagina.[26]

Wijdeveld took a theatrical approach to designing the decorative schemes for the double-height grand hall aboard *Nieuw Amsterdam*. Using a predominantly grey and silver palette, the space was to function as a backdrop to the colour and animation brought to it by the passengers themselves. The bas-reliefs and sculptures for this room were created by John Raedecker, and were influenced by his monument at Wassenaar, itself inspired by *The Tempest*'s immortal lines, 'we are such stuff as dreams are made of.'[27] The solid forward and aft walls were adorned with murals by Gerard V.A. Roling, conveying an abstract vision of the interplay between harmony and disharmony. The room's furnishings, particularly the chairs, in contrast, were in the characteristically Cubist manner of De Stijl.

The ceiling vault in the First-Class dining saloon was clad in padded leather with Murano-glass light fittings, the bulkheads featuring modern stained and engraved glass treatments by Joep Nicolas (1897–1972). These used a patent *vermurail* process, developed by the artist, whereby designs were traced onto the glass in metallic oxides. The pastoral scenes created for *Nieuw Amsterdam* had a warm, dusky glow.[28]

The architect J.J.P. Oud (1890–1963), who was a member of the De Stijl group and is now perhaps best known for his worker housing schemes in Rotterdam, where he was the city architect, and Shell headquarters building in The Hague, was responsible for a number of the *Nieuw Amsterdam*'s Cabin- and Tourist-Class public rooms. Perhaps the most remarkable of these was the Tourist-Class cocktail bar on the main deck – where bright colours, whimsical cocktail-glass and bottle motifs on the bar front, and ribbon windows with rounded ends set an atmosphere of cheerful informality. Thus, although Holland America made sure that the *Nieuw Amsterdam*'s passengers in all classes were well cared for in the design of their accommodations, those in Tourist Class arguably enjoyed a more progressive form of Modernist design – and modern living – than their First-Class counterparts.

In the decade following the Paris Exhibition, America had lagged somewhat behind Europe, its passenger ships being neither outstanding in terms of speed, nor scale, nor even in the modernity of their appointments. Worse still, as a result of Prohibition, American ships were dry – a situation which led to the United States Line lamenting that its flagship, the *Leviathan* proved nothing so much as the fact that 'The *Aquitania* [owned by Cunard] is the most popular ship in the world and it cost us nine million dollars to find out.'[29]

By the mid-1930s, however, America arguably had taken the lead with regard to modern technology in passenger ship design and construction. In terms of aesthetics, however, American liners still emulated their foreign competitors. 'Moderne' was, after all, an international style with little to distinguish the bleached veneers of the American *President Coolidge* from, say, the British *Empress of Japan*, the German *Bremen* or the Italian *Conte di Savoia*. What really came to distinguish American ships – in method, materials and mode – was typically practical. No other country put such emphasis on fire safety through prevention than did the United States at a time when liner fires all too often made the headlines. Fire at sea has always been the most fearsome accident that can befall a passenger liner. Those acres of wood panelling and wide-open vistas of public rooms, with stairwells piercing through several decks, made them all potential floating charnel houses – as the premature fates of *l'Atlantique* and the *Normandie* had demonstrated.

Having few ships of its own to be rendered obsolete by the adoption of a radical new order for fireproofing standards, America pioneered a new concept: vessels constructed entirely of fire-retardant materials, as opposed to the British method of fighting fires using sprinklers. This created two rival camps in ship design that endured until the 1990s: fireproofing versus fire fighting. Today, a combination of both techniques is mandated in ship construction. The 1930s American approach, however, transformed the way in which ships were designed and constructed and, indeed, how they were decorated. Arguably, this, more than any other factor, defined American liner aesthetics in the ensuing decades. So far as the American authorities were concerned, ornate historicist interiors were not only dated, but also positively dangerous. Logically, modern design was safe design, rational and comprehensive in all its elements. Thus, although American maritime Modernism was late in evolving, it was truly more than skin-deep.

The Americans' championing of the benefits of fireproof ships was a result of bitter experience as even their newest vessels were not immune from the tragedy of fire at sea. The 1930-built *Morro Castle* of the New York & Cuba Mail Steamship Co., designed by Theodore E. Ferris, was technically a modern ship. A bulbous bow, gravity davits (the first on an American liner) and turbo-electric machinery made the ship very progressive. Inside, alas, it was panelled throughout in varnished and stained plywood. On the night of 8 September 1934, an arsonist set the *Morro Castle*'s writing room ablaze and the fire was allowed to spread from stem to stern through a combination of ineptness, deficient design and flammable materials. No one bothered to close a single fire-resisting door. Panic, poor seamanship and a lack of command conspired to kill 133 people, almost all passengers.

The *Morro Castle* fire burned like a beacon through the American shipping

*Below: A corner of the America's bright and spacious Cabin-Class dining room. Note the abundance of polished metal details and the use of concealed lighting, not only at ceiling height but also forming a door frame.*

*Below (right): Sweeping curves in a Cabin-Class lounge on the America: here again concealed lighting has been used to dramatic effect, this time reflecting off a smooth expanse of white ceiling. The wall murals with their sprayed-on cloud effects and compass roses are also typical period details.*

industry. The result was a Federal law dictating fireproof construction which also coincided with a wholesale re-examination of American marine policy under the new economically interventionist administration of Franklin D. Roosevelt.

The leading proponent of this new approach to ship design (which came to be known as 'Method One') was the prominent naval architect George G. Sharp, who also wholeheartedly embraced the idea of cohesive shipboard design aesthetics. As chairman of a special committee appointed by the National Fire Protection Association to recommend regulations governing fire-resisting construction, Sharp investigated ship fireproofing methods and materials. This culminated with fire tests conducted in January 1936 aboard the steamer *Nastasket*. Existing fireproof sheeting, for example Haskelite, was found not to be sufficiently resistant to heat and distortion and led to the development of a new asbestos-based sheeting, called 'Marinite', which was far cheaper, lighter and easier to work with than another alternative – solid steel. Sharp's desire to incorporate the safest possible construction technology was matched by his desire to transform how ships looked, inside and out.

America, meanwhile, had been without a flagship trans-Atlantic liner since its second-hand *Leviathan* – a war reparation from Germany – had been withdrawn in 1934. Towards the end of the decade, with the world economy largely recovered from the Great Depression, the United States Line felt sufficiently confident to try again.

William Francis Gibbs was appointed to coordinate the design of the new ship. Gibbs had been born in Philadelphia in 1886, earning a science degree from Harvard, and subsequently graduating from Columbia in 1913. In 1922, he formed the naval architecture and marine engineering consultancy Gibbs Bros, which became Gibbs & Cox in 1929. During the 1930s, he designed or converted a succession of passenger and cargo liners for America's leading shipping companies – including United States Line, Matson Line and Grace Line. Subsequently, from 1942, Gibbs was the Controller of Shipbuilding for the War Production Board and then Chairman of the Combined Shipbuilding Committee of the Combined Chiefs of Staffs. Unusually for a naval architect, Gibbs was a commanding figure and an iconoclast with a very singular vision of how ships ought to be designed. To him, a liner was a piece of

*Below (top): The* America *features on the cover of a mid-1950s United States Lines cabin-plan brochure.*

*Below (bottom): As with most flagship trans-Atlantic liners, the* America's *First-Class dining saloon was a double-height affair. Colours are muted and accented with polished metal inlays.*

floating technology, which should be designed to be as safe, effective and visually impressive as possible. He was completely disinterested in – indeed, disdainful of – architectural theory and he believed that interior decoration was strictly women's work. This notwithstanding, his designs were highly acclaimed and – despite his protestations – the technological progressiveness of his output arguably was far less superficial than that of many European designers who claimed wholeheartedly to embrace the Modern Movement. As Gibbs proved, theory and practice were not the same thing – nor were they even necessarily in any way linked.

Certainly, the 33,961-ton *America* synthesised the best of American maritime design of the period. 'She blends very nicely restraint with progress; she incorporates a modern approach to problems with the just right touch of respect for the old school.'[30] Yet, the *America* was the first three-compartment, fireproof liner on the North Atlantic and the first with automatic closing fire screen doors.

In appearance, the liner represented a natural evolution of Gibbs' earlier *Santa Paula* quartet with the same 'sampan' funnels, combining a teardrop body, oval cap and square soot shield. The arrangement of the funnels, foremast, kingposts and short foredeck made the *America* look as though it was rather in a hurry. As with several inter-war liners, however, its funnels were too short by half and had to heightened before the maiden voyage. A raked bow and cruiser stern completed a thoroughly modern, yet pleasing, silhouette.

By entrusting the interior decoration to Smyth, Urquhart and Marckwald, Gibbs imparted another novelty: the *America* was the first major North Atlantic liner decorated by women. They produced Moderne interiors that were both pragmatically up-to-date, yet soothingly homelike. As the travel writer C.M. Squarey observed, 'They have done a truly creative job that is fresh and stimulating and essentially American in body and spirit. Foreign period styles, however excellent, have no place on such a ship. While there is a comparative absence of elaborate ornamentation in the decoration of the *America*, the use of metals in structural and decorative details is a modern note that adds much lustre to these interiors.'[31]

Moreover, the *America* coyly hid its essentially fireproof construction with a warm and inviting collection of rare woods so thin one could reach the asbestos core underneath with a dull penknife: soft oak, walnut, mahogany, prima vera and white maple in the staterooms and, in the public rooms, Macassar ebony, curly maple, quartered oak, harewood and zebrawood. So thin were these finishes that the damage wrought by soldiers carving graffiti when the liner was used as a World War II troopship resulted in all of the stateroom veneers being patched and painted over when the *America* was refitted for post-war service.

Until the advent of the *America*, art had not played any significant role in US-flag liners and, where it was found, it tended to be conservative and hung on walls as an afterthought, rather than assuming any place in the decorative whole. By the time the *America* was being designed, the United States had finally caught up with progressive European practice in that respect:

'While recent press descriptions of liners as 'floating palaces of art' would seem extravagant, the importance of the fitting out and decoration of a new passenger ship is not to be minimalized. In many instances the finest talent of the country is recruited and every effort made to reflect the best in national taste and culture. Certainly this was true of the French Line's *Normandie* and of the more recent Dutch and Norwegian ships, the *Nieuw Amsterdam* and *Oslofjord*. So far, however, the United States has been curiously indifferent to the possibilities in this field, with the result being that American artists and designers have had little opportunity to show what they could do. Certainly, the success of competitions for the decoration of public and private buildings, efforts along the same lines for our forthcoming new passenger ship might bring the same worthwhile results.'[32]

Indeed, the *America* displayed a fine selection of the country's artists and artisans. Moreover, their works formed an integral part of the décor: Charles Baskerville's intricate gesso relief with bronze-leaf background depicting an Everglades foliage scene at the entrance of the Cabin-Class lounge; Barry Faulkner's decorative map charts in the Cabin-Class smoking room; exquisite carved lacquer on linoleum murals by Pierre Boudelle in the Cabin-Class dining room; and André Durenceau's heroic 20ft (6m) Cabin-Class ballroom mural depicting Neptune driving four steeds through the waves. Rather more wistful was Constantin Alajalov's (famed for his *New Yorker* covers) ceiling paintings of shipboard life in the Cabin-Class cocktail lounge. Tourist-Class meals were enjoyed beneath Hildreth Meire's stylised murals of the skylines of San Francisco, New York, Paris and London.

Alas, the new flagship was launched on 31 August 1939 – the day German armed forces invaded Poland. Thus, upon completion, the ship was unable to enter trans-Atlantic service and, instead, was sent cruising until being requisitioned as a troop transport.

While the trans-Atlantic liners wowed travellers and the general public alike with their luxury and statistical superlatives, just as with Le Corbusier's and Melnikov's architectural contributions to the Paris Exhibition, it was in ships that were smaller, more peripheral (and, therefore, far less contentious in terms of national identity) that the most radical design innovations emerged in the 1930s. While the great liners, such as the *Normandie* and the *Queen Mary* have since then attracted a great deal of scholarship – and individual monographs – until now, these smaller, arguably more innovative, ships have been left largely outside of the canons of maritime and design literature. On such vessels, a more open-ended experimentation could take place, unhindered by political interference and with less fear of public ignominy. Thus, while Britain, Germany, France and Italy battled for honours on the North Atlantic with ever faster, more prestigious and luxurious tonnage, Denmark produced a series of quite revolutionary small passenger ships for domestic services. An important technical innovation which gave Danish vessels a competitive advantage was the development by Burmeister and Wain (B&W) of the marine diesel, first installed in the 1912 passenger-cargo liner *Selandia*.

*Below (left): The dining saloon on the Rotna featured a remarkable – but short-lived – wavy plywood ceiling, bowing upwards between the ship's structural framing. The reason it was removed and replaced with a flat ceiling was that the waves made some passengers feel nauseous.*

*Below (top): Upon delivery in 1936, the little Danish motor ship Hammershus brought considerable comfort and modern interior design to the short overnight service from Copenhagen to the island of Bornholm in the Southern Baltic. The all-white livery treatment of the hull and superstructure gave something of the allure of a tropical liner or cruise ship.*

*Below (bottom): The dining saloon on the Hammershus by Kay Fisker featured robust leather-upholstered chairs and veneered wall and ceiling panels secured with chromed metal fixing strips. The dark woodwork of the outboard walls contrasted with the lighter ceiling finish and with the white table linen.*

*Above (left): All of the fixtures, fittings and furniture on the Kronprins Olav were bespoke items, specially designed by the architect Kay Fisker. Here, we see a group of leather-clad armchairs in a corner of the semi-circular First-Class smoking saloon.*

*Above (right): A subsequent view of the same space, taken after post-war refurbishment (note that the furniture is now upholstered with moquette). The slightly abstract composition of this image of lady smokers is typical of progressive trends in the architectural photography of Modernist buildings and interiors during the mid-20th century.*

In 1934, the Dampskibsselskabet paa Bornholm af 1866 (popularly known as the '66' Company), which traded between Copenhagen and the island of Bornholm in the Southern Baltic, ordered a new passenger ship from B&W. The previous year, Thorkil Lund, an enterprising Bornholm businessman, had joined the '66' Company's board of directors and he set about steering the firm in a forward-looking direction. Dissatisfied with the shipyard's own design proposals, in 1935 the '66' Company contacted the distinguished and progressive Copenhagen architect Kay Fisker for assistance. Fisker had previously designed the Danish Pavilion at the Exposition des Arts Décoratifs and was also well-known on Bornholm as he had designed stations and other buildings for the Gudhjembanen railway and the Handelsbanken in Rønne, completed in 1921.

While International Modernism appeared to advocate a revolutionary approach, linked with scientific analyses and the exploitation of new technology, Fisker sought to reconcile history and civilisation, community and society, nature and culture. Indeed, to him, Denmark's vernacular architecture of bricks and tiled pitched roofs was nature transformed into culture, born of a clear sense of the Danes' place in history and the world. Fisker designed on a readily accessible, human scale and with an egalitarian social outlook, emphasising deep-rootedness, significance and sobriety.[33] Perhaps his greatest skill lay in composition as he had an unwavering ability to create visually stimulating, yet harmonious, facades through judiciously related areas of unadorned brick and simple fenestration. Moreover, his methodology closely mirrored that of naval architects, refining existing precedents and building on prior knowledge.

As Fisker had been appointed late in the design process, time was unusually tight and the keel for the new ship was shortly due to be laid on the slipway. Early on in the process, it became clear that strict limitations had been placed on Fisker's creative freedom as B&W had already agreed a tightly budgeted contract price. Besides, the yard had its own drawing office, which also prepared interior designs. So, had Fisker's proposal been too outlandish or expensive, the project could easily have been given back to B&W.[34]

Fisker, however, had his own strongly held views about how the new ship should look. In designing its interiors, he closely followed the rational principles which

The 1937 Copenhagen–Oslo motor ship Kronprins Olav *had a semi-streamlined forward superstructure. The black hull livery stepped down towards the stern, creating an impression of forward movement. This photograph shows the vessel in the mid-1950s.*

governed all of his architectural and design endeavours – the use of traditional, hard-wearing materials which had been shown to stand the test of time, in a stripped back, unadorned manner, emphasising their intrinsic beauty. The detailed outfitting required particularly careful thought as the ship was intended to sail in all weathers on what was a lifeline service. The furniture and fixtures would, therefore, have to withstand punishing usage in rough winter weather when some passengers might be seasick. Thus, almost every fitting had to be purpose-designed by Fisker and his colleagues. (In Denmark, following Arts and Crafts traditions, it was then accepted practice that architects should design the furnishings for their buildings to achieve visual harmony and coherence.)

The *Hammershus* was delivered to the '66' Company in June 1936 and, although very small at only 1,726 tons, it provoked much interest on account of its striking modernity.[35] While the architecture and design press enthused over the interior design, the *Hammershus* was hailed in the Copenhagen newspapers as 'et helt lille *Queen Mary*' (a proper little *Queen Mary*).[36]

Later, in 1938, the '66' Company required Fisker's assistance to help with the design of a sister ship named the *Rotna*. Although this was very similar to the *Hammershus*, one obvious innovation was the remarkable wavy plywood ceiling in the First-Class hall and dining saloon. Unfortunately, 'this proved to be contrary to the well-being of the passengers as in rough weather there appeared to be waves both inside and out, so after a couple of years, it proved necessary to get flat ceilings installed.'[37]

Not far from the Bornholm terminal in Central Copenhagen stood the handsome headquarters of Det Forenede Dampskibs Selskab (The United Steamship Company) – one of Denmark's most prestigious shipping lines, whose services then reached all over the western hemisphere. The new *Hammershus* must have provoked much curiosity amongst DFDS's senior management – especially the firm's managing director, J.A. Kørbing. The company had recently ordered a new ship for its premier Copenhagen–Oslo service from the Helsingør Shipyard, which was also a DFDS subsidiary. Thus, a few months after the *Hammershus* entered service, Kay Fisker was invited to meet Kørbing as he wanted Fisker's assistance to design the new ship's passenger accommodation.

*Below (top): The First-Class writing room on the Kronprinsesse Ingrid: even overnight vessels such as this required spaces for businessmen to work at desks while in transit. Kay Fisker's design used a mixture of direct and indirect lighting to achieve an atmosphere of calm.*

*Below (bottom): The* Kronprins Frederik *in Esbjerg harbour in the early 1950s. The design was obviously a development from the* Kronprins Olav.

*Below (right): The* Kronprins Frederik's *elegant First-Class entrance hall featured a Y-shaped staircase. The vertical ribbed panelling on the balustrades is repeated in the adjacent wall finishes. The armchairs with winged headrests were a bespoke design by Fisker which prefigured the famous Egg and Swan chairs designed by his former pupil Arne Jacobsen in the latter 1950s.*

A great advantage to Fisker was the fact that Kørbing had involved him much earlier on in the design process than in the *Hammershus* project, and so he had the possibility of making a greater input to the new ship's overall layout. Better still, he would now be working in close collaboration with the highly regarded young naval architect, Knud E. Hansen, who was then employed by the Helsingør Shipyard. Ever since the *Hammershus* had entered service, Fisker and Hansen had corresponded to learn more from each other about innovations in naval architecture and interior design.

Born in 1900 in Helsingør, Knud E. Hansen had studied naval architecture at the Polyteknisk Læreanstalt in Copenhagen. Following his graduation in 1925, he gained practical experience in shipbuilding at a number of yards, both in Denmark and abroad. Working together, the two men were to produce for DFDS one of the most significant small passenger ships of the 1930s and Fisker was closely involved in both the external and interior design.

The *Kronprins Olav* was sleek and streamlined with a high bow profile, a cruiser stern and a long, low superstructure with a tapering funnel. In the interior, Fisker developed the design principles he had first introduced on the *Hammershus*. The walls in all the First-Class saloons were lined with matt-varnished sycamore with ceilings in similarly finished hazel. Joints between the panels were matt-chromed metal. Throughout, the lighting was indirect, either concealed behind coves or around

the perimeter of floating suspended ceilings. Fisker designed a new range of furniture for the *Kronprins Olav* – high-backed armchairs with winged headrests and long curved banquettes. In the semi-circular First-Class smoking room, these were in red leather, which contrasted with the black linoleum flooring used throughout and also referred to the DFDS livery. In its First-Class hallway adjacent, the *Kronprins Olav* had a Y-shaped staircase with a portrait of the Norwegian Crown Prince strategically placed in the void.[38]

With almost everything specially designed – from the ship's overall profile down to clocks and ashtrays – the *Kronprins Olav* was also a wonderful advertisement for modern Danish design. At the 1938 Spring Exhibition at the Royal Academy in Copenhagen, Fisker, by this time also the professor of architecture there, mounted a display of photographs and architectural drawings of his firm's ship design schemes. Knud E. Hansen also found success as he set up his own naval architecture consultancy in Copenhagen, which went on to become a leading designer of passenger ships in the post-war era.

In the winter of 1938, meanwhile, DFDS placed an order for another new passenger ship, this time for its important Esbjerg–Harwich route in order to cope with the growing tourist and business traffic between Denmark and Britain. Before construction of the 3,895-ton *Kronprins Frederik* could commence, World War II broke out in September 1939. At first, work proceeded as planned and the keel was

*A DFDS publicity photograph showing the First-Class dining saloon on the* Kronprins Frederik: *the ceiling lights were designed for the ship by the architect Poul Henningsen, who had previously worked with Fisker on the interior for the Danish Pavilion at the Paris Exhibition.*

laid that November. When Denmark was invaded in April 1940, the ship was already well advanced and, after a short break due to materials shortages, the construction was completed by the summer of 1941. By this time, any possibility of using the ship for its intended purpose had vanished and so it was laid up in Copenhagen's South Harbour basin. After Denmark's liberation, it was towed back to Helsingør for completion, finally entering service in 1946.

Within, the *Kronprins Frederik* had very high-quality accommodation for 311 passengers, spread equally between First and Second Class. A semi-circular First-Class smoking saloon filled the forward part of the ship and, to the rear, there was a small curving cocktail bar, entirely covered in cream padded leather. Immediately aft of the hallway was the First-Class dining saloon, panelled in teak. From the largest components to the smallest details, the *Kronprins Frederik* had a great sense of visual cohesion and harmony. The curvilinear forms of the saloons, staircases and the bar counters were echoed in the furniture – from long banquettes and high backed lounge chairs, to plywood restaurant chairs and even the dressing tables in the First-Class suites. Fisker commissioned Poul Henningsen, an up-and-coming young architect, to design the lighting scheme. This included partially recessed glass ceiling fixtures of various kinds and also pressed metal table lamps to create a warm and relaxing atmosphere.[39]

The *Kronprins Frederik* was such a success that an identical sister ship, to be named *Kronprinsesse Ingrid,* was ordered in 1947. This entered service in June 1949 just in time for the busy summer tourist season.

In America, meanwhile, the need for commercial advantage combined with New Deal consumer confidence to bring about a generation of streamlined consumer goods – ranging in scale from electric toasters and Hoovers to automobiles. It seemed inevitable that the practice would be readily adopted by ships where, unlike household gadgets, the wind-cutting qualities of streamlining would have a practical application. Indeed, wind tunnel tests were undertaken using models of the *President Hoover*, both as built, a 'semi streamlined' version and a full streamlined model:

| | |
|---|---|
| ship required to produce | 18 knots |
| as built | 14,500 |
| semi-streamlined | 14,110 |
| streamlined | 13,900 |

The less wind resistant streamlined model appeared to show a potential fuel saving of $284 a day over the conventional version of the *President Hoover* actually built.[40]

This notwithstanding, by the mid-1930s, the majority of practically minded ship owners regarded streamlining not as a sensible engineering device, but one of pure style – even whimsy. Nevertheless, the streamlined output of the industrial designers Raymond Loewy and Norman Bel Geddes across a wide range of consumer products amply demonstrated that the style was commercially viable and so, perhaps not surprisingly, America also led the way in streamlined ship design. In August 1936, the naval architecture journal *Marine Engineering* observed that:

> It is fairly admitted that the speed of the vessel operating under normal circumstances did not warrant the application of streamlining with a view to reducing wind resistance and increasing propulsive efficiency. The main object of the owners in applying this mode of construction of the new vessel was to produce a design that embodied something different and daring which would appeal to the tastes and attention of the traveling public, already quite familiar with the application of artistic air-flow design in rail and motor transportation.[41]

An aesthetic precedent already had been set – not in some glamorous trans-Atlantic liner, but in a humble car ferry, which puttered back and forth between Seattle and Vancouver Island.

The *Kalakala* was actually a radical reconstruction of a fire-damaged steam-powered ferry called the *Perlata* which had originally entered service in 1926, connecting San Francisco with Oakland in California. Indeed, along with a sister, the *Yerba Buena*, it was one of the last steam ferries on the route. Disaster struck in 1933, however, when an arsonist destroyed the wooden ferry terminal and the *Perlata* too caught light.

The wreck was sold to Capt. Alexander Peabody, the chairman of the Puget Sound Navigation Co. of Seattle, otherwise known as the Black Ball Line, and towed to the Lake Washington Shipyard for reconstruction. Captain Peabody was something of a radical in the otherwise conservative world of American coastal shipping and, reputedly at the suggestion of his equally forward-looking wife, he employed a Boeing engineer called Louis Proctor to construct a large model to show how the ferry might look with a streamlined superstructure. At the shipyard, the naval architect Helmuth W. Schmitz translated Proctor's radical proposal into a full set of construction drawings and, meanwhile, the fire-ravaged hulk of the *Perlata* was scrapped down to the belting.[42]

Proctor's new design took the form of a spectacular streamlined silver superstructure with large porthole windows and viewing galleries; truly, it was 'the shape of things to come', gone to sea. William Thorniley, the Black Ball Line's publicist, chose the name *Kalakala*, which means 'flying bird' in the local Chinook Indian language and an advertising campaign was launched to promote the world's most futuristic-looking ship.

The *Kalakala*'s maiden sailing was attended by a crowd estimated at over 100,000, such was the curiosity about the ship. In regular service between Seattle and Bremerton, the *Kalakala* was a great success. The saloon deck contained comfortable lounges with upholstered bench seating, a fashionable circular cocktail bar and a dance saloon, featuring 'The Flying Bird Orchestra' to entertain passengers. Nothing of this kind had previously been attempted on a car ferry and soon the *Kalakala* became a national sensation, featuring in newsreels, magazines and Sunday supplements.

Yet, notwithstanding its seductive curves and shimmering silver topsides, the *Kalakala* embodied a paradox which, from the perspective of a true Modernist, appeared to typify concerns about American industrial design in general. The

*Below (left): The remarkable streamlined ferry* Kalakala *brought Boeing aircraft aesthetics and technology into ship construction. As nearly all of the resistance faced by ships comes from the water, the design did nothing to increase speed, but it made the vessel an icon in the Puget Sound area.*

*Below (top): A colour-tinted postcard of the* Kalakala *('The World's First Streamlined Ship'); this was one of many postcard images produced of the ferry – suggesting that the design did indeed capture the public's imagination.*

*Below (bottom): Commuters read their newspapers in one of the* Kalakala's *saloons. Primarily intended to carry passengers and vehicles en masse, the ferry also contained a dance saloon and a cocktail bar to provide a secondary leisure function.*

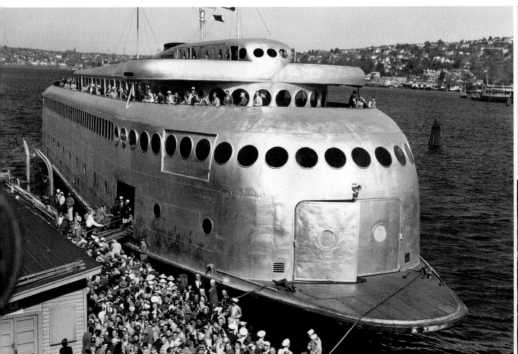

*Less unorthodox than the* Kalakala *was Raymond Loewy's styling of the Virginia Ferry Corporation's* Princess Anne. *Again, this steam-powered ferry was primarily a transport ship but with the added entertainment attractions of dining and dancing. Unlike the* Kalakala, *which remained a one-off, the* Princess Anne's *aesthetic profoundly influenced ferry design in Europe and North America in the 1950s. The subsequent use of motor propulsion meant that passengers on the after decks did not get covered in soot.*

streamlined superstructure arguably was mere fancy dress, designed for commercial advantage, rather than to exemplify any deeper logic. Below the surface, the *Kalakala* remained essentially a rather primitive craft, the hull of which really was little more than a motorised barge.

Modernism, on the other hand, sought to distinguish itself from mere repackaging for commercial expediency by emphasising the need to design from the inside outwards, rather than the other way around. European and American design critics, such as Nikolaus Pevsner, Henry Russell Hitchcock and Philip Johnston, could all agree that American streamlining had nothing more than surface appeal and that there were no more fundamental principles than the need to distinguish a product in the marketplace. Whatever modern American design represented, it was certainly not any kind of fundamental social and cultural re-ordering of the kind proposed by Le Corbusier et al.

Yet, while accusations of mere 'styling' – rather than technological and social engineering – were applied to Raymond Loewy's streamlined re-packagings of household goods, the case of the *Kalakala*, was not so straightforward. For starters, the streamlined upperworks were of lightweight monocoque construction, inspired by Boeing's aircraft design. This form saved weight and allowed the ferry a greater deadweight capacity to carry a larger payload of cars and trucks than would otherwise have been the case. Secondly, although streamlining did not help the ferry to sail any faster than its existing 17.5 knot service speed, it had the potential to make maintenance easier. Essentially, a streamlined exterior on a ship had far fewer awkward corners for salt water to gather and cause corrosion. Above all, however, the *Kalakala*'s long service life can, in part, be attributed to its being an iconic design, with passenger facilities in excess of 1930s standards. Leaving ideological judgements aside, it appeared that a modern-looking ship could perhaps be a wise long-term investment proposition, giving that vital 'edge' over the competition.

The *Kalakala* continued in service until 1967, after which it was sold for static usage as a crab processing vessel in Alaska, where it remained until 1998 when it was rescued for preservation. American ship design, meanwhile, never looked back and one sensational ship after another was delivered from the latter-1930s onwards.

Only one year after the *Kalakala* first entered service, Sun Shipbuilding delivered the *Princess Anne* to the Virginia Ferry Corporation for service between Norfolk and Cape Charles. Although designed by W.R. Elsey, superintendent of floating equipment to the Pennsylvania Railroad, Raymond Loewy 'was consulted with reference to the superstructure streamlining.' (Loewy, incidentally, also styled the remarkable GG1 electric locomotives for the PRR, introduced in 1935).[43] Of more conventional appearance than the *Kalakala*, the *Princess Anne* had a domed funnel with the navigation bridge, forward superstructure and bow styled to match.

Loewy, who was never shy to publicise his own achievements, observed that:

The results surprised a lot of people, both in the shipbuilding and business worlds. People liked the unusual appearance and some of its peculiar appointments. A small band, at my request, was placed onboard in the lounge; passengers boarded the ferry now as much for fun as to get from one point to another. They danced, went to the snack bar, and made the round trip as though they were taking a short pleasure cruise… it was all very gay and romantic, a long way from a boring ferry crossing… The elongated openings on the promenade deck made the ship look longer and, when illuminated at night, the *Princess Anne* looked like a giant liner ready to cross the Atlantic… From then on, ocean liners were influenced by the *Princess Anne*'s streamlined approach. Besides better appearance, the new silhouette had valuable repercussions in the public-relations area, and… the smooth, flowing lines of the superstructure facilitated maintenance.[44]

Loewy, however, went on to condemn rival imitators of this new look:

Carried away with the *Princess Anne* look, naval engineers in America and overseas went on a binge which produced floating monstrosities. I wonder sometimes whether I should have designed the *Princess Anne* and thereby become an accessory before the fact of such seagoing infractions of good taste.[45]

Ironically, though, the *Princess Anne* proved to be anything but practical in daily ferry service. Its funnel was too short and so sooty smoke was dragged down onto

*Below (left): The* Panama's *veranda cabin plan enabled sitting areas to be shared between four adjacent inboard and outboard cabins.*

*Below (right): The cocktail bar on the* Panama *by Raymond Loewy featured robust furnishings, clean lines and strong contrasting colours.*

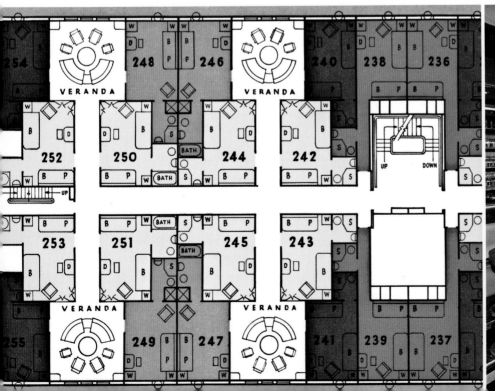

the after decks. Additionally, the curved bow plating made the job of the deck crew difficult as it was less easy to see overboard when throwing and catching ropes. Consequently, during its career, the *Princess Anne* was gradually de-streamlined and ended its days in the 1970s working on the Delaware River as the *New Jersey*. By then, nearly all evidence of its streamlining had gone.

Back in the mid-1930s and, doubtless, also inspired by the *Bremen*, the *Europa* and the *Normandie*, Norman Bel Geddes created a fantastic vision of the ocean liner of the future. Rendered in model form or in air-brushed illustrations, this captivated readers of *Scientific American* and the *Saturday Evening Post* but, tellingly, not the shipping journals.[46] Naval architects and ship owners appreciated the vision, but rejected it as not being sufficiently practical. Instead, in Paramount's *The Big Broadcast of 1938*, cinema-goers were treated to the Hollywood fantasy of a *Normandie*-esque liner racing a Bel Geddes-esque one. The film, like the Bel Geddes design, had no greater effect on modern liner design – but it did introduce Bob Hope to the world.

The way ahead for liner aesthetics was not signposted by futurist fantasies or film fiction, but in the bureaucracy of Washington and on a subsidised American secondary liner route, serving that supreme symbol of American enterprise: the Panama Canal. Panama Line carried nothing more extraordinary than government supplies and army staff from New York to the Canal Zone, but its new trio of liners – designed by George G. Sharp, named the *Panama*, *Ancon* and *Cristobal* and delivered in 1939 – were remarkable. Seldom have three ships introduced more new and novel features, inside and out.

The 'Panamas', as they were known, threw tradition aside in external appearance, but managed to be modern without being freakish, sleek yet business-like. Their design emphasised simplicity and harmony of line, coordination and rationalisation of elements, and concealment of clutter. The beamy hulls were capped by a long, low superstructure and a streamlined funnel. These were the first liners without sheer; having level decks throughout did away with expensive shipboard joinery. Among the first mast-less ships, they had only two uprights carrying lanyards and navigation lights on either side of the bridge-mounted vent posts and the aft kingposts. The funnel was internally guyed, another first for an American liner, which avoided the need for tensioned cables cluttering the upper decks, as on the *Queen Mary*.

Predictably, fire safety was unprecedented. Four insulated steel fire screen doors divided the ships into five fire zones, each with its own enclosed stairwell leading to centreline passageways. Each zone had its own fire station equipped

*Below (left): The main lounge on the Panama was of double height. Thanks to the use of fireproof finishes and the ingenious concealment of retractable bulkhead doors, a spacious atmosphere was achieved while maintaining the strictest safety standards.*

*Below (right): The Panama's stylish funnel livery with chrome bands looms in the background in this Panama Line publicity image.*

Panama Line

*at ease*.. **for a delightful two weeks' vacation**

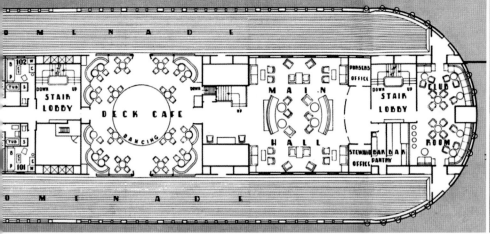

with extinguishers, alarms, gas masks and two hose points. A fire control room was adjacent to the wheelhouse. All interior partitions were constructed on the fireproof 'Sharp system' of hollow steel panels with asbestos core fitted flush from deck to deck head with no false ceilings. Furniture and fittings were made of metal or alloy, eliminating wood except for sheathing open passenger decks, rail tops, cargo hold battens, reefer gratings and steamer chairs.

A maximum of 202 First-Class passengers were accommodated in 70 staterooms, all with private facilities. Of these, 38 were outside cabins and the remaining 32 were arranged on the 'Sharp Veranda System' – taking its name from the naval architect, George C. Sharp. Everything was made of anodised or enamelled metal or alloy and there was carpeting underfoot. Three pastel colour schemes were used: tones of beige or light blue for walls, pale yellow for ceilings and blue-grey for furniture – or apple-green walls, coral ceilings and sea-green furniture.

For vessels rigidly subdivided by watertight and fireproof bulkheads, their 'wide open' feeling was a remarkable accomplishment. To facilitate the fire zone concept, as well as spaciousness, these were the first American liners with divided funnel uptakes. As the funnel was far forward, the amidships engine hatch was sited on the port side and the staircase on the starboard side so as not to break the vista aft. Raymond Loewy's interior design comprised pastel or neutral grey tones, clean, uncluttered surfaces, an emphasis on structural elements, rather than on decoration, and superbly designed and comfortable furniture. According to Loewy, 'Planning the interior of a ship is not a matter of 'interior decoration', but of design.' The New York Times praised his 'avoidance of period encumbrances and decorative claptrap'.[47] As Loewy later recalled, to ensure that the Panama and her sisters remained pristine and uncluttered by incongruous additions, 'Each time a ship returned to her New York berth, one of our specially assigned designers would spend two or three days onboard to see that everything we had designed remained shipshape. It was part of our services for more than 10 years.'[48] Modernist interiors were very sensitive to even slight interventions by non-experts and so Loewy was right to insist that the Panama-class liners remained as he and his colleagues had intended.[49]

From being so lacking in confidence about its ability to make any kind of contribution of its own to modern architecture and design at the 1925 Paris Exhibition, by 1939, America had become a style leader in its own right. American liner design never looked back and, from being regarded as conservative – even puritanical, due to Prohibition laws – ships flying the Stars and Stripes came to be viewed as being amongst the most glamorous of the post-World War II era.

003: **FASCISM AND THE MODERN LINER**

**M**odernism is a complex term, but it is often portrayed as left wing and liberal in outlook – however, that is to ignore its adoption by Fascist Italy, following the 1922 March on Rome. Some leading Italian artists and writers, who were members of the Futurist movement, espoused a nationalistic rhetoric of newness, youth, war fever and dynamism. This went hand in hand with the country's rapid industrialisation and imperial ambitions, themselves imaged in a burgeoning national infrastructure and in a collective cult of the youthful, healthy body. Much Modernist theorising, indeed, lent itself to such interpretations.

One potential problem for such new and radical political systems in embracing the avant-garde was the inevitable gulf between the progressive aesthetics favoured by the design literate intelligentsia and the sometimes reactionary conservatism of the masses, who felt much more comfortable with aesthetics embodying a sense of history and tradition. Just such a situation had occurred in the post-revolutionary Soviet Union, where Modernism, in the form of Constructivism, had become the official collective design style in the early 1920s. Firstly, the economy had contracted in real terms since 1917, meaning that large-scale architectural commissions could not be afforded in quantities sufficient to make a cultural impact in so vast a country. Secondly, the peasantry – who were in the majority – simply could not understand either the theoretical arguments for Modernism or the abstract forms of Modernist art, design and architecture. Consequently, when Josef Stalin came to power in the latter 1920s, Modernism ceased to be the aesthetic of Soviet Communism and, instead, realism and revived Neo-Classicism became favoured by the state as these styles were utterly didactic and, unlike Constructivism, required no specialist prior knowledge or understanding.

Thus, the Soviet experience of the Modern Movement exemplified a number of paradoxes. On the one hand, a dictatorship had the potential to impose a uniform aesthetic upon all levels of society – something which would not be impossible to achieve in the same way in a liberal democracy. On the other hand, however,

*Opposite: Lloyd Triestino's white-hulled Victoria was a significant vessel in terms of design and propulsion. Fitted with four Sulzer diesels, the liner was briefly the fastest motor ship in the world.*

*Below: The Cosulich-owned motor liner Vulcania was one of a number of notable Italian-built vessels of the mid-1920s, symbolising the country's increasing industrial prowess.*

even the most fearsome dictator could only govern with the consent of the majority and so, then as now, politicians were wont to ingratiate themselves with 'ordinary people' through rampant populism and the denigration of anything too avant-garde or intellectually challenging. Yet, there remained a need to signify to the masses that the regime was progressive, and so Modernist aesthetics – when used sparingly and carefully targeted in certain areas and not others – could usefully serve propaganda purposes.

It was in Fascist Italy and Nazi Germany, however, that such tensions between Modernism and historicist propaganda were most evident. Being technologically charged icons of modernity and national pride, ship designs inevitably were very sensitive barometers of taste, which came simultaneously to represent both conservative and progressive agendas.

Integral to Mussolini's vision of the new Italian nation were the expansion of shipbuilding, and of the country's liner services to the Americas and to an Italian empire in East Africa, that had first been envisaged decades earlier. To that end, the Genoa-based Lloyd Sabaudo and the Navigazione Generale Italiana were merged in January 1932 under a national programme to save Italian industry in the wake of the Great Depression. Through this process, Finmare – the parent company of the Italian state shipping line – became one of the largest and most powerful in Europe. Previous to this, each firm had ordered a single new flagship liner with the aim of capturing the Blue Riband for Italy. Since 1928, there had been an agreement to cooperate between the two companies and a third, the Trieste-based Cosulich Line, in which Lloyd Sabaudo owned a significant stake.

Mussolini himself delivered a lecture in 1926 at Perugia's University for Foreigners with the title *Roma antica sul mare* [the seapower of ancient Rome], and believed that Italy's imperial destiny required the Mediterranean to be 'converted from an Anglo-Saxon lake into a Latin sea.'[1] As with other aspects of Italian industry and culture, such as cinema, civil engineering, and – especially – sophisticated road technology, the investment and training instituted during the Fascist period to realise

*Below (left): Unlike previous Italian motor ships, which invariably contained grand historicist decorative schemes, the Victoria was of progressive design. Here we see the First-Class dining saloon with geometric leaded windows by Pietro Chiesa, bas-relief panels by Augusto Cernigoi and sculpture by Libero Andreotti.*

*Below (right): The cocktail bar in the First-Class smoking saloon, adorned with mirrors and chromed details.*

such aspirations bore different fruit long after the virtual end of Mussolini's regime in July 1943.

The 1931 Lloyd Triestino motor ship *Victoria* brought the 'Littorian' style – the Italian form of 'Moderne' – to the high seas. In contrast with the earlier Cosulich liners *Saturnia* and *Vulcania* of 1927–28, which were richly decorated in a florid Baroque idiom, the *Victoria* was the first fully modern passenger ship built in Italy; it is also still regarded as one of the most beautiful vessels ever built, the product of a very progressive team assembled under the direction of Nicolò Costanzi (1893–1967) at the Cantieri San Marco at Trieste.[2] Costanzi had graduated in naval architecture from Trieste University, becoming the technical director of the Cantiere Navale Triestino at Monfalcone, where the first important passenger ship he designed, the *Saturnia*, had been completed in 1927.[3]

The *Victoria*, was designed in cooperation with the distinguished Trieste architect and interior designer, Gustavo Pulitzer Finali (1887–1967). A graduate of the Munich Polytechnic in 1911, he was a student of Theodor Fischer, the founder and first president of the Deutscher Werkbund, and his contacts with shipping circles came through friendship with the prominent Trieste-based Cosulich family. Indeed, Pulitzer's earliest shipboard design commissions included the smoking room on the *Saturnia* and the vestibule and grand staircase on the *Vulcania*. These spaces, whilst in line with the overall historicist aesthetics of these ships, were rather more restrained in manner and set the tone for his subsequent work.[4] On the *Victoria*, both the hull and superstructure design (by Costanzi) and the internal planning and décor (largely by Pulitzer) set new standards for coherent, pleasing and efficient design. A fast but modestly sized luxury vessel built for services in the Eastern Mediterranean, the *Victoria* had a service speed of 21 knots – although 23 knots was attained on trials.

The year the *Victoria* was launched, Pulitzer wrote of his approach to naval architecture and, in retrospect, his words can be seen as characterising what was to become an Italian tradition in ship design:

*The Second-Class hallway featured abstract murals by Augusto Cernigoi. Although less generously proportioned, a similar harmony of finish was achieved in both First- and Second-Class accommodations.*

*Above (top): A charming rendering showing First-Class passengers in evening dress about to enter the ballroom on the Rex.*

*Above (bottom): The Rex was distinguished by sweeping hull lines and a counter stern. The vessel was built to signify Italy's transformation into a modern industrial nation, capable of challenging for the Blue Riband.*

*Above (right): By the 1930s, most liners had extensive fitness facilities. On the one hand, public health issues and claims of racial superiority became politically important; on the other, clothing fashions became more revealing and thus required a toned body to show them off to best effect. Here we see an impression of the gymnasium on the Rex.*

Not architecture overlaid on that of the ship, not structures with no purpose. Architecture must find its harmony in the congenial nature of the décor, without altering the spaces that are offered by the structure of the ship itself. Endless exquisite effects can be achieved in every detail through studying the appropriate, and at the same time hidden, possibilities all materials offer for decorative expression. [5]

Modestly sized and operating in Mediterranean and Far Eastern service, the *Victoria* was not subject to the same international scrutiny as the great 'national flagships' employed on the trans-Atlantic routes to America. To compete with the finest of these vessels, Italy would have to build on a far grander scale.

The commissioning, design and 1931 launch in Genoa of the trans-Atlantic liner *Rex* in August, followed in 1932 by that of the *Conte di Savoia* at Trieste, demonstrated the role of politics and personalities – and, of course, finance – in the creation of such large and expensive vessels. Honouring King Vittorio Emmanuel III – but in Latin, not Italian – the *Rex* also evoked that earlier Roman empire with which Mussolini encouraged comparisons. The hull designs of both vessels owed much to the technically advanced German liners *Bremen* and *Europa*, and extensive research on their design was undertaken in Austria and Hamburg.[6]

The two liners were designed for the southerly route across the Atlantic, and featured very extensive open decks and lido facilities to exploit the better weather this offered. In this respect they marked a departure from the concept of 'floating cities' that concealed the maritime nature of the voyage. Indeed, the 1932 poster by Giovanni Patrone for the new vessels used the phrase 'six wonderful days' to stress the enjoyable experience of 'the sunny route'.[7] Good weather notwithstanding, the *Conte di Savoia* was also fitted with massive Sperry gyroscopes to minimise rolling motion. These were of great publicity value, but proved largely ineffective at sea.

With their handsome raked bows and funnels – and especially through having the latter both set well forward – both the *Rex* and the *Conte di Savoia* conveyed an impression of urgent pace and energy which was more than matched by their performance. They attained over 30 knots on trials, although they were intended to operate at only 25 to 26 knots. In 1933 the *Rex* became the only Italian liner to take the Blue Riband, with an average speed across the Atlantic of 28.92 knots, taking four days, 13 hours and 58 minutes – over two hours better than the previous record.

Both liners offered very high standards of accommodation, although there were four classes of passengers; for example, all First-Class cabins were equipped with telephones. The interior of the *Rex* was in 18th-century style by Casa Ducrot of Palermo, with cabins by Enrico Monti of Milan, and represented the last example of the old-style 'floating palace' passenger ship (only the gymnasium was, to some extent, modern in appearance). The *Conte di Savoia*, by contrast, had interiors coordinated by Pulitzer, fresh from his acclaimed work on the *Victoria*, and so his work looked decisively to the future, though Studio Coppede of Florence contributed the decidedly anomalous Sala Colonna, a replica of the ballroom in Rome's Palazzo Colonna, complete with frescoed ceiling.[8] The contrast between the period atmosphere of this one room and that of the First-Class dining room, main lounge and Bar Fumoir – all designed by Pulitzer in a strikingly spare and elegant style – must have been quite startling for passengers. Despite this oddity, the overall role assumed by Pulitzer was then unusual, having, as he did, responsibility for the planning, execution and coordination of every interior detail. Though rather overshadowed by the legend of its sister ship, the *Conte di Savoia* embodied many technical advances over the *Rex*. Certainly both deserved a longer and more successful career than history granted: the *Conte di Savoia* was set ablaze by German bombers and scuttled by its crew in September 1943 while anchored in the Venice lagoon, just after the Armistice that month. The *Rex* was destroyed by allied bombers in September 1944 while moored off Capodistria, and the wreck was given to Yugoslavia to be scrapped as a war prize.[9]

In addition to its building up of Italy's own merchant fleet, the Fascist Government made the expansion of the country's industrial base as a whole one of its top priorities. Crucial to all of this was the shipbuilding industry, upon which many other supply businesses were contingent. To secure orders, Italy offered foreign shipping lines very competitive prices. Indeed, it was even possible to pay for ships in commodities, rather than money.

Of course, national pride dictated that established shipping nations – such as Britain, France and the Netherlands – would favour their own domestic builders. Countries with emerging and more peripheral merchant fleets had no such compunctions, however, and the lure of being able to finance tonnage with raw export

*Below (left): The* Conte di Savoia *was an altogether more modern looking liner than the* Rex*. As with the earlier* Victoria*, the interiors were generally progressive, being largely the work of Gustavo Pulitzer Finali. Only in the First-Class Sala Colonna was it decided to revert to a grand historicist idiom.*

*Below (top): Viewed side-on, the* Conte di Savoia *made a fine impression of speed and modernity at sea. Here, the liner passes the coast outbound from Genoa.*

*Below (bottom): Smooth surfaces and strong horizontal accents increase the sense of spaciousness in the First-Class hallway on the* Conte di Savoia*.*

goods was irresistible. Hence, the Italian 'Littorian' style found its way onto passenger ships built for Norwegian, Polish and Swedish operators before Italy joined the Axis with Germany.

In 1933, Polish Ocean Lines decided to construct a pair of 18-knot ships, measuring 14,000 tons, for its trans-Atlantic trade from Gdynia to the USA. As Poland was suffering from the ongoing effects of the Depression, it could only afford the 62 million lire cost by supplying an equivalent value of coal for use by Ferrovie dello Stato, the Italian State Railways. The new ships were to be constructed by the Cantieri Riuniti dell'Adriatico of Monfalcone – a major coup for the Fascist government. The first of the sisters, named the *Pilsudski*, commenced its maiden voyage in September 1935 and, meanwhile, construction gathered pace on the second of the two, named the *Batory*.

These vessels were of similar design and appearance to the recent Lloyd Triestino liner *Victoria* and they could accommodate 280 in Tourist Class, 75 in 'Interchangeable' Class and 415 Third-Class passengers. Intended as symbols of a vibrant and progressive Poland, the passenger accommodation was designed in a progressive manner with contributions from some of the country's most forward-looking artists and architects, Stanislav Brukalski and Barbara Sokolowska-Brukalska, coordinated by the Italian Nino Zoncada. At the shipyard in Monfalcone, their work was re-interpreted by Gustavo Pulitzer Finali and, no doubt, the outfitting process made use of Italian materials for wall, ceiling and floor finishes. There was relatively little woodwork and, instead, metal, glass, rubber and ceramic finishes were employed, along with chromed tubular steel furniture and indirect lighting. The *Pilsudski* and the *Batory* were highly successful ships – so much so that plans were afoot to construct a further, larger, sister when World War II broke out in 1939 and Poland – which had achieved a great deal in difficult circumstances during the 1930s – was plunged into darkness.[10]

Norway's Bergen Line, which ran a network of services from West Coast ports

*The Polish trans-Atlantic liner* Batory *was reputedly financed through the export of coal to Italy. The liner and its sister, the* Pilsudski, *were popular intermediate-sized vessels, the similarity between their design and that of the* Victoria *being notable.*

across the North Sea to Britain and the near continent, also signed a contract with Cantieri Riuniti dell'Adriatico at Monfalcone for a new motor ship for its Bergen–Stavanger–Newcastle route. This was to be paid for using dried Norwegian codfish, which the Roman Catholic church required for its religious rituals. The *Vega* was delivered in 1938 and, at 7,300 tons, it eclipsed in size any passenger liner yet seen in North Sea service.[11] This time, Gustavo Pulitzer Finali had sole control over the interior design and, consequently, the ship more closely resembled a miniature Italian liner than a Scandinavian one.[12] The First-Class dining saloon was most impressive, with a double-height ceiling and concealed perimeter lighting. Sadly, the *Vega* only saw service for two seasons and was destroyed by Allied bombing during World War II.[13]

The Swedish American trans-Atlantic liner *Stockholm* of 1938 promised to be a most innovative vessel, yet it suffered a protracted building process. It too was ordered in the mid-1930s from the Cantieri Riuniti dell'Adriatico at Monfalcone.[14] The design involved cooperation between a number of forward-looking architects and naval architects both in Sweden and Italy. Eric Christiansson, Swedish American Line's technical director, carried out the principal design work. He had been born in 1901 and went to sea at the age of 14. In the 1920s, while studying marine engineering, he worked as a plater at the Lindholmens Shipyard in Gothenburg. Upon graduation, he joined the Broström group, Swedish American's parent company, serving as its technical director between 1934 and 1965 and designing a succession of important passenger liners and cargo ships. In an article written for the shipbuilding trade press in the early 1950s, he explained that there were no short cuts to the design process and little opportunity to make corrections if a vessel fell short of expectations: 'A lady's hat that does not turn out exactly as the milliner had visualised it is easily altered. An unsuitable type of car will disappear from the market quite quickly, the cost of the experiment falling gently on a large number of customers. Even an unattractive house can be made beautiful by screening trees. The ugly part is called the back of the house, and no one expects it to look as well as the front,' he pointed out,

*Below (left): The Norwegians bartered fish to pay for the North Sea motor ship* Vega. *In this rendering of the First-Class hallway, it is obvious that Pulitzer's interior design again followed the* Victoria's *precedent.*

*Below (top): A typically 1930s advertising poster for the Bergen Line's North Sea service to Newcastle, operated by the 1931-vintage Danish-built* Venus *and by the newer, larger Italian* Vega.

*Below (bottom): The* Vega *is seen during its brief career in North Sea service, when the liner was the largest sailing regularly between Britain and the Continent.*

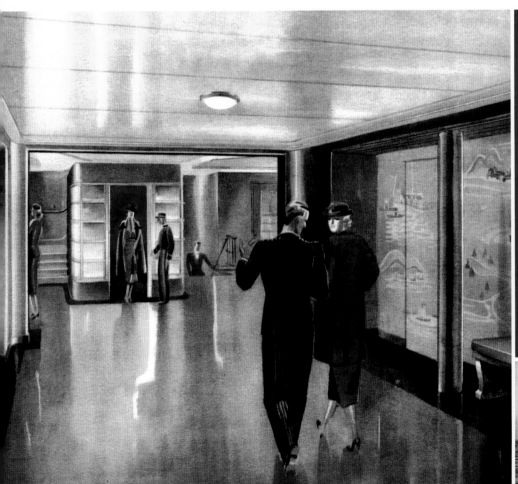

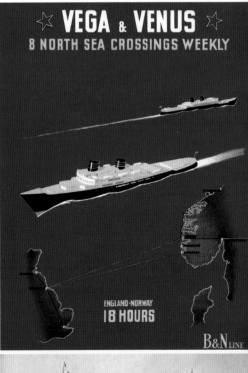

VEGA & VENUS
8 NORTH SEA CROSSINGS WEEKLY

ENGLAND–NORWAY
18 HOURS

B&N LINE

adding: 'But a ship cannot have a back. Neither can she be covered by any protective disguise. Besides, she should, if possible, look as attractive to people 30 or 40 years from now as she does to the present generation.'[15]

In light of this perceived need for a liner to stand the test of time, Christiansson's approach was evolutionary, rather than revolutionary, in that his designs were clearly rooted in established naval architectural traditions. From the 1938 *Stockholm* to the 1966 *Kungsholm*, each had a well proportioned silhouette with two funnels (even though, on the post-war Swedish American Liners, the forward of these was a dummy, fitted purely for aesthetic reasons). Where Christiansson was notably innovative was in layout planning and in his specification of powerful diesel motors, rather than steam propulsion.

The *Stockholm*'s principal public rooms were the work of Nils Einar Eriksson, one of the architects previously involved in the Stockholm Exhibition and the designer of Gothenburg's famous Concert Hall. He was assisted by another Gothenburg architect, Gustav Alde, and the detailed execution of their work was supervised at Monfalcone by Nino Zoncada, who also contributed the connective spaces and hallways. Even so, as Eriksson, Alde and Zoncada worked in a similar manner, a high degree of coherence was achieved. Significantly, the *Stockholm* was specifically designed as a dual-role cruise ship and trans-Atlantic liner. In terms of layout and external appearance, the innovative 1938 German Kraft durch Freude liner *Wilhelm Gustloff* heavily influenced the design and, in many ways, the *Stockholm* was a two-funnelled version of that vessel.

Most unfortunately, while nearing completion, the *Stockholm* was virtually destroyed by fire at the shipyard and so it was partially scrapped, then rebuilt in a slightly enlarged form. It now measured 30,390 tons and so was the largest Swedish American liner ever. The ship eventually ran trials in the Gulf of Trieste in 1941. Frustratingly for Swedish American, it proved to have serious stability problems and delivery was postponed until sponsons were fitted on either side of the hull below the waterline. The ship was intended to carry 1,350 passengers in three classes on Atlantic line service between Gothenburg and New York but, when cruising, the First- and Tourist-Class accommodations were to be amalgamated and the Third-Class areas closed off entirely, reducing the passenger capacity to a mere 620. Among the

*Below (top): The newly launched* Stockholm *awaits tugs to move the incomplete vessel for outfitting. Unfortunately, before this work was finished, a serious fire destroyed most of the upper works.*

*Below (bottom): After considerable rebuilding, the* Stockholm *was finally completed and documented for posterity. Here, we see a chair and desk-cum-make-up table in a typical cabin.*

*Below (right): The* Stockholm*'s interior design involved collaboration between Swedish and Italian architects, as shown here in the writing room. The liner's axial planning enabled a centreline vista to be opened from space to space.*

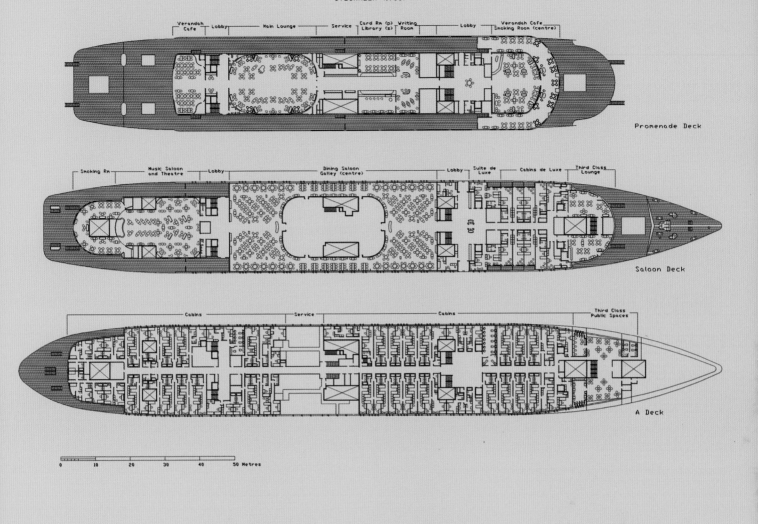

STOCKHOLM (1938)

Promenade Deck

Saloon Deck

A Deck

special provisions made for the ship's cruising role were an open-air swimming pool (most unusual for a Scandinavian trans-Atlantic vessel at that time) and spacious sun decks. All cabins and public rooms to be used in cruise service were completely air-conditioned. This, in itself, was noteworthy at a time when many liners designed exclusively for tropical services offered this comfort only in their First-Class dining saloons and, perhaps, one or two other major public rooms.[16]

As with a number of recent trans-Atlantic liners – most notably the *Normandie* and the *Nieuw Amsterdam* – the exhaust uptakes were split, enabling an open plan central circulation axis on both public room and cabin decks. The *Stockholm*'s accommodation was most notable for the 250 spacious First- and Tourist-Class cabins intended for cruise service. Perhaps the most remarkable feature of the cabin arrangement was that the majority of rooms were arranged either side of a single wide central hallway extending the full length of each deck. By developing the traditional 'bibby' cabin (which gave even inside rooms a narrow space leading to a porthole) into a repeat arrangement of interlocking U-shaped spaces, almost every cabin could be sold as an 'outside'. Furthermore, all were equipped with full-size twin beds, spacious wardrobes and, in most cases, a separate sitting area. The majority of the en-suite bathrooms had full-size baths and twin washbasins. They were arranged in such a way that the beds and baths all oriented fore and aft in the interest of passenger comfort and safety. However, the *Stockholm*'s divided funnel

*A general arrangement drawing showing the Stockholm's main public room decks plus a cabin deck: here, the liner's centreline circulation plan is particularly evident. On the cabin deck, the rooms are L-shaped so as to interlock and thus giving most passengers at least one porthole to let in daylight.*

casings, stairways and hatch trunkways, which made the central circulation passages possible in the first place, increased the overall complexity of the design. With this in turn driving up the cost of building and maintaining such an arrangement, it seems hardly surprising that schemes of this type were not more widely used, in spite of their apparent attractiveness from the passengers' point of view.

Sadly, due to the delay in delivery, Swedish American Line was again thwarted as Italy entered World War II on the German side and its fine new flagship remained at the builder's yard. Later, it was sold to the Italian Government who placed it under the management of the Italian Line and had it converted into the troopship *Sabaudia*. In May 1945, the ship capsized at Trieste following allied aerial bombardment. Yet the *Stockholm* had survived in pristine condition just long enough to leave a deep and lasting impression on both the owner and builder. That influence would be seen in many post-war Scandinavian and Italian liners.[17]

Notwithstanding his important work on the *Conte di Savoia*, after Fascist Italy's 'Pact of Steel' with Germany in 1939, it became imperative for Gustavo Pulitzer Finali, who was a Jew, to leave. So, like many other progressive European architects, he moved to America, finding work there with the industrial designer Henry Dreyfuss. The post-war European Recovery Plan, however, gave the reconstruction of the Italian liner fleet new impetus and so Pulitzer returned, taking once again a leading role.[18]

In Germany, meanwhile, the retreat to conservative positions was very clear; both Norddeutscher Lloyd and Hamburg-Amerika continued to develop their fleets with government subsidies, obedient to the politics and prestige of the National Socialist regime. In order to ingratiate itself with 'the ordinary man in the street' and to claim to govern in the interests of the masses, rather than those of the intelligentsia, the Nazis adopted a populist approach to art and design. As Joseph Goebbels observed, using ominous nautical terminology, so far as aesthetic matters were concerned, it was 'necessary to move at the speed of the slowest in the convoy'.[19] This meant that

Modernism was largely banned. Additionally, the fact that many of Germany's most progressive designers – and their clients – were Jewish made them all too easy targets for destructive propaganda.

In practice, although the Nazi approach to design may have been carried out through fear and intimidation, it was not so different from concurrent approaches elsewhere in the differing contexts of public building, housing and new technology. As in much of Europe and the United States, stripped back Neo-Classicism was favoured for government buildings to convey a sense of logic, order and inner strength. For housing, German vernacular styles – however spurious – were preferred to suggest the continuation of deep-rooted folk traditions. This approach was analogous to the 'Tudorbethan' aesthetic used by housing developers in the UK, based on selling a fake romanticised view of the past. Where modern technology was involved, however – for example, factory buildings and consumer goods, such as the Kraft durch Freude (KdF) wagen car and the Volksradio – a modernistic aesthetic was tolerated. Even the usage of large choreographed casts and effects lighting at political rallies and emotive propaganda imagery may have taken more inspiration from contemporary Hollywood than anything else.

That the National Socialists' official design styles did nothing so much as reflect mainstream popular taste throughout most of the Western World at that time was not as surprising as it might seem. At the point of experience, for the majority of Germans, the regime appeared to be reassuringly banal. This wilfully conventional and mundane approach was reflected in German liner interior design of the era.

It was at this point that Woldemar Brinkmann (1890–1959) came to prominence; a student of Paul Ludwig Troost, he had worked with him on several ship interior design projects, as well as overseeing the Bremen Deutsche Holzkunst-Werkstätten. In 1931, he formed his own consultancy, specialising in interior design. Brinkmann was first commissioned by Norddeutscher Lloyd to design the interiors of two vessels, the *Scharnhorst* and *Gneisenau*, built at Bremen in 1932 and 1935

*The German Kraft durch Freude vessel* Wilhelm Gustloff *was arguably the first ever purpose-built mass-market cruise ship. Although built partly to address propaganda purposes, the high-density layout prefigured the requirements of today's cruise industry.*

*The ballroom on the* Wilhelm Gustloff *typifies the rather conventional design of the KdF fleet. Vessels of this type were intended to have widespread popular appeal and so they were required to appear simultaneously traditional and modern – just as cruise ships today must equally address the same diverse impulses.*

respectively for Far Eastern routes. The third ship in the class, the *Potsdam*, was built at Hamburg with the architect Max Wittmaack as interior designer. In the general design of his two vessels, Brinkmann was indebted to Troost's work, but with less historical quotations and excessive decoration. After Troost's death, Brinkmann's contacts with Albert Speer brought him numerous important commissions. In 1937, he was responsible for the interior of the German Pavilion, designed by Speer, at the Paris Exposition Internationale des Arts et des Techniques dans la Vie Moderne. The grand central hall of this building made reference to the First-Class central lounge of Hamburg-Amerika's *Europa* and could be considered an amplification of it. Brinkmann subsequently obtained the commission for the new Munich Opera and, later, for the gigantic opera house that was to have been built under plans by Hitler and Speer for the new city of Germania (formerly Berlin).

Brinkmann also designed the interiors of the motor vessels *Wilhelm Gustloff* and *Robert Ley*, built for the Deutsche Arbeitsfront (German Workers' Front) and its leisure and propaganda division, Kraft durch Freude (Strength through Joy). This organisation had been founded by Robert Ley with the aim of structuring and controlling the free time of German workers and, equally, of providing pleasure cruises to the Baltic, Norway and the Mediterranean, sold at modest prices. Having first used various NDL liners, such as the steamer *Sierra Ventana*, Ley drew up a new ambitious programme that envisaged the completion of 30 vessels specifically for cruising, with the declared objective of accommodating at least two million German workers each year.[20]

Notwithstanding their sinister associations with the Nazi indoctrination programme, Brinkmann's two cruise vessels were particularly innovative. In fact, they were nothing less than prototypes of a new kind of cruise ship, the general arrangement of which was adopted in other countries after the war. The ships offered two- or four-berth cabins, all outside, with a single, logically arranged deck of public rooms for one class only, and generous outdoor spaces for sports activities. Moreover, the standard of crew accommodation matched that for passengers.[21] The external profile of the two ships, while not identical, was quite compact, simple and clean: a single funnel of elliptical form being placed centrally on a long superstructure distinguished by the absence of ventilators and other cluttering elements.[22]

The arrangement of communal space was based on locating all the public rooms along the promenade deck, with the aim of accommodating all passengers without additionally using the restaurant, located on the lower deck. A succession of five large rooms ran from bow to stern. These included the theatre and the Wilhelm Gustloff Halle. The style adopted by Brinkmann was based on his experience of working with Troost: strictly symmetrical Neo-Classicism rendered in traditional materials, using light colours, ceilings of simple geometrical design and walls divided by pilasters

*Below (top): A plan of a cabin deck in the Robert Ley's hull shows the interlocking arrangement of the cabins outboard of parallel corridors to give each a porthole window. Just as on today's purpose-built cruise ships, all services were located along the centreline.*

*Below (bottom): Requiring only a moderate service speed for cruising duties, the Robert Ley had more bluff fore and aft lines than typical of passenger ships built for liner service. This increased the deck area inboard, enabling higher densities of passengers to be carried on pleasure and indoctrination trips.*

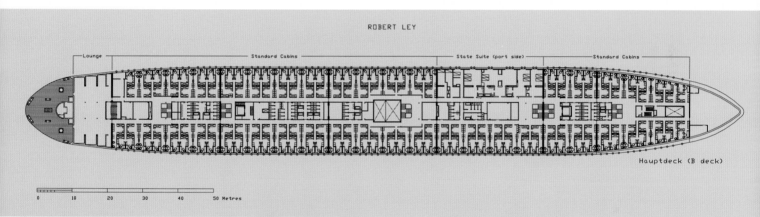

ROBERT LEY

Hauptdeck (B deck)

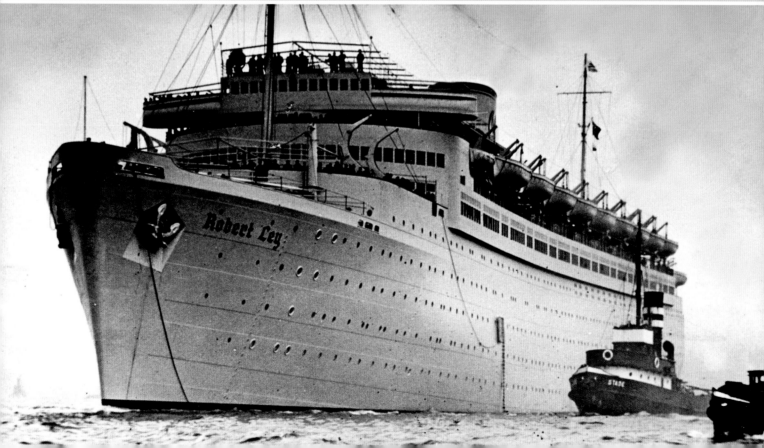

and decorative framing. Furniture consisted mostly of traditional seats and armchairs made of wood, while the decoration of the rooms, entrusted to German artists of romanticist outlook, featured folk costumes and bucolic landscapes.[23] The exception was the Wilhelm Gustloff Halle, in which the panelling was of dark wood with gilded bronze lamps, dominated by a portrait of Adolf Hitler, whose gaze was unavoidable. Certainly, the advanced structural and technical design of the ship was not reflected in its interior design, which slavishly followed the directives of the Nazi regime. (Indeed, such conservatism continues to be exemplified in the design of the 'mass market' cruise-ship interiors of the present era.) Furthermore, the KdF cruise ships were painted overall in white with an emblem of propeller blades, containing a Swastika, on their funnels and this symbol was deployed throughout the KdF cruise operation. Such usage of a universal brand image was also an early manifestation of the kinds of corporate identity strategies nowadays widely used in passenger shipping – and, indeed, throughout the contemporary hospitality and leisure industries.

In designing the *Robert Ley*, Brinkmann placed greater emphasis on decorative

*A remarkable colour image showing the Robert Ley's ballroom with its restrained Rococo detailing as designed by Woldemar Brinkmann.*

elements. The ship's two main public rooms, the *Theatersaal* and the *Tanzsaal*, differed from those on the *Wilhelm Gustloff* in being two decks high with galleries, one square and the other circular. Both rooms had large dance floors of polished wood and featured decorative reliefs set into the walls. Balustrades, in the form of crossed swastikas, and impressive lamps completed the décor.[24] Speer chose these two rooms to represent the regime's interior architecture, illustrating them in his 1941 book *Neue Deutsche Baukunst* which, as a celebration of anti-modern architecture, opened with the Munich buildings of Troost. The two ships shared a violent fate with the regime that had commissioned them; both were bombed by allied aircraft with substantial loss of life. Brinkmann never completed his drawings for the interior design of a great trans-Atlantic liner for Hamburg-Amerika, the new *Vaterland*, which was launched at Hamburg in 1940 and would have entered service in 1942, the German intention being to capture the Blue Riband from Cunard's *Queen Mary*.

The violent fates of the Fascist liners were arguably seen as a reflection of the violent and destructive political ideology that had brought them into being. Yet, ironically, during the 1930s, Le Corbusier himself had pondered the possibility of using aircraft to unleash a 'blitzkrieg' on existing cities in order to clear space as quickly as possible for his 'Plan Voisin'. In practice, blitzkrieg certainly did clear urban sites as effectively as Le Corbusier had imagined – but the human cost was incalculable and those who survived were scarred for life.

Aerial bombardment, mines and torpedoes, meanwhile, devastated the world's merchant fleets and so, just as on terra firma, in the post-war era, there came an urgent need to build anew.

*Above (left): Viewed from one side of the proscenium, a musical recital with singing to piano accompaniment takes place in the* Robert Ley*'s Theatersaal, designed by Brinkmann.*

*Above (right): Hitler poses on a steamer chair on the* Robert Ley*'s promenade deck. Upon the outbreak of World War II, the KdF cruise ships were given over to military purposes. Both vessels met violent ends – the sinking of the* Wilhelm Gustloff *when carrying refugees in the Baltic being a particularly tragic event.*

004: **BUILDING ANEW**

The destruction wrought by World War II both decimated Europe's merchant fleets and disabled its economies. Germany and Italy lost nearly all of their pre-war passenger vessels – while France suffered the cruel blow of losing the *Normandie* to fire in New York harbour. Moreover, the totalitarian regimes in Germany and Italy had subverted history for propaganda purposes, meaning that the past was tainted. Only Modernism, it was argued, stood in opposition to the extreme conservatism and jingoistic visions now inextricably associated with Fascism and the Holocaust (this notwithstanding Mussolini's embracing of Modernist aesthetics prior to joining the Axis). In the post-war era, Modernism came to dominate design debates, both on terra firma and at sea.

At the start of the conflict, Britain's merchant fleet had dominated the world's sea lanes – but many ships had been sunk by torpedoes, bombardment and sabotage in the interim and so the priority was to build afresh. Yet, Britain was bankrupt and the post-war settlement did not favour her imperial interests. Necessity won, however, and so Britain's post-war rebuilding programme represented a continuation of pre-war design practice. The prestigious new Cunard liner *Caronia* of 1948 typified the situation; built as a dual-purpose trans-Atlantic liner and luxury cruise ship, it was intended to earn dollars from wealthy American dowagers, and so the interior design followed Cunard's pre-war formula, as demonstrated so successfully by the *Queen Mary*, which had entered service 12 years before. Britain's other major passenger shipping lines – P&O, British India and Union-Castle all followed suit.

The emigrant trades from Europe to Australia and New Zealand offered other possibilities, however, and on these routes, a number of innovative ships entered service in the latter 1940s and early 1950s. The Port Line's refrigerated combination passenger-cargo liners *Port Auckland* and *Port Brisbane* of 1949 had streamlined superstructures, the design of which reflected the most modern naval architectural practice of the period. Later, in 1955, Shaw Savill Line introduced its one-class 'tourist' liner *Southern Cross* on a round-the-world routing via New Zealand. Built by Harland & Wolff in Belfast, the *Southern Cross* was one of a number of post-war liners to have boilers and turbines located aft in the superstructure, thus opening up uncluttered expanses of sun deck and freeing the public rooms from being divided by casings containing exhaust uptakes. The *Southern Cross* had an impressive streamlined silhouette and, as with the *Caronia*, the superstructure was painted in pale green to reduce glare when sailing in tropical waters. Notwithstanding such

*Below (top): The British liner* Southern Cross *offered a one-class round-the-world service via New Zealand. The machinery-aft layout enabled more efficient use to be made of the hull and superstructure at the widest point amidships. By emphasising the bridge structure and officers' accommodation, an effective counterpoint was made to the aft-located funnel, helping to balance the profile.*

*Below (bottom): A rendering of the superstructure of Delta Line's three 'Del' passenger-cargo liners, topped by a large dummy funnel containing the officers' accommodation with an observation deck above. The boilers exhausted instead through slender twin smokestacks to the rear of this.*

*Below (right): The double-height lounge on the three 'Dels' was surrounded by tall windows. A glazed partition opened onto an adjacent outdoor veranda deck.*

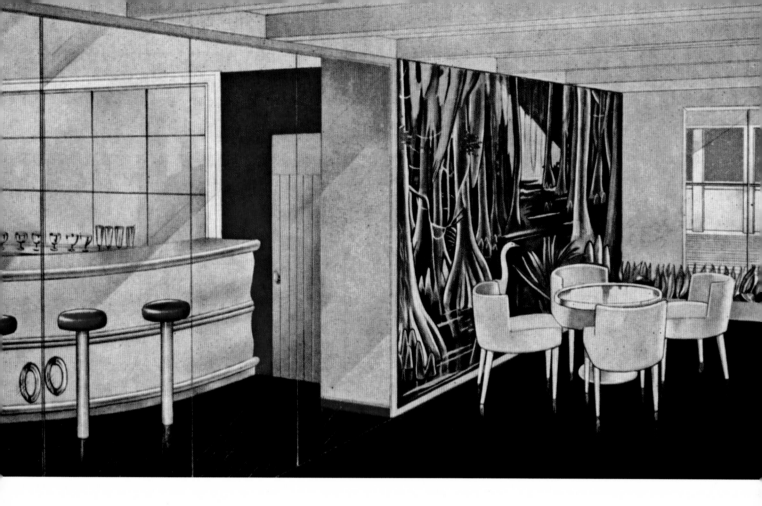

forward-looking naval architecture, the *Southern Cross* was otherwise moderately conservative in terms of interior design – but, as in the past, British liners were commissioned to earn money for their owners, rather than to represent the avant-garde at sea. Indeed, in the post-war era, it was from countries whose ships benefited from generous government subsidies to cover building and operational costs that the most glamorous and innovative designs appeared. America, Italy and a newcomer – Israel – looked to the future with confidence and built or converted armadas of passenger ships which, one way or another, reflected a new era for Modernism at sea.

America may have been a late entrant into World War II, but it not only helped win the conflict, it also decisively won the peace thereafter. So far as shipping was concerned, Britain's giant *Queen Mary* and *Queen Elizabeth* had been vital in securing victory, thanks both to their great speed and their ability to carry whole divisions of troops at a time (albeit in severely cramped conditions). America, of course, felt duty-bound to outdo even these great Cunarders. Hitherto, the United States had not had much success in the trans-Atlantic trade; its first superliner in the 1920s, the *Leviathan* (originally the German *Vaterland*) had suffered due to Prohibition and, later, the *America* of 1939 was only getting into its stride on the North Atlantic when war was declared and it was converted to the troop ship USS *West Point*.

In the mid-1940s, with the conflict in Europe barely won, the United States confidently began to build a new post-war fleet. It was spared the physical scars of war and, as masters of the new age, Americans could not help but view the future with confidence. It was a world defined by science and shaped by atomic power, jet propulsion, plastics and synthetics. The passenger liner, itself suddenly threatened by jet aviation, would also be reshaped, reflecting the American dream, when the country's culture would come to prominence in ways undreamt of only a decade before (it will be remembered that the United States did not even participate in the 1925 Paris Exhibition).

The first of the new generation of American liners was for the Delta Line's New Orleans–South America route and announced just as World War II ended. In November

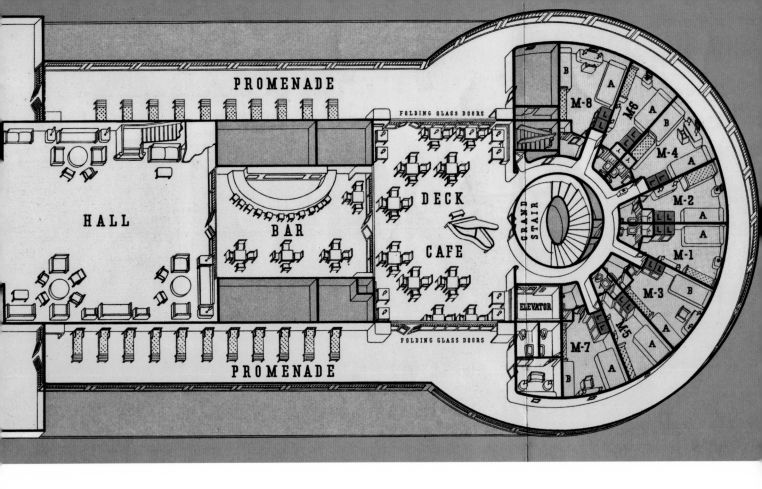

PROMENADE

HALL

BAR

DECK

CAFE

FOLDING GLASS DOORS

FOLDING GLASS DOORS

PROMENADE

GRAND STAIR

ELEVATOR

B · M-8 · M-6 · A · B · A · M-4 · A · M-2 · A · M-1 · M-3 · B · A · M-5 · M-7 · A · B · A

*Part of a deck plan of Delta Line's 'Del' class passenger-cargo liners, showing the unusual circular forward cabin plan with a spiral staircase at the core.*

1945, it was revealed that the vessels would be 'air-conditioned throughout, the first passenger-cargo ships to have this feature for all aboard, including the crew.'[1] When the first of the three ships – and first post-war American liner – the 10,723-ton *Del Norte,* was launched at Pascagoula on 11 January 1946, it was reported that, for the first time on a commercial vessel, 11 tons of Alcoa's new 6051 structural aluminium had been used in the construction. The funnel structure, lifeboats and davits were all made of the alloy.[2] The very large, squat, oval-shaped funnel was, in fact, a dummy and the actual uptakes for the boilers were well aft and arranged as twin kingposts. The ship's 121 passengers were accommodated in outside en-suite staterooms, none of which had upper berths. The *Del Norte* introduced another novelty: the 'radial' arrangement of staterooms in a semicircular deckhouse, the 'wedge' shape of the rooms giving maximum light and space while concentrating electrical and plumbing systems in a central inner core. Even the crew accommodation was on the George C. Sharp 'veranda' system.

Nine years after he gained prominence by designing every aspect of the New York Central Railroad's new 20th Century Limited, the industrial designer Henry Dreyfuss finally came to ship 'styling' in 1948 with American Export Lines' post-war 'combi' passenger-cargo liners, popularly known as the 'Four Aces' – the *Excalibur*, *Exochorda*, *Exeter* and *Excambion* (9,644 tons).[3] As with so many of America's immediate post-war liners, these were converted from wartime tonnage, in this case four 'Duchess' class Navy attack transports. For Dreyfuss, this was a 'dry run' for America's first big North Atlantic liners in a decade – the 23,719-ton *Independence* and *Constitution* of 1950 – for the service from New York to Mediterranean ports.

In July 1949, American Export Lines announced that 'we have engaged Dreyfuss to provide distinctive interiors that represent the best features in Modern American Living. We wanted to make sure that our passengers will be able to enjoy the comfort and convenience that the best skills and ingenuity of American industry can provide for years to come. It's that kind of advanced thinking that Dreyfuss can contribute to the big ships just as he did to the new Four Aces.' Dreyfuss's belief was that everything connected with a company or a concept, be it a train or ship or hotel chain, should reflect a consistent 'look' and, in so doing, create an immediately identifiable 'lifestyle' to which the prospective customer could aspire.

In his styling of the ships' exteriors, Dreyfuss both looked forward and nodded to tradition. Thus, the *Independence* and *Constitution* were the last liners with graceful counter sterns. The funnels showed Dreyfuss's styling in that even American Export Lines' 'E' markings were usurped for an elegant buff with dark blue tops and white bands set off by red stripes. Even the ships' names were rendered in Futura type.

Inside, the *Independence* and *Constitution* managed to be different from previous trans-Atlantic liners, yet reassuringly familiar to their mainly American passengers. To achieve this end, an unprecedented degree of testing was undertaken, and elaborate mock-ups of practically every fitting constructed to try out the deck arrangements, basic staterooms groups, colour schemes, locations of furniture, lighting fixture patterns on ceilings and ventilators. While these models were primarily for design planning, they were also used by the shipyard and joinery personnel for visualisation of rooms and special features to facilitate construction work.

The accommodation for all three classes – First, Cabin and Tourist – was not only of a uniformly high standard but also continued Dreyfuss's penchant for practical innovation and the refinement of details:

> In his approach to the *Independence* problem, Dreyfuss sought these simple goals: (1) luxury without ostentation; (2) blending of modern design concepts with tradition; (3) ease of maintenance; (4) economy in construction and in utility of space… Every bed, lower or upper, folds back flush with the wall, whilst settees, by doing a neat somersault act, become excellent beds. Every basin has hot, cold, and iced water, all from the same tap. Room temperature is at your own control over a range of 60–80 deg. F. Port-holes are permanently sealed, but fitted with a polarised lens, the object of this ingenious device being to banish glare. Bed lamps are the same as those used over aeroplane seats.[4]

Indeed, no detail was too small or insignificant to escape Dreyfuss's attention:

> Many accessories aboard the *Independence* and the *Constitution* were designed specially to fit in with the overall design concept. Included are three sets of

*Below (left): Designed by Henry Dreyfuss, the dining room on the* Independence *made extensive use of indirect lighting. Neatly concealed ceiling ventilators point to the growing sophistication of hidden servicing – such as air-conditioning – on American liners such as these.*

*Below (top): Unusually for post-World War II liners, the* Independence *and the* Constitution *had counter sterns. Dreyfuss must have thought that this aft-body form would give the vessels a romantic image. Here, the* Independence *is in her subsequent all-white linery.*

*Below (bottom): As with the dining spaces, the lounges on the* Independence *emphasised comfort rather than decoration. Furnishings invited relaxation and the lighting scheme created an atmosphere of calm.*

*The record-breaking* United States *is manoeuvred by a tug during one of the liner's regular Southampton calls.*

chinaware (dining room, stateroom and deck service), silverware, glassware, napery, ashtrays, stewards' uniforms, blankets, soap wrappers, match covers, menus and other printed matter...[5]

The *Independence* and *Constitution* were usurped, in size and speed, if not in style, by a vessel conceived and created to be America's first and only true 'ship of state'. Less the creation of a nation than of a man, William Francis Gibbs, the liner was as intensely a personal statement as has ever been built to sail the seas. Having nurtured the idea of building the ultimate ocean liner for most of his 40-year career, Gibbs succeeded magnificently. As the British satirical magazine *Punch* grudgingly observed 'after the loud and fantastic claims made in advance for the liner *United States*, it comes as something of a disappointment to find them all true.'[6]

With William Francis Gibbs and President Truman's daughter among the passengers, the *United States* left New York amid stirring scenes on 3 July 1952. When it returned on the 14th, the band played 'I'm Just Wild About Harry', not for President Truman but Commodore Harry Manning, who now commanded the fastest passenger ship ever built. Eastbound, the *United States* sailed from Ambrose Light Ship to Bishop Rock in an astounding three days, 17 hours and 48 minutes at an average speed of 35.59 knots and, westbound, it crossed from Bishop Rock to Ambrose in three days, 12 hours and 12 minutes. In so doing, the *United States* bested the *Queen Mary's* record by a good 10 hours. Even so, the Cunarder's homeport of Southampton gave the new flagship one of the greatest receptions ever afforded any liner. America and William Francis Gibbs finally had a record breaker.

The *United States* was a remarkable creation as well as a unique one. Not only was the liner conceived to be the fastest ship in the world, but also the safest. The shadow cast by the *Morro Castle* fire was still long and dark. On the *United States*, it was claimed, only the butcher's block and the pianos were made of wood. Much of this was showmanship, of course, as Sharp had already proven that thin wood veneers on Marinite cores did not impact upon fire safety, but it made for good

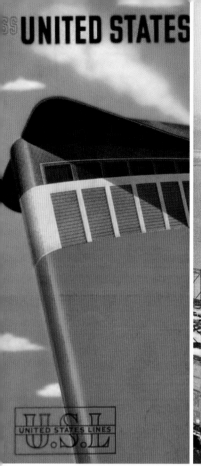

UNITED STATES LINES
U.S.L

copy when Steinway refused Gibbs' request for aluminium pianos.[7] Lest American taxpayers begrudge the *United States'* $70-million cost, it was often reported that the liner could be readily converted into a troop transport, capable of conveying an entire army division to Europe in three days. Alas, the 'troop ship masquerading as ocean liner' moniker dogged the *United States* to the end.

It has been asserted that the *United States* was the fastest ocean liner ever built because Gibbs crammed the most horsepower in the lightest displacement hull that would hold the machinery – and it is an irrefutable argument. For years, every technical aspect of the vessel was cloaked in the kind of Cold War military secrecy that Gibbs revelled in. This, in itself, nurtured the myth that its speed was the result of some wonderful development below decks. In fact, the *United States* had the same steam turbine machinery installation as a United States Navy *Independence*-class aircraft carrier. Gibbs, it appeared, had accomplished the near-impossible with the unremarkable.[8] What made the *United States* unique was neither revolutionary engineering, nor technical innovation, but the sheer bravado and determined will that only Gibbs could bring in constructing a passenger liner around a warship's power plant. Even so, as an economic proposition, the *United States* was a spectacular failure – but the liner was never built to balance books. Instead, its role was to project American prestige, technical supremacy and, possibly, military might across the Atlantic. No ship had more expected of it than the *United States* and no other vessel subsequently made a crack at breaking the speed record because no other country could have afforded to do so. Gibbs was building a machine that could cross the most unforgiving ocean in the world in three-and-a-half days with 2,000 passengers in considerable comfort and utter safety or, alternately, 15,000 troops.

Gibbs, however, viewed himself solely as an engineer and was unconcerned about issues of 'harmony' between naval architect and interior designer; one cannot imagine him sitting through a single meeting discussing his vessel's 'lifestyle' or deferring to a mere 'decorator' in adopting divided uptakes to achieve some open-plan 'vista effect' from space to space. His job and passion was to design the strongest, safest

*Above (left): The* United States' *giant funnels painted in the American national colours featured regularly in United States Lines' publicity imagery.*

*Above (right): The* United States *manoeuvres in the Hudson River while the* America *lies at United States Lines' pier.*

and swiftest ship in the world. Having done that, he turned over the frills and finery to others. To him, this aspect was 'women's work' and so, as with United States Lines' earlier America, decoration of the interiors was consigned to Smyth, Urquhart & Marckwald.

For Dorothy Marckwald, this was not only her biggest and most important project, but also one with even more self-imposed constraints than her previous Gibbs assignments. Not only did she have to work around a set of empty voids, the design and scope of which she had little or any input in determining, but she had to cope with the most stringent safety regulations ever imposed on a liner. Even though Gibbs had no interest in design theory, one can be sure that a cushion or drapery which did not meet or exceed his precise technical specifications would have drawn his wrath. Thus, safety, structural soundness and seaworthiness produced the parameters around which Marckwald was required to work. Consequently, although the United States' passenger spaces were slick, comfortable and commodious, with full air-conditioning, their expanses of painted Marinite and aluminium-framed furniture lacked the visual richness of Cunard's Queens. As with the America, the best parts of the ship were the foyers with their crisp contrasts of oyster white bulkheads, aluminium handrails and glistening black lino. The First-Class ballroom was also impressive, with its sculptured ceiling, etched glass panels and pale gold walls, set off against red carpeting and upholstery. Equally, the double-height First-Class dining saloon tried hard to replicate the grandeur of the liner's trans-Atlantic rivals. Decorative modernity notwithstanding, however, the United States was an oddly formal, class-conscious ship inside, especially for an American one – but Gibbs had practically dictated to United States Lines that its flagship would be laid out along traditional lines with three classes, not two – and the ship owner apparently had little choice but to agree with its forceful naval architect.[9]

The same year as the United States entered service, the first jet airliner, the Comet 1, was introduced. After the fuel-guzzling flourish on the maiden voyage, however, the United States was just another 'five-day boat'. Even so, the engine room was off-limits for 'security reasons' and, when it was drydocked, tarpaulins masked the propellers. Even the Revell plastic model of the ship was cut-off at the waterline, lest eight-year-old boys discover the hull form. With the commencement of the Cold War, such precautions added to the liner's mystique.

Notwithstanding its technological brilliance, the *United States* arguably represented the beginning of the end of the trans-Atlantic express liner – indeed, it was to be the last ever 'proper' holder of the Blue Riband (subsequent winners have been high-speed small craft, not ocean liners, designed to carry thousands in comfort). In such a context of progress and change, a largely forgotten earlier design by Gibbs & Cox was actually far more prophetic in terms of post-war passenger ship development.

The *Chinook*, delivered in 1947, was a moderately sized roll-on/roll-off car ferry which, as with the pre-war *Kalakala*, was built for the Puget Sound Navigation Company – this time to serve on a triangular overnight routing between Seattle, Victoria and Port Angeles. Making good use of twin diesel engines which had been ordered for US naval ships, the *Chinook* was both economical and highly manoeuvrable – indeed, it was a forerunner of the typical overnight short-sea vessels of the 1960s. The passenger accommodation was of a very high standard with a mix of 100 cabins and couchette berths and there was a remarkably extensive range of lounges, shops and restaurants. William Francis Gibbs called the *Chinook* 'the *Queen Elizabeth* of the Inland Seas'[10] and its ability to carry 100 American-sized cars, loaded through the stern and sides, was remarkable for that time. It was not for another decade until more vessels of this size and type came to be introduced in appreciable numbers and, meanwhile, European shipping lines re-equipped themselves with conventional passenger liners.

Italy emerged in 1945 from the ravages of World War II with her passenger fleet almost completely destroyed, including the trans-Atlantic liners *Rex* and *Conte di Savoia*, launched only a decade earlier. The *Saturnia* and *Vulcania* had survived, together with the *Conte Biancamano* (1925) and *Conte Grande* (1928), and it was necessary to make the most of these elderly vessels in order to reinstate both the prestigious North Atlantic route from Italian ports to New York and services to South America – less glamorous, certainly, but socially and commercially vital. Indeed, Italy's fraught situation made this latter service essential, as many Italians sought new lives abroad for a variety of economic and political reasons.[11]

In the overall context of Modernism at sea, Italian architects and designers paid informed attention not only to selection of materials and to details of interior design, but also to the key issue of ensuring the graceful and harmonious appearance of the ships themselves. This issue is less discussed, although in comparable design

*The First-Class lounge on the* United States, *featuring a concentric cove-lit ceiling to focus attention on the dance floor and etched-glass screens.*

fields – such as cars, luxury coaches and motorcycles, as well as buildings proper, all areas in which Italy excels – it is taken for granted. From the role played by the 'oversize' funnels of the *Augustus* and *Giulio Cesare* to the daring twin lattice stacks of the *Raffaello* and *Michelangelo*, Italian ship design reflects a sure and practical understanding of the complex relationship between functionality and beauty. Donato Riccesi has explored these issues in relation to the designs by the Trieste architect and ship designer Nicolò Costanzi for *Augustus* and *Giulio Cesare*:

> The most original feature of these two ships consisted of the funnel: single, central, and perhaps too large, which suggested a new aesthetic for the 'dead mass' [*opera morta*] of a ship, in this instance perfectly resolved by an element that eluded any functional criteria…[12]

Serious research and debate on such essential issues was first promoted by the naval architect Nicolò Costanzi, who, after World War II, was responsible for merchant ship design at the Trieste head office of Cantieri Riuniti dell'Adriatico, with yards at nearby Monfalcone. For over 50 years, he designed most of Italy's important vessels, and also actively promoted scientific research into hull hydrodynamics. Significantly, he was additionally a talented painter, and some of his striking, semi-abstract, studies of ship profiles hang today in the offices of Fincantieri in Trieste, and are reproduced in their publicity material in acknowledgement of the tradition of ship design he established. Costanzi's last project was the 1966 *Eugenio C.*, but he is widely regarded as having led by example in laying down secure scholarly foundations for that blend of engineering and aesthetic talent that still characterises vessels from Italian yards.

The most prolific contributor to post-war Italian shipboard design at sea was,

*The Puget Sound ferry* Chinook, *also designed by William Francis Gibbs, was prophetic in terms of post-war passenger-ship design developments. With car ownership increasing sharply, ferries such as this became commonplace from the latter-1950s onwards. The* Chinook *was innovative in terms of propulsion, having diesel electric machinery consisting of compact motors powering generators so as not to break the clear span of the garage space.*

however, Giovanni (Nino) Zoncada (1898–1988), who graduated from the Accademia di Belle Arti in Venice in 1922. A painter by vocation, he joined the technical team of the Monfalcone shipyard where, in the mid-1930s, he became head of the interior decoration department. There, Zoncada interpreted designs by other architects as well as implementing his own plans for ship interiors. Although his greatest influence was undoubtedly Gustavo Pulitzer Finali, he also worked with other forward-looking European architects – such as the Polish Stanislaw and Barbara Brukalski on the *Pilsudski* and the *Batory*, and with Swedes Nils Einar Eriksson and Gustav Alde on the *Stockholm*.

In March 1948, Zoncada moved to Genoa, where he was asked to work in tandem with Giò Ponti on producing a successful bid for the complete refurbishment of the liner *Conte Grande*, and some of the rooms on the *Conte Biancamano*. Their proposals were successful and this marked the start of a collaboration between the two men. At the same time, he began his long association with the Costa family. Led by Angelo Costa, the firm built up a fleet of passenger liners which nowadays is the largest flying the Italian flag. Thereafter, Zoncada, whose attention to continuity and consistency is unparalleled in the field of Italian shipboard design, was to furnish the majority of Costa ships.[13]

The other major presence in Italian ship design, albeit of an earlier generation, was the Milanese Giò Ponti (1891–1979); not only a talented architect, but also an artist, craftsman, planner and designer. His vision of a world in which good design should be available for all was argued in many publications, and reflected in his long editorship of the eminent design journal *Domus*. Ponti espoused Modernist design with enthusiasm, believing that it could bring about a second Italian Renaissance. Indeed, he went on to be commissioned by many leading Italian manufacturers in a key period which saw both the growth of mass production and the exploitation of

*Above (top): The First-Class smoking saloon on the rebuilt* Conte Biancamano *– one of a number of surviving older liners which re-opened Italian trans-Atlantic services in the post-World War II era. The decorative ceiling panels were sculpted by Marcello Mascherini.*

*Above (bottom): The* Conte Grande *in the 1950s when operating between Italy and South American ports.*

*Above (right): The First-Class smoking saloon on the* Conte Biancamano.

new materials in Italy's post-war building and industrial manufacturing boom. Typical of how his design approach spanned practicality, aesthetics and new technologies was his extensive use of gold anodised aluminium, often grooved to conceal joints, for both wall and ceiling surfaces, and he was similarly enthusiastic about the possibilities offered by new coverings such as Formica:

> Italian ships should be dedicated to…the honour of Italy, in two ways. One is figurative, represented in the decorations, pictures and ornaments, and it is the restatement of the…legendary Italy of art and history… The other way of honouring Italy is to make Italian ships superior to all the foreign ones, even if we conceive of a ship only as a 'functional means of transport' and not as propaganda. Do you not want to achieve the maximum elegance and decisive unity?[14]

The 23,842-ton *Conte Biancamano* had been built on the Clyde in 1925 by William Beardmore and Co., a company that built several ships for the Genoese firm of Lloyd Sabaudo, of which Beardmore himself had been for a time a director.[15] The *Conte Grande* (23,562 tons) was built three years later by the Stabilimento Tecnico Triestino in Trieste and, in 1932, both ships became part of the Italian Line under Mussolini's integration of all major shipping companies. The *Conte Grande* was the last of the liners of the 1920s to have grandiose historicist interiors, but its construction inaugurated a new era for Italian shipbuilders, and it was also the first liner to represent Mussolini's regime that began in 1922 – a role later famously occupied by the *Rex* and *Conte di Savoia*. Massive government subsidies covered the costly building and operation of the ship, and interior décor by Adolfo Coppedè of Florence and Armando Brasini of Rome outdid all previous Italian vessels in richness and eclecticism.

Lacking experience of constructing large passenger vessels, the Trieste shipyard engineered the *Conte Grande* closely on the earlier Clyde-built sister, and the typically British exterior profile remained an oddity for an Italian-built vessel.[16] Popular with passengers despite (or, probably, because of) their old-fashioned glamour, both ships

The Giulio Cesare *looks resplendent berthed in Buenos Aires in the latter 1960s.*

spent the latter years of the war as hard-working troop transports for the United States Government and, on their return to Italian ownership in 1947, it was decided to rebuild them completely, with a government grant meeting half the cost. The need for ships to carry emigrants of all kinds was urgent, and even major rebuilds were quicker and cheaper than ordering new vessels.

The *Conte Biancamano* was rebuilt at Monfalcone, and the *Conte Grande* at Genoa; nothing remained of their original interior décor after war service, and the extensive work on these rather elderly vessels – which included remodelling the bows, superstructure and funnels of the *Conte Grande* – provided the first opportunity in naval interior design for younger architects who would become well known in post-war decades. Work on the Second-Class interior of the *Conte Grande* was carried out by the Milanese architect Matteo Longoni (1913–84), who went on to design many liners for both Italian and Greek owners, and by Gustavo Pulitzer Finali. On the *Conte Biancamano*, Pulitzer worked alongside Zoncada, and Ponti, in collaboration with other architects: Umberto Nordio's group from Trieste (Aldo Cervi, Vittorio Frandoli, Romano Boico), and Alessandro Psacaropulo.

The two *Conti* emerged from their two-year rebuilds completely transformed: ornate interiors calculated to impress through richness of decoration and evocations of a wild gamut of period styles were replaced by well-lit elegant spaces with modern furniture and murals by contemporary Italian artists. This was a remarkable shift, especially given the constraints under which the work was carried out. That this change was first seen in the remodelling of two liners built in the 1920s reflects the difficulties faced by the Italian shipping industry at the time – but also the talents upon which it could call.

Italy's first new post-war trans-Atlantic liners, the sisters *Augustus* and *Giulio Cesare* were built in 1949 for the long-established year-round service from Italy to the east coast of South America, although in 1956 the *Giulio Cesare* was switched to the New York run (returning to the South America route in 1960, with the arrival of the *Leonardo da Vinci*). The *Augustus* also ran to New York from 1957 until 1961, after which it too operated only on the South American route.

The *Augustus* was built at Trieste, the *Giulio Cesare* at nearby Monfalcone. Their construction was highly symbolic not only in marking the rebirth of the national fleet through new vessels but also asserting Italy's economic ties with Trieste and its surroundings which, at the time, were still under United Nations administration.[17] It was a further sign of the times that the 12-cylinder Fiat diesel engines for the two new liners, then the most powerful motors ever installed in a ship, had been built in 1939 for the re-engining of the 1926 steamer *Roma* and the 1927 motor vessel *Augustus*, projects never realised because of the war, but whose wider planning influenced the design of the new ships.[18]

The new twin liners were handsome ships in the emerging post-war idiom, immediately recognisable by their raked bows, curved-fronted superstructures, and single masts. Above all, their dramatic centrally placed funnels owed more in scale and profile to aesthetics than to mere practicality. Designed by Nicolò Costanzi, they were ships of 27,000 tons each, with interiors very much in the style of the rebuilt *Conti*. Passenger accommodation was designed to a very high standard. Cabins, for example, contained a maximum of four-berths, even in Third Class. There was full air-conditioning and each ship boasted three swimming pools and four cinemas – meaning that there was plenty of entertainment. On the *Giulio Cesare*, Ponti and Zoncada were responsible for First-Class areas, with Pulitzer designing the dining room; on the *Augustus* the group of Trieste architects – Boico, Cervi, Frandoli and Nordio – undertook extensive design work, with Pulitzer again responsible for the First-Class dining saloon. As with the rebuilt *Conti*, not only the décor, but also the architectural fabric of public spaces, was decidedly modern, with clean surfaces, indirect lighting and straightforward layouts. Original works by contemporary Italian artists contributed to a strong sense of national identity.[19]

Next, Italy began to add new tonnage to the prestigious New York service, on which American Export Lines' *Independence* and *Constitution* were now the main rivals. The name of Italy's new trans-Atlantic flagship – *Andrea Doria* – is, however, synonymous with maritime tragedy. Launched in 1951, the liner sank with the loss of 43 lives off Nantucket Island only five years later, following a collision with the 1948-built Swedish American passenger-cargo liner *Stockholm*, an accident caused by a misreading of navigation instruments on the latter vessel.[20]

Her sister ship, the *Cristoforo Colombo*, was launched in 1953 from the same Ansaldo Genoa Sestri shipyard. The entry into service of the two marked the completion of the first phase in the post-war reconstruction of the Italian passenger fleet, confirming Italy's leading position on the sunny mid-Atlantic routes from the Mediterranean to the Americas. The new ships owed much in general design to the *Augustus* and *Giulio Cesare*, with handsome proportions and more streamlined hull forms. Interior design was by a group of outstanding architects; on the *Andrea Doria*, Cassi, Rossi and Parenti, Ponti and Zoncada, Pulitzer, Giulio Minoletti and Carlo Pouchain were involved.[21] On the *Cristoforo Colombo*, the design skills of Pulitzer were predominant, working with the Milanese Guglielmo Ulrich, although several other designers also contributed, including Attilio and Emilio La Padula, Nino Zoncada and Luigi Carlo Daneri.[22] Of the two, the *Andrea Doria* was the more glamorous ship, outfitted with shiny rubber floors, abstract murals, mirrored walls, three-dimensional ceilings and contemporary sculpture. Pulitzer's treatment of the *Cristoforo Colombo* was more demure, with gentle colours and indirect lighting.

Whereas the Italian Line enjoyed state-sponsored largesse, the Costa family was known for its financial shrewdness and initial Costa vessels were ingeniously converted from some quite elderly freighters. Within these limitations, Nino Zoncada became adept at designing fresh, stimulating interiors, highly suited to tropical sailing on Costa's warm weather routes from Italy to South American ports. The 'Zoncada look' was entirely practical and utilised polished vulcanised rubber flooring, aluminium and thin plywood wall veneers, cove-lit pegboard ceilings, plate-glass partitions and brushed stainless-steel details. His own bespoke furniture designs were manufactured by Cassina specifically for each project. The liberal use of murals and decorative panels by contemporary artists enlivened the spaces.

By the mid-1950s, Costa's fleet comprised the *Luisa C.* (1919), the *Andrea C.* (converted from a 1942 American-built standard 'ocean' type cargo vessel), the *Anna C.* (1929) and the *Franca C.* (1914). Remarkably, the latter remained in service until 2009 as the Christian missionary ship *Doulos* and was for a long time the world's oldest operational passenger vessel. Elderly though many of these initial Costa liners may have been, thanks to Zoncada, their interiors were exceptionally modern.[23]

With post-war recovery continuing apace, in 1958, Costa took delivery of its first purpose-built passenger liner from the Ansaldo shipyard in Genoa – the *Federico C.* This was a commodious three-class steam turbine vessel of 20,416 tons with purposeful lines and extensive lido decks, featuring three outdoor pools set in abstract mosaic surrounds. For Zoncada, its outfitting was a prestigious commission and great care was taken with the details. Perhaps the most notable space was the

*Below (left): The* Cristoforo Colombo *in all-white livery towards the end of the liner's service for the Italian Line.*

*Below (top): Adriatica Line's* Ausonia *operated between Venice, Piraeus, Beirut and Alexandria. The liner was essentially a miniaturised version of the* Cristoforo Colombo *and the* Andrea Doria.

*Below (bottom): The First-Class cocktail bar and lounge on the* Cristoforo Colombo.

oval First-Class ballroom, dominated by a painted panel by Massimo Campigli. The adjacent First-Class lounge featured a bronze sculpture of a flute player by Marcello Mascherini. Other significant areas were the chapel, the Cabin-Class ballroom and the First-Class staterooms – which had dark wood veneer panelling and silk bedspreads.[24]

The arrival of the *Federico C.* made Costa Line a serious and competitive player on the routes from Europe to South America – but Italian involvement was greater still on the Eastern migrant trades to Australia, where a succession of ever-larger vessels was introduced. The established operator was Lloyd Triestino, founded in 1837, which began its post-war revival with three new 13,100-ton sister ships, built at Trieste in 1951. The *Australia*, *Neptunia* and *Oceania* sailed at monthly intervals from Genoa, Naples and Messina to Port Said, Suez, Aden, Colombo, Djakarta, Fremantle, Melbourne and Sydney.[25] These were followed by a similar, though slightly smaller, quartet comprising the *Africa*, *Europa*, *Asia* and *Victoria*, delivered in 1952–53. The *Africa* was partly the work of Giò Ponti, whilst Gustavo Pulitzer Finali designed the *Victoria*'s interiors in their entirety and contributed individual rooms to the *Australia* and *Europa*.[26] The *Victoria*, incidentally, survived until recently in largely intact condition as a Christian missionary and hospital ship, named the *Anastasis*.

Not only did Finmare's reconstruction plan involve trans-Atlantic liners and emigrant ships, but also new ships for Italy's short sea routes across the Adriatic, Tyrrhenian and Mediterranean Seas. The former were operated by Adriatica, a Venice-based subsidiary split off from Lloyd Triestino in 1937, with routes from Venice and other Italian East Coast ports as far as Beirut and Alexandria. The company's first post-war vessel was the *Esperia* – actually salvaged at the end of the war from the bombed out hulk of the incomplete *Ausonia*, which had been laid down at the Cantieri Riuniti dell'Adriatico shipyard at Monfalcone in 1940. Finally delivered in 1949, this – and other smaller Adriatica new buildings – had strikingly modern interiors by Gustavo Pulitzer Finali. The company's finest liner, however, was a new *Ausonia*, delivered in 1957 from Cantieri Riuniti dell'Adriatico.[27] In almost every respect, this vessel was a miniaturised *Andrea Doria*; designed internally by Zoncada, it was, as with all his work,

*Below (left): The First-Class lounge on the* Cristoforo Colombo *by Gustavo Pulitzer Finali, featuring an irregularly shaped back-lit ceiling composition.*

*Below (right): The First-Class writing room on the* Cristoforo Colombo, *with lounge chairs arranged around an irregularly shaped table.*

liberally adorned with modern artworks. Highly popular as a Mediterranean liner and, later, as a cruise ship, the *Ausonia* remained in seasonal operation for Greek-Cypriot owners until 2008, sailing from Cyprus and Greece on short Mediterranean cruises to the Aegean Islands.

The *United States'* winning of the Blue Riband had signalled to the world that America was now an economic and military superpower and, simultaneously, the new Italian liners were conceived as floating ambassadors for Italy's post-war 'Renaissance' identity as a progressive, style-conscious industrial nation. For the new state of Israel, however, passenger ship design also became an important way of signalling cultural ambitions to the world. Moreover, when Israel was formally declared a nation state in May 1948, it came under attack by Arab armies on all fronts. Once a centre of regional communications, the country was now isolated in a hostile environment, locked in on all its land frontiers, leaving its international airport and its one developed and accessible deep-sea harbour – Haifa – as its only links to the outside world. Israel had, to all intents and purposes, become an island and, as with all island nations, it depended on sea communications for the transportation of both goods and passengers.

It was against this background of war and isolation that the expansion of the Zim Israel Navigation Company's fleet took place. Initially consisting of veteran second-hand ships, in the early post-war years, Zim brought thousands of Jewish refugees and immigrants to Israel. With the cessation of hostilities, there was a new source of passengers, with the beginning of a tourist trade from other Mediterranean ports and from the USA and so Zim required new tonnage. When, in September 1951, Germany apologised for the Holocaust and announced its determination to make substantial reparations, the possibility of expanding of the Zim fleet emerged.

Between 1953 and 1955, with purchase credits received under the reparations scheme, Zim ordered 18 new ships from German shipyards. There were four new passenger liners in all: the *Israel* (1955), *Zion* (1956), *Theodor Herzl* and *Jerusalem* (both 1957). Attractive steam turbine vessels of moderate size, they were distinguished mainly by their outstanding interior appointments, which were:

*A First-Class stateroom on the Cristoforo Colombo by Nino Zoncada, featuring velour-upholstered chairs, satin bedspreads and matching padded-wall panelling.*

Consciously Israeli, in that they sought to express in symbolic terms the character of the country and what it stood for. The interiors were all designed by Israeli architects (and) they were all consciously designed in the spirit of the Modern Movement in architecture, in accordance with the forward-looking policy of Zim, and as a natural expression of the architects' own design direction. Modern architecture had been universally accepted in Israel since the 1930s, and consequently influenced the approach of the architects in designing these ships.[28]

The Jewish resettlement of Palestine had increased in pace between the wars as Jews sought to escape persecution in Europe and the USSR. In the 1920s and 30s, many Jewish architects and their clients had come to embrace the Modern Movement, the socialist ideals and internationalist outlook of which appeared to mirror their own hopes and experiences as a people without a state. Moreover, as numerous Jewish cultural commentators – from Walter Benjamin to Clement Greenberg – had observed, European history had been rendered kitsch by Fascist regimes and its visual imagery subverted to become Anti-Semitic propaganda. Thus, even in 1930s Palestine, Modernism was the favoured aesthetic of Jewish architects and designers engaged in constructing the fast-expanding cities of Tel-Aviv and Haifa. In Palestine, moreover, the 'new' architecture was closely related to the local vernacular, the indigenous domestic architecture of the Middle East. Thus, in Israel, International Modernism, when suitably adapted to suit local imperatives of economy, technology and climate, arguably was not perceived as being a revolutionary movement but, rather, a popular expression of the national will. Indeed, it was viewed as being entirely appropriate to the Zionist enterprise, and expressive of the youth, the pioneering spirit, the austerity and puritanism of a frontier society. Well before the architects of Israel designed the first Zim passenger ships, the ethos and the language of the Modern Movement was widely accepted.[29]

The architects initially entrusted with designing Zim passenger ships were two well-known Israeli firms: the partnership of Al Mansfeld and Munio Weinraub in

*Below (top): The graceful* Andrea Doria *at sea, early on in the liner's short career.*

*Below (bottom): The* Andrea Doria's *First-Class cocktail bar by Giò Ponti, featuring a decorative panel by Romano Rui.*

*Below (right): Part of the First-Class lounge on the* Andrea Doria, *designed by Giò Ponti with murals by Salvatore Fiume and a sculpture of Andrea Doria by Giovanni Paganin.*

Haifa, and the husband and wife team of Dora and Yeheskiel Gad of Tel-Aviv. Alfred (Al) Mansfeld was born in St Petersburg in 1912, but after the Soviet revolution, in 1922, the family moved to Germany, where he was educated. Between 1931 and 1933, he studied architecture at the Technische Hochschule in Berlin but, with the rise of the Nazis, he moved to Paris, where he completed his studies at the Ecole Speciale d'Architecture in 1935. He then emigrated to Eretz Israel, initially working as an architect for the celebrated Levant Fair in Tel-Aviv, which was a showcase of Modernist architecture and design. His talent was immediately recognised and, in 1935, he won first prize in a competition for the design of the central square of the coastal city of Netanya.[30]

Munio Weinraub came from Szumlany in Silesia in 1909, but was raised in Bilitz in German-speaking Poland.[31] Like many Eastern European Jews facing the restrictions of entrance to the local universities, he chose to study in Germany itself. In April 1930, he was accepted as a student in the Bauhaus at Dessau, which was then experiencing a period of political turmoil. After one semester, Hannes Meyer, the school's director, was dismissed, to be replaced by Ludwig Mies van der Rohe. Although Weinraub was one of five students expelled by Mies for their active political support of the left-wing Meyer, Mies obviously approved of Weinraub's talents, if not his socialist politics, and invited him to work in his Berlin office. The approach of Mies to architecture was to be the dominant influence in Weinraub's career and he rejoined the Bauhaus after eight months with Mies. Due to the rise of Nazism in Dessau, however, he left without graduating.[32]

Weinraub, one of seven *Bauhauslers* to leave Hitler's Germany and settle in Eretz Israel, came to Palestine in June 1934, and made his home in Haifa. In 1936, Al Mansfeld moved from Tel-Aviv to Haifa, where he began to practise. The following year, he and Weinraub set up in partnership in Haifa. This continued until 1959, embracing the critical first phase of the Zim new building programme.

Dora Gad, originally from Bukovina in Romania, studied architecture at the Technische Hochschule in Vienna, before coming to live in Palestine. The pattern

*The forward part of the Andrea Doria's First-Class promenade contained a winter garden space, the curved bulkhead of which was adorned with ceramic panels by Guido Gambone.*

is strikingly similar in all three cases: architects born in Eastern Europe, moving westward to study, and then settling in Palestine. She at first worked with Oskar Kaufman, the well-known Viennese architect, on the design of the Mograbi Theatre in Tel-Aviv, and then with Alexander Klein on various planning and housing projects. In 1942, Dora and her husband, Yeheskiel Gad, set up practice in Tel-Aviv. Their major contribution was in the field of interior design, and among their more prestigious projects were the interiors of the Israeli Parliament (the Knesset), several Israeli embassies, the residences of the President and the Prime Minister, and the interiors of luxury hotels, including the Hiltons in Tel-Aviv and Jerusalem, and the Boulevard Hotel in Singapore. These latter projects gave them particular expertise in modern hospitality design.

When Zim decided to appoint Israeli architects to design their passenger ships, they approached these two well-established but independent firms, and suggested that they collaborate on the project. In about 1957, Yeheskiel Gad gave an account of how the appointment of the architects had come about:

The Architects and their assistants started their ship-building career three years ago, when Zim Navigation Co. invited them to design their ships' interiors. This invitation came some time after the boats had been ordered from the yard, when their first sketches were submitted and the Managers of Zim were offered to their surprise interiors of a rich operatic pseudo-oriental style. Then it became clear to them that these 'floating ambassadors' of Israel should in their atmosphere have something in common with their home country, and for this reason the next idea – to call for the help of experienced Italian or Scandinavian designers – also was abandoned. Zim entrusted the job to four architects, known in Israel for their 20-year long varied successful activities in building and interiors – though their combined experience in ship-building was nil.[33]

As Mansfeld later commented, 'For the Israeli architects involved…this meant not just getting rid of psychological inhibitions, but also acquiring skills that we had never practised before.'[34] The success of the operation depended firstly on the compatibility of the architects and their willingness to work together in harmony. Two of Zim's directors, Dr Naftali Wydra and Zvi Yehieli, supervised the planning and construction of their new ships by setting up a Ship Planning and Building Division, headed by Gershon Yoran, Zim's own naval architect.[35] During the construction period, the Gads divided their efforts. Yeheskiel Gad maintained the Tel-Aviv office, while his wife, Dora, spent much time in Hamburg, where the Howaldswerke Deutsche Werft AG built the *Israel*, *Zion*, *Theodor Herzl* and *Jerusalem*.

German payments under the Reparations Agreement of 1952 were made to the Israeli government which, in turn, loaned money to Zim, who chose the shipyard. Thereafter, all technical issues were settled directly between Zim and the builder. Measuring only 6,695 tons and capable of maintaining 19 knots, the ships were designed to carry grain and bales, as well as refrigerated cargo. There was accommodation for 47 First-Class passengers, 33 in what was called 'Changeable Class', and 233 in Tourist Class, served by a crew of 147. These vessels were intended to serve the Zim trans-Atlantic line from Haifa via Naples to New York.

The first of the new sisters, the *Israel*, was indeed a microcosm of the Jewish State. The food was kosher and, naturally, there was a synagogue with a tented ceiling, focusing on a colourful stained-glass screen masking Torah scrolls. The cabins – even in Tourist Class – were simple, functionally organised and comfortably furnished with Scandinavian-designed furniture, but of Israeli manufacture. An article

*The oval-shaped First-Class ballroom on the Federico C. was a notable design success for Nino Zoncada – full-length curtains and a mural by Massimo Campigli adding to the refined elegance.*

*Previous pages: The minimalist elegance of the First-Class lounge on the* Federico C.*, featuring a sculpture by Marcello Mascherini.*

*Above: A hallway onboard the* Israel*, featuring an open-tread stairway enclosed by frameless plate-glass panels.*

in the *Architectural Review* noted, 'the architects wanted passengers to feel that they were in a ship, not in a poor imitation of the Waldorf Astoria'.[36]

The *Israel* and *Zion* were followed by the larger *Theodor Herzl* and *Jerusalem*, which had more extensive passenger accommodation. On the *Theodor Herzl*, the First-Class lounge (called the Altneuland, after Herzl's famous novel) was located forward on the boat deck, its sweeping form reflecting that of the superstructure. Other facilities – including the Tourist-Class lounge (the Miriam Hall), another large lounge (the Haifa Hall), reading room (housing a permanent exhibition commemorating Herzl), the gallery (which served as a games room and art exhibition space), children's dining room, cinema, synagogue and lido pool – were accessible to all passengers. As with the latest Italian liners, the new Zim ships were distinguished by their extensive displays of contemporary art. On the *Theodor Herzl*, boarding passengers were greeted in the entrance hall by a sculpture in wrought iron by Itzhak Danziger, an eminent Israeli sculptor; entitled 'And the Burning Bush was Not Consumed', symbolising the perpetual regeneration of the Jewish Nation. Melamine plastic panels designed by Naphtali Bevem formed a mural in the main lounge, which was also decorated by a colourful transparent screen, by Zahara Schatz. A panoramic view of Haifa Bay, by Jean David, decorated the Haifa Hall, while a photographic enlargement of an antique map of the city formed the backdrop to the bar. The major differentiation between the two ships was in colours: the *Theodor Herzl* ranged from cool blue to purple, while the *Jerusalem* featured the yellows, browns and olive greens of the Jerusalem landscape and the Judean Hills. The décor was light, colourful and elegant; frameless glass doors and suspended staircases, with open risers, enhanced the feeling of space. Indirect ceiling lighting was complemented by wall and table lamps, designed by the architects and manufactured by Louis Poulsen in Copenhagen.

Zim's new passenger fleet was widely admired and the Scandinavian influences upon the interior design were in line with wider design trends in the 1950s. Since the Stockholm Exhibition of 1930, Denmark, Sweden and Finland had become style

The First-Class lounge on the Theodor Herzl features a ceiling composed of tightly packed bamboo rods forming a canopy above the dance floor.

leaders in Northern Europe. Indeed, the cosy domesticity, vernacular materials and high level of craftsmanship associated with progressive Scandinavian design made it, for many, the most acceptable face of the Modern Movement. Where the New Brutalism appeared carnivorous, overturning the past and replacing it with structures alien in form, scale, materiality – and politics – the Scandinavian approach was more pragmatic and, for many critics and observers, it signalled cultural continuity.

The occupation of Denmark and Norway by Germany during World War II – and Finland's ongoing struggle to remain independent of Russia – suspended the development of Scandinavia's merchant fleets until liberation came in 1945. Then, the priorities were to build up denuded fleets of cargo liners and also to construct new overnight passenger vessels for Scandinavian domestic routes.

The *Kongedybet*, owned by the Dampskibsselskabet af 1866 paa Bornholm (The Steamship Company of 1866 on Bornholm – or '66' Company) and delivered in 1952 from the Burmeister and Wain shipyard in Copenhagen, was a fine example of Danish Modernism in a small overnight ship. As with the pre-war *Kronprins Olav*, the design was drawn up by the naval architect, Knud E. Hansen, working in collaboration with the builder and with his old friend, the architect and academic Kay Fisker. Since the end of World War II, the '66' Company had experienced a significant upturn in passenger numbers – especially summer tourists. Externally, the *Kongedybet* reflected modern trends with its domed funnel and curvaceous superstructure – but its interiors were the most notable aspects of its design. The smoking saloon was given an oval shape which Fisker visually strengthened through a corresponding grouping of the furniture. He also devised a remarkable ceiling design, which was an enigmatic composition of back-lit abstract curvilinear forms. As the *Kongedybet* was to be fitted with stabilisers, it was also possible for Fisker to design fixtures and fittings that were much lighter in style than in previous vessels for the Bornholm trade. As with other progressive ships of the era, plate-glass doors between the saloons created a very open layout in what were, in reality, quite compact and potentially claustrophobic spaces.[37]

The *Kongedybet* was to be Kay Fisker's final ship design. By then, he was approaching 60 and was much occupied with architectural projects on terra firma. At the Royal Academy's School of Architecture, however, one of his students, Kay Kørbing, went on to become arguably the best known Scandinavian architect involved in ship interior design. Kørbing, who graduated during World War II, had, like many of his generation, become interested in the theories of Ludwig Mies van der Rohe. Mies's strictly formal and constructionally determined architecture utilised completely open planning and emphasised the interplay of interior and exterior.

Born in 1915, Kørbing was the son of J.A. Kørbing, who was the technical director of DFDS from 1921, its managing director from 1935 until 1955, and subsequently its chairman. Initially, he had planned to follow in his father's footsteps but, perhaps fearing claims of nepotism or possible conflicts of interest, Kørbing senior did not encourage his son to become involved with shipping. He worked instead as a builder in Copenhagen – a beginning which he says first interested him in the raw materials of building, and which taught him the importance of good architectural detailing. His interest in design led him to join first Det Tekniske Selskabs Skole in 1938 to gain admittance to the Royal Academy, where he studied until 1942. When Kørbing graduated in 1942, Denmark was under German occupation and work was scarce, and so he left for Sweden, finding employment with the highly respected architect and urban planner Cyrillus Johanson. There, he produced the competition-winning design for a church in the Storä Essingen district of Stockholm. He returned to liberated Denmark in 1945 and his first job was the rebuilding and interior design of Denmark House in London's Piccadilly, the headquarters of the Danish Tourist Office.[38]

Kørbing's first ship design was a smoking room for the DFDS cargo liner *Naxos*, built in Frederikshavn in 1953–55, which could carry 12 passengers. Next Kørbing designed the cabins and saloons for two DFDS passenger and cargo liners for the North Atlantic trade – the *Oklahoma* and the *Ohio*, both built at Helsingør and delivered in 1956.

After the cargo liners, Kørbing was asked to design the passenger vessel *Prinsesse Margrethe* for the Copenhagen–Oslo route:

My godfather asked me to do general arrangement drawings for the new Oslo ship 'and we'll do the rest', but knowing how important good detail was, I refused unless I could do all the interiors and design them down to the smallest details… I was also very determined to be my own man, so with what might be called youthful enthusiasm, I analysed all the aspects of the design and

*Below (top): The* Theodor Herzl *shortly after delivery to Zim Lines.*

*Below (bottom): A hallway on the* Theodor Herzl, *separated from adjacent saloons by plate-glass partitions.*

*Below (right): The cocktail bar on the* Theodor Herzl *with concealed lighting, polished rubber flooring and abstract murals on the bulkhead.*

*The Zim passenger-cargo liner* Zion *arrives in New York harbour.*

outfitting of such ships to find out what the design possibilities were. That both my father and godfather were in senior positions in DFDS certainly helped as I got business advice from one and detailed technical information from the other. This enabled me to be really quite clinical in my analysis of the design problems, so I think that the *Prinsesse Margrethe* represented a big leap forward in design terms.[39]

The engine room was located two-thirds aft and the exhaust uptake was in fact routed through the ship's rear mast. The funnel, slightly forward of amidships, actually contained the air-conditioning plant. Thus, the First-Class public rooms, which occupied the forward half of A deck were well away from any engine noise. Aft, the Second-Class cafeteria (also on A deck) and the dining saloon, on B deck below, were divided into two smaller sections by the casing surrounding the exhaust uptake. This was a most ingenious layout and, indeed, the *Prinsesse Margrethe* was perhaps the ultimate development of the small motor liner for overnight service before the advent of car ferries. According to Kørbing:

The *Prinsesse Margrethe* had truly open-plan interiors and we had to work carefully round the existing design regulations. I wanted fully glazed bulkheads between the saloons to make a greater feeling of space, so we developed retractable fire doors which folded away into the ends of the stair towers. When you looked along the length of the ship, there was a continuous vista from one space to the next. In addition, the *Prinsesse Margrethe* had a modern fire sprinkler system throughout, so she was much safer than many another passenger vessels of her era. Neither the Americans nor the Italians used sprinklers, wrongly believing that it was better to use fireproof materials – but that couldn't stop clothing, food, bed linen or luggage from catching alight. I also designed a whole new range of furniture for the ship and special lighting, which was manufactured by Lyfa, using Swedish Örrefors crystal to give a subdued effect.[40]

One of the outstanding features of the *Prinsesse Margrethe,* and of subsequent ships designed by Kørbing, was the range of artworks integrated into its interior design to finish off vistas from one space to another. Colours were carefully selected and the judicious use of subtle shades of green, blue and grey for furnishing in the forward saloon was accentuated by reflections of the sea and sky through the generous expanses of windows. Equal attention was paid to the atmosphere of the ship at night. Indeed, each armchair was placed below an individual ceiling light, while each grouping around the perimeter had its own table light. At night, these gave a soft glow which reflected warmly in the veneered wall panelling. While the flooring, wall finishes, lighting and furniture design were the same throughout, different palettes of colours were used to give each space a distinct character.[41]

Introduced in 1957, the *Prinsesse Margrethe* was immediately hailed as being among the finest of its type and it was followed by a near-identical sister ship, the *Kong Olav V*, ordered from the Aalborg Værft for delivery in 1961. (A significant

*Serving Bornholm, the* Kongedybet *was a small overnight passenger and cargo vessel whose design built upon the established success of the pre-war* Hammershus *and* Rotna *on the same route.*

The forward-located smoking saloon
on the Kongedybet, *designed by
Kay Fisker, was oval-shaped and the
ceiling had an abstract arrangement of
concealed lighting.*

difference was that, whereas the *Prinsesse Margrethe*'s shell plating was riveted to
the frames, the *Kong Olav V* was of all-welded construction.) Yet, these two vessels
exemplified a paradox. In terms of their interior design, they appeared to represent
the latest thinking, yet, as each could only carry small numbers of cars, they were to
be outmoded and replaced by new roll-on/roll-off ferries with the same names within
less than a decade of having entered service. The world changed rapidly during the
1960s and the shipping world was forced to change with it.

Nowhere was this change felt more strongly than Britain; a nation which, in
the mid-1950s, was in many respects – housing, industry, transport – stuck to the
past with decaying infrastructure on the home front and a fragmenting empire. The
destruction and misery of World War II and the ensuing hardships endured through a
period of severe post-war austerity were interrupted by the joyous events of 1951's
Festival of Britain – and by the coronation of a young and glamorous Queen Elizabeth
II in 1953. Both occasions were enthusiastically embraced as new beginnings with
the promise of better things to come. The festival was planned to mark the centenary
of the 1851 Great Exhibition and as a morale booster, showing off what a bold new
Britain had to offer her people and the world in an age of post-war recovery.

The festival's London site on the South Bank of the Thames was, to some degree,
modelled on the Stockholm Exhibition of 1930, likewise promoting the contemporary
socialist-biased values of the Welfare State in such things as comprehensive education,
affordable new housing and the scientific and technological advancement of domestic
life. The exhibition's principal architects had been proponents of Modernism in the
1930s and of the humanistic values it embodied. Hugh Casson was responsible for
coordinating the People of Britain exhibit, a friendly and 'homely' perspective of the

*Above (top): A stern-quarter view of the Prinsesse Margrethe at sea, shortly after delivery to DFDS in 1957. Comparison between this vessel and the same company's Kronprins Olav, completed 20 years previously (see page 75) is instructive. The Prinsesse Margrethe represented the ultimate development of the overnight passenger liner prior to the advent of car ferries.*

*Above (bottom): The First-Class cocktail bar on the Prinsesse Margrethe, with decorative panels by Aagard Andersen and Svend Dalsgård.*

*Above (right): In the First-Class hallway there was a striking black and white photo mural by Keld Helmer Petersen.*

nation's populace in various walks of life at work, home and leisure. Misha Black handled the Land of Britain exhibits, presenting the United Kingdom's agriculture, industry, scientific and technical achievements. James Gardner, who had designed the Britain Can Make It exhibition in 1946, was responsible for the Festival Pleasure Gardens amusement park at nearby Battersea in a tongue-in-cheek 'Victorian' style, recalling the festival's predecessor of a century earlier.[42]

Ultimately, the nation's shipowners, along with their own design and technical departments, would look to the festival's principal architects, their colleagues and associates for the way ahead.[43] Yet, the shipowners recognised that they themselves also needed to adapt to the new trading conditions and service standards of a radically altered post-war world. (British shipowners would never have entrusted this work to such radical iconoclasts as Alison and Peter Smithson, Ernö Goldfinger or Denys Lasdun as a sense of 'good taste' and moderation also was required.)

Shortly after World War II, Sir Colin Anderson, by then knighted and also President of the Design and Industries Association, made a trip to North America with Brian O'Rorke and Orient Line's naval architect, Charles F. Morris, to see what they could learn from the new hotels and advances in railway sleeping car designs. The *Orion* had set the terms of reference for Orient Line's policies on passenger ship architecture from 1935 onwards. Brian O'Rorke was commissioned to design interiors for *Orcades*, completed in 1948 as the line's first large post-war passenger liner, as well as the larger *Oronsay* and *Orsova* of the early 1950s and, finally, the *Oriana*.

Other British lines tended to be less advanced in the architectural design of their first new post-war ships. For example, the four-ship 'Saxonia' class of intermediate North Atlantic liners, built between 1954 and 1957 for Cunard's Liverpool–Montreal services, seemed to be a step backwards, even from the architecture of the pre-war *Queens*. In official Cunard publicity material, their design approach was explained as, 'recreating the past in terms of the present by using modern methods of construction to interpret some of the gems of historical interior design and construction'.[44] What this really amounted to was retaining a traditional arrangement of public spaces, with Victorian and Edwardian era decorative frills and embellishments being replaced by a veritable panopticum of whimsical forms, colours, textures, patterns and motifs, supposedly representing someone's conceptions of modern British design.[45]

With the exception of Orient Line, which had maintained a systematic approach to passenger-ship architecture since the *Orion*, most British shipping lines appeared to be satisfied that whatever identity they had already built up through service experience would suffice to carry them forward for as long as they wished to transport passengers. There were many factions in the industry that foresaw a more lucrative future in their cargo operations and would have been content to abandon passenger service altogether.

By comparison, long-range air travel was emerging as a virtually new phenomenon, faced with the challenge of setting, rather than modernising, its image and standards of service British Overseas Airways Corporation (BOAC) foresaw that the creation of a distinctive design identity was crucial to its role of developing and promoting air travel as fast, safe and reliable to those with greater disposable income and more free time to travel and enjoy their prosperity. In 1946, the airline's chairman, Viscount Knollys, established a BOAC Design Committee, with Kenneth Holmes, principal of the Leicester College of Art, as its creative director. The committee was mandated to assert a design identity appreciable by everyone coming into contact with its facilities, services and representatives. The policy was also aimed at fulfilling the Council of Industrial Design's objectives of creating worldwide goodwill through promoting British industrial production and goods, including aircraft and other equipment and

*A corner of the First-Class smoking saloon on the* Prinsesse Margrethe, *featuring a mural on the rear bulkhead by Ole Schwalbe.*

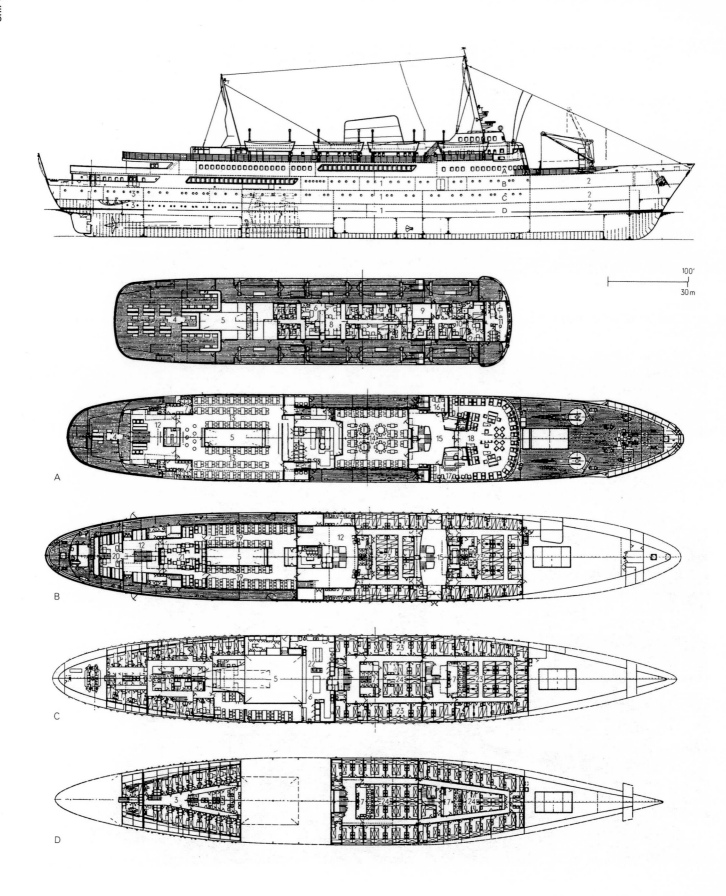

100'

30 m

A

B

C

D

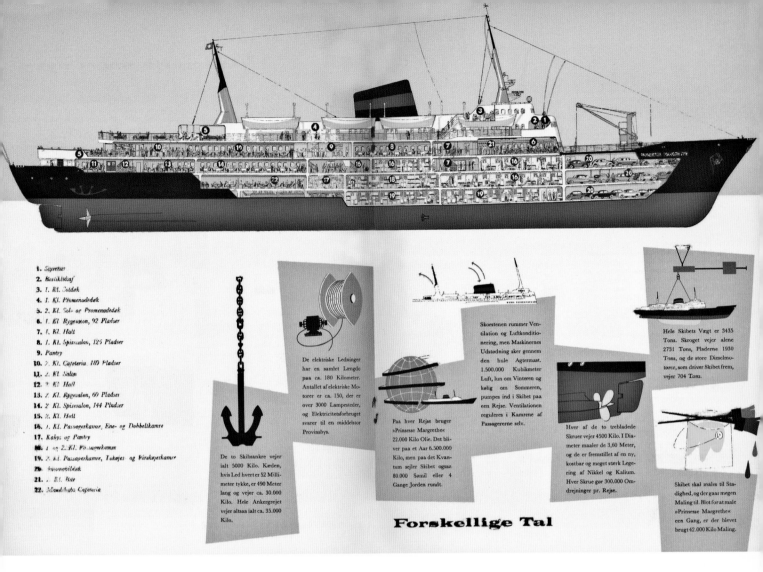

1. Styrehus
2. Bestiklukaf
3. 1. Kl. Soldæk
4. 1. Kl. Promenadedæk
5. 2. Kl. Sol- og Promenadedæk
6. 1. Kl. Rygesalon, 92 Pladser
7. 1. Kl. Hall
8. 1. Kl. Spisesalon, 125 Pladser
9. Pantry
10. 2. Kl. Cafeteria 189 Pladser
11. 2. Kl. Salon
12. 2. Kl. Hall
13. 2. Kl. Rygesalon, 60 Pladser
14. 2. Kl. Spisesalon, 144 Pladser
15. 2. Kl. Hall
16. 1. Kl. Passagerkamre, Ene- og Dobbeltkamre
17. Kabys og Pantry
18. 1 og 2. Kl. Passagerkamre
19. 2. Kl. Passagerkamre, Tokøjes og Firekøjeskamre
20. Automobildæk
21. 2. Kl. Bar
22. Mandskabs Cafeteria

De to Skibsankre vejer ialt 5000 Kilo. Kæden, hvis Led hvert er 52 Millimeter tykke, er 490 Meter lang og vejer ca. 30.000 Kilo. Hele Ankergrejet vejer altsaa ialt ca. 35.000 Kilo.

De elektriske Ledninger har en samlet Længde paa ca. 180 Kilometer. Antallet af elektriske Motorer er ca. 150, der er over 3000 Lampesteder, og Elektricitetsforbruget svarer til en middelstor Provinsbys.

Paa hver Rejse bruger »Prinsesse Margrethe« 22.000 Kilo Olie. Det bliver paa et Aar 6.500.000 Kilo, men paa det Kvantum sejler Skibet ogsaa 80.000 Sømil eller 4 Gange Jorden rundt.

Skorstenen rummer Ventilation og Luftkonditionering, men Maskinernes Udstødning sker gennem den hule Agtermast. 1.500.000 Kubikmeter Luft, lun om Vinteren og kølig om Sommeren, pumpes ind i Skibet paa een Rejse. Ventilationen reguleres i Kamrene af Passagererne selv.

Hver af de to trebladede Skruer vejer 4500 Kilo. I Diameter maaler de 3,60 Meter, og de er fremstillet af en ny, kostbar og meget stærk Legering af Nikkel og Kalium. Hver Skrue gør 300.000 Omdrejninger pr. Rejse.

Hele Skibets Vægt er 3435 Tons. Skroget vejer alene 2731 Tons, Pladerne 1930 Tons, og de store Dieselmotorer, som driver Skibet frem, vejer 704 Tons.

Skibet skal males til Stadighed, og der gaar megen Maling til. Blot for at male »Prinsesse Margrethe« een Gang, er der blevet brugt 42.000 Kilo Maling.

**Forskellige Tal**

facilities. The airline's corporate identity covered everything from the graphic design of timetables, brochures, menu cards and other printed items – including, luggage tags, match-book covers and playing cards – to the interior design of airliner cabins.[46]

As long-established as railway travel was, British Railways also foresaw the need to establish a strong corporate identity as part of its massive modernisation programme, announced in 1955. A design panel was created to assist the railway in its conversion from steam to diesel traction and the introduction of new rolling stock, and to assert modern standards of comfort, service and corporate identity in an industry whose worldwide direction was being set by the examples of Trans Europe Express (TEE) and the new Roma Termini railway station in Italy. Leading British architectural firms, including Sir Hugh Casson, Professor Misha Black's Design Research Unit (DRU), Ward & Austin and others, were commissioned to design everything from locomotives and passenger coaches to graphic items and ferries operated by the railway. The famous 'double arrow' symbol, created by DRU, was subsequently introduced as the logo of British Rail and of Sealink, as its ferry division was later to become known.[47]

Since 1948, ferries connecting Britain's rail services across the Irish Sea and with Europe via the English Channel and North Sea were designed essentially as mini ocean liners. This aesthetic was retained as car decks were introduced on the Dover–Boulogne service aboard the *Lord Warden* in 1951. The *Maid of Kent* joined the *Lord Warden* and its French-owned counterparts on the same route in early 1959 as the first ship completed under the Railway Modernisation Programme. The traditional lines of the ship's exterior belied the attractive modernity of the Ward & Austin-designed interiors, praised by the architectural press as having an appropriately workmanlike, but graceful, style with clean lines, simple forms and solid

*Above: This cut-away drawing of the* Prinsesse Margrethe *was part of the very extensive publicity material produced by DFDS to promote the ship. The funnel amidships is a dummy, only containing the ship's ventilation plant, with engine fumes being exhausted instead via the aft mast. Considered the last word in overnight passenger ship design in 1957, the vessel was quickly rendered obsolete by growing car ownership.*

*Opposite: A general arrangement drawing of the* Prinsesse Margrethe *illustrating how the placement of the engine room towards the stern enabled the forward two thirds of the cabin and public room decks to be free of blockages, opening up vistas from space to space.*

Above (top): The British Railways steam turbine car ferry Maid of Kent operated between Dover and Boulogne. The vessel was the first to be completed under the railway's Modernisation Plan.

Above (bottom): The Lord Warden was British Railways' first large car ferry on the Dover Strait and, not surprisingly, the design was developed from the railway's existing fleet of packet steamers. Nearly all were delivered from the same Clyde shipyard – William Denny & Bros in Dumbarton.

Above (right): An artist's rendering showing part of the lido area on the Brasil. Sailing into tropical waters en route to Rio, the Moore-McCormack liners offered cruise-style amenities, rather like those of contemporary tropical hotel resorts in Miami.

colours in soft tones. The hard-wearing and easily serviceable finishes and interior fittings throughout the passenger accommodations were carefully chosen and coordinated to be as attractive as they were functional.[48]

The *Maid of Kent* became the prototype for other British Rail and Sealink ferries built throughout the 1960s for various routes, as well as being a reference for the larger ships of the decade to follow. Ward & Austin's involvement in these included the design of custom-made furnishings and fittings, restaurant tableware, and a complete system for standardised cabin fabrication throughout British Rail's fleets. The firm's other shipboard work included some of the Tourist-Class interiors of the *Oriana* (1960) and the complete design of all accommodation on the Blue Funnel passenger-cargo liner *Centaur* (1964).

DRU, meanwhile, designed the owner's, passenger and crew accommodations, wheelhouse, service areas and overall silhouette of the East & West Steamship Company of Karachi's passenger-cargo liner *Ohrmazd*, as well as working with Brian O'Rorke and DRU on the *Oriana*'s interiors. Sir Hugh Casson later served as coordinating architect for the *Canberra* and was involved, both directly and indirectly, in the design of the *Queen Elizabeth 2*. These forthcoming liners – and their foreign competitors – would be among the finest yet seen, reflecting Modernism's ascent as the new orthodoxy for 1960s art, design and architecture in Britain.

In America, however, alternative approaches already were emerging and ornament was making a comeback on ships, just as it already had done in new resort hotels in Las Vegas, Atlantic City and South Miami Beach. The new 14,984-ton *Brasil* (which adopted the Portuguese spelling) and *Argentina*, built by Ingalls shipyard at Pascagoula and delivered in 1958, were the largest liners ever built in the American South. Designed by Bethlehem Ship Design to the specifications of

Moore-McCormack's vice chairman of the board, Admiral Robert E. Lee, their interior design and overall external styling was entrusted to Raymond Loewy Associates.

Their engines were sited 35ft (10.7m) further after than would otherwise be the case, dispensing with a central funnel for a pair of uptakes right aft. To balance their profiles, Loewy designed dummy 'funnels', conventionally located amidships. These were unusual in having winged observation platforms and, remarkably for American ships, private solaria for 'overall tans'. They were also the first US-built ships with Denny Brown stabliser fins and they were also the first American liners with a fully open-plan arrangement for all of the promenade deck public rooms.

Raymond Loewy's décor anticipated the forthcoming shift away from Modernism to Post-Modern revived Baroque as he used ornate grillwork and, most notably, modern interpretations of Louis XVI period furniture and candelabra in both the main lounge and deluxe suites. Some of the rooms were striking, however, especially the Deck Café, with its two-deck-high windowed wall overlooking the pool and lido. The Moore-McCormack twins were, of course, too late to matter. By the time *Brasil* was delivered on 5 September 1958, the jet age had arrived and the sea routes to Central and South America were amongst the first to suffer from this new competition.

*Above (top): The white-hulled* Argentina *shows Raymond Loewy's styling to good effect; as the exhaust uptakes were towards the stern, the funnel structure amidships actually contained a solarium for topless sunbathing.*

*Above (bottom): The aft-facing lounge on the* Brasil *had a flat white ceiling and full-length curtains, but Raymond Loewy introduced ornate brass table lamps and decorative partition screens – much as in American luxury hotels of the period.*

005: **SPACE SHIPS**

Before jet travel came to dominate, however, a final generation of passenger liners entered service. Against a backdrop of economic growth, nuclear technology, air and space travel, these vessels arguably reflected the apotheosis of the Modern Movement in ship design. Ironically, they also represented the end of an era. Generally larger – and more spacious – than the 1950s generation, they were also more egalitarian in terms of layout so that they could combine the roles of two-class trans-Atlantic liners with operating as seamless one-class cruise ships. Such planning innovations, however, depended upon commercial imperatives. While France, Italy and the United States continued generously to subsidise their trans-Atlantic flagships, Britain, the Netherlands and the Scandinavian countries were more commercially minded and it was arguably from these nations that the most progressive designs emerged – at least so far as the passenger experience was concerned.

Had World War II not intervened, the Holland America Line would have ordered a sister ship to its highly acclaimed 1938 *Nieuw Amsterdam*. The project was postponed, however, until post-war recovery and rebuilding in the Netherlands had taken place. The nation's immediate passenger shipping needs were otherwise met with smaller passenger-cargo ships and Intermediate-Class liners. These were designed with a predominance of Tourist-Class accommodation to handle the large numbers of people leaving the Netherlands – and the rest of Europe – to make new lives for themselves in the Americas and elsewhere around the globe. Most significant among these were the 15,000-ton *Ryndam* and *Maasdam* of 1951 and 1952 respectively, and the larger 24,000-ton *Statendam*, delivered in 1957 for service between Rotterdam and New York.[1]

Holland America Line confirmed in July 1952 that a new flagship liner with the flexibility to be suitable also for cruising would be built, though another three years were to pass before an order was finally placed with the Rotterdam Drydock Company in October 1956. To be named the *Rotterdam*, the new ship was to reflect a similar style of design and service as the *Nieuw Amsterdam*, by then in full stride at mid career. The new Holland America flagship was also to represent the City of Rotterdam's remarkable rebuilding and re-emergence after the inner centre was all but completely destroyed by German Luftwaffe bombardment on 14 May 1940, only five days before the Netherlands was occupied by Nazi forces.

The new post-war city centre, with its then ultra-modern port facilities, railway station, the Lijbaan shopping and commercial centre – with an exclusively pedestrian

*Below (left): An early 1950s vintage Holland America Line poster, advertising Tourist-Class trans-Atlantic services by the intermediate-sized* Maasdam *and* Ryndam. *These vessels had elliptically shaped 'Strombos' funnels – a design solution made popular by French liners of the preceding period and supposedly more efficient in dispersing smoke.*

*Below (right): Holland America Line's* Rotterdam *of 1959 had her machinery spaces aft of amidships. Where a funnel would ordinarily have been, there was instead an observation lounge with viewing platforms. The liner made a boldly modern impression in a livery of grey and white.*

Holland-America Line

S.S. MAASDAM S.S. RYNDAM
Comfort with Economy

Holland-America Line
s.s. ROTTERDAM

"It's good to be on a well-run ship"

high street – and immediately adjacent residential buildings, was an exemplar of modern post-war architecture and urban planning. The traffic-free Lijbaan quickly became a prototype for other urban commercial centres around the world. The essence of this city's rebirth as a modern European metropolis, with its forward-looking design, was also to be embodied in the new Dutch liner that would also take its name.

Moreover, having come through the destruction of war, the Dutch believed that Internationalism was infinitely preferable to jingoism and conflict. Rotterdam's harbour, at the mouth of the Rhine, was marketed as 'Europort' and overlooked by the 'Euromast' – a 'space needle' observation tower. Continuing in this vein, the theme of the new flagship was to be a grand tour of contemporary Europe. To design cultural cohesion reflected the abstract aim of De Stijl in the 1920s – and also the very real commercial imperative of attracting American passengers. While France and Italy could promote their very resonant high cultural traditions through shipboard design, the Netherlands was best known for being a flatscape, punctuated with windmills, and for producing cheese, clogs and tulips. By designing a European ship, however, Holland America would be able to offer potential passengers the best of everything – from French cuisine served on Delft porcelain to an Italian ice-cream parlour, all arranged within an abstract Modernist framework.

While Holland America's new *Rotterdam* was to sail in tandem with the *Nieuw Amsterdam* in North Atlantic service and, likewise, cruise during the winter months, the new ship was designed from the outset for dual-purpose service without compromise to her functionality in either role. The key decision was made to build the *Rotterdam* with two – rather than three – classes of accommodation for line service, with the flexibility for these to be fully integrated when cruising. This would overcome the shortcoming of three-class ships, where the perfunctory Third-Class accommodation was generally less suited for cruising than the more easily combined First and Cabin classes.

In contrast, the *Rotterdam* was planned with a consistently high standard of public amenities throughout both classes, with the delineation between the two being asserted more by a difference in scale, than by their overall quality. Thus, the First-Class domain offered larger cabins and suites, and its public spaces reflected the *Nieuw*

*Above (left): The* Rotterdam's *Odyssey Dining Room was for the use of First-Class passengers when in liner service. This magnificent double-height space was decorated with ceramic bas-relief panels by Nico Nagler showing scenes from Homer's* Odyssey, *while the ceiling was covered in rows of Delft porcelain stars and atoms. The Second-Class La Fontaine Dining Room, adjacent, was of similar design.*

*Above (right): Another consequence of the* Rotterdam *having exhaust stacks towards the stern was that an expanse of deck space atop the superstructure was available to sunbathers, as this brochure cover shows.*

143

Aboard our fabulous flagship ROTTERDAM, you'll enjoy cuisine (from many lands) that few of the world's great restaurants can equal ... gracious and attentive Old World service ... decor of breath-taking artistry ... and an exciting round of festive social activities. The ROTTERDAM truly sets a *new standard* in Continental shipboard luxury!

...one of the world's great ships!

*The First Class Smoking Room — perfect spot for a demi-tasse.*

*A soda bar, ping pong and other games make the Atlantic Promenade a favorite with the 'teen set.*

*Superb cuisine becomes even more satisfying when it's enjoyed in a setting of splendor: a ROTTERDAM dining room.*

*Comfortable furnishing, handsome decor, a sense of graciousness — these are features of all ROTTERDAM accommodations.*

IMPORTANT NOTICE

*Above (left): Promoted as 'one of the world's great ships!' the* Rotterdam *may neither have been so large nor so fast as some trans-Atlantic rivals, but the liner's design was equally suitable for crossings and cruising duties. This fold-out brochure shows the smoking room,* La Venezia, *the ice-cream parlour, a corner of one of the dining rooms and a First-Class cabin.*

*Above (right): Steamer chairs are lined up adjacent to the outdoor swimming pool on the* Rotterdam's *fantail. Above, the decks rise in tiers towards the liner's distinctive twin exhaust stacks.*

*Amsterdam*'s grandeur, while Tourist-Class featured open planning and bright colours, hopefully to appeal to younger people. Thus, as on the *Nieuw Amsterdam*, those paying less arguably experienced a more progressive form of design. Even so, nearly all cabins throughout both classes featured en-suite toilet facilities, baths or showers.[2]

In plan, the *Rotterdam* represented a significant departure from established traditions. Hitherto, the First-Class domain on trans-Atlantic liners was isolated as an exclusive 'island' amidships and the remaining accommodations and facilities were split fore and aft. In complete contrast, onboard the *Rotterdam*, First- and Tourist-Class spaces were divided horizontally on alternate decks. This meant that each class had its own promenade, boat and sun decks, a complete run of public rooms from end to end of the superstructure and cabin decks extending fully fore and aft. As a result, each class was given the impression of having the complete run of the ship to itself without being made aware of the other's existence.

A key feature of this arrangement was the *Rotterdam*'s unique central double staircase. This adopted a 'scissors' arrangement of interleaved stairways, following the example of a typical department-store escalator installation, providing interleaved access from one deck to the next. Rather than being used to segregate up and down movements, aboard the *Rotterdam*, this was adopted to allow the passengers of either class to access their respective decks, without coming into contact with those of the other class. Concealed sliding panels could be closed on each deck lobby to segregate the two interleaved stair spirals during Atlantic crossings. With the panels opened for cruises, all passengers had the complete run of the ship without any apparent evidence of the ship's decks being segregated at other times.

The inspiration for this came from a visit made to the Château de Chambord near Paris by Holland America chairman, Willem de Monchy, who was intrigued by the Renaissance palace's overlapped spiral grand staircase, designed by Leonardo da Vinci, that allowed entering and departing guests to access the king's chambers without encountering each other.[3]

The *Rotterdam* was designed with a fairly conventional steam turbine propulsion plant, located about three-quarters aft, rather than amidships, so as to allow for a greater amount of open space throughout the passenger accommodation. This was less extreme than the machinery arrangements of other modern passenger ships of the time, such as the *Southern Cross*, in which the boilers were fully astern. Although the *Rotterdam* featured divided steam and exhaust uptakes, Holland America chose to develop a more open and cohesive plan for the passenger spaces, rather than to pursue the idea of a *Normandie*-style axial plan. The great advantage of the *Rotterdam*'s machinery being located aft in this regard was that it allowed the main staircase, with its spacious deck lobbies and banks of passenger lifts arranged on either side, to be located directly amidships, where the funnel casing would have been on a conventional liner.

The dining rooms for both classes were on B deck forward and aft of the main staircase, which provided access to each separately in Atlantic service, or to both rooms while cruising. Both dining rooms aboard the *Rotterdam* featured central ceiling vaults extending up through A deck above, where these were flanked by Tourist-Class cabins to port and interchangeable rooms to starboard. The main suites of public rooms were arranged with those on the upper promenade deck allocated to First Class in trans-Atlantic service and the lower promenade deck suite serving as the corresponding Tourist-Class domain, or both strata complementing each other in cruise service. The upper promenade deck rooms more closely followed the style and ambience of the *Nieuw Amsterdam*'s First-Class interiors. Most remarkable among these were the Ambassador Club and Ritz Carlton ballroom.

*The* Rotterdam's *circular Ambassadors Lounge was an intimate First-Class nightclub. Strikingly decorated in tomato red (including a red baby grand piano), gold and midnight blue, set against dark veneer, the space was a popular venue for late-night jazz music. The furniture designs were by the Danish architect Kay Fisker. Over the years, the liner's interiors remained much as built, as this image shows.*

The Ambassador Club was circular in plan with rich palisander panelling and an ingenious concentric arrangement of a central star-shaped dance floor, ringed by an orchestra podium and cocktail bar on diagonally opposite quadrants. These focal elements were surrounded by outer lounge areas, extending off into intimate alcoves. This space, along with the dining rooms, the main staircase and central deck vestibules, was designed by an Amsterdam architect, J.A. van Tienhoven. Apart from the dining rooms, the *Rotterdam*'s Ritz Carlton was perhaps most evocative of *Nieuw Amsterdam*'s architecture, it being a double-height space with an upper balcony and a wide, curved staircase. The continuous panelled sweep of this room's forward and side walls was adorned with a mural by Cuno van den Steene in lacquered teak, depicting scenes of the Aegean Sea. The Ritz Carlton, along with the adjoining Tropic Bar cocktail lounge, were designed by the firm of Mutero & Son, who were also responsible for the library. The smoking room, by Carel L.W. Wirtz of Rotterdam, had a gently undulating ceiling, panelled in two-tone leather and wood rectangles. Full-height windows overlooking the open deck on either side and banquettes with swing backs allowed passengers to either face into the room or to gaze outwards. This ability to convert from an outward to an inward focus made the space popular both during the day and in the evening.[4]

The promenade deck spaces, intended for Tourist-Class use in Atlantic service, consisted of a spacious main lounge of asymmetrical layout which extended the full width of the ship. The floor was slightly terraced around a commodious kidney-shaped dance floor, itself set slightly off the centreline. Furniture of varying colours and shapes was arranged in irregular groupings following the varied pattern of the room's overhead lighting fixtures. To port, the adjacent Ocean Bar continued the lounge's full-height windows.

The forward part of both public decks was occupied by an egg-shaped cinema auditorium, with balcony seating for First-Class passengers and the flexibility to serve cruise passengers universally on an open ship basis, with two internal staircases joining its balcony and main levels. This was designed by the architect Cornelius Elffers, whose work ashore in Rotterdam included a bank headquarters building along the City's Blaak thoroughfare. The elegantly tiled indoor swimming pool on D deck was designed by H.A. Maaskant, who had previously designed the Rotterdam Business Centre on Stationsplein, and some of the apartment houses adjacent to the Lijbaan and the National History Museum extension in Westzeedijk. Indeed, the work of these architects helped to establish a definite architectural link between *Rotterdam* the ship and city.[5]

*Below (left): A stern view of the* Leonardo da Vinci, *the Italian Line's trans-Atlantic flagship liner of the early 1960s.*

*Below (right): The First-Class Arras Lounge on the* Leonardo da Vinci, *by Vincenzo Monaco, Amadeo Luccichenti and Nino Zoncada, had a lattice ceiling to diffuse light and a very formal arrangement of furniture.*

Indeed, the *Rotterdam*'s interiors have probably endured better than development in the city of Rotterdam from the same era, much of which has since been reworked and, in some instances, completely replaced by newer structures. Throughout its entire service life of some 40 years, the *Rotterdam* was little altered and retained the original 1950s élan. At the time of writing, the magnificent liner has been substantially restored and converted to take up a static role as a hotel and tourist attraction in Rotterdam.

Following the tragic loss of the *Andrea Doria*, Italian pride was restored with the ordering of a new national flagship, the *Leonardo da Vinci*, from the Ansaldo shipyard at Genoa-Sestri. The keel was laid on 23 June 1957 and the ship was launched and named one year later with delivery in June 1960. In nearly every respect, this was an enlarged and improved version of its short-lived predecessor and, not surprisingly, safety was the top priority. With this in mind, the four boilers were split between two separate engine rooms, each pair supplying steam to Parsons turbines, connected via gears to one of the two propeller shafts.[6] This meant that a great deal of redundancy was built in – but also that both sets of boilers were required to be fired up for the ship to operate, meaning that it was best suited to sail at a 25-knot maximum speed, rather than a slower and more economical cruising speed. In addition, the hull was immensely robust – so much so that it drew slightly more water than its designers had intended. This notwithstanding, technically and aesthetically, the *Leonardo da Vinci* was truly a Ferrari of the high seas – an extraordinarily beautiful, glamorous floating showcase for the newest and best in Italian shipbuilding, art and industrial design.

The ship had 11 decks; the superstructure – surmounted only by a single forward mast and an aerodynamic funnel – receded gracefully in a series of tiers towards the rounded spoon-shaped stern. The hull lines were fairly straight, but the bow soared upwards towards a slender clipper-shaped prow, making a striking composition. The *Leonardo da Vinci* was every inch an ocean greyhound – but it was also a most expensive ship to operate and it has been alleged that it burned more fuel tied up at the quay than many another lesser vessel used in service and, as we shall see, this had a negative impact on its long-term profitability. In the early 1960s, however, the Italian Line was less concerned by the jet age than its more northerly competitors as its lengthy sun-drenched Mediterranean route had always attracted a more leisured, cruise-orientated clientele, as well as many students and migrants in the less glamorous, but inexpensive, Third-Class accommodation. All that was to change – but, for the time being, the service was immaculate, the pasta was flawless,

*Below (left): The* Leonardo da Vinci*'s First-Class Capri Dining Saloon by Nino Zoncada featuring sculptures by Marcello Mascherini.*

*Below (right): The Paintings Cocktail Lounge on the* Leonardo da Vinci *by Monaco and Luccichenti: again, the furniture layout is rigorously formal, unlike the informal arrangements usually favoured by Pulitzer or Zoncada.*

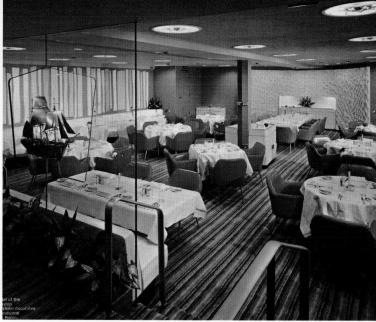

the red wine flowed and the dance bands played. So confident was the line that it even suggested that, in future, the *Leonardo da Vinci* might be converted to nuclear propulsion.

Passengers were accommodated in three classes with vertical subdivisions, forward and aft of amidships. The deck layout was designed for open-air activities, including three swimming pools, one for each class. An architectural competition was held to design the interiors with a panel of judges chaired by the art historian and critic Giulio Carlo Argan and consisting of Italian Line executives. Perhaps not surprisingly, the selected designs were mainly the work of architects with previous shipboard experience – Gustavo Pulitzer Finali, Matteo Longoni, Mario Gottardi and Nino Zoncada. Giulio Carlo Argan, however, supported Vincenzo Monaco and Amedeo Luccichenti's design proposals and they devised some of the most striking and unusual spaces. Previously, the two had designed a number of Modernist buildings in 1930s Rome, where they had continued to work during the 1950s on numerous architectural projects.[7]

On the *Leonardo da Vinci*, they produced a series of geometrically planned formal saloons for First-Class passengers. The main feature of the Arras Room was its slatted ceiling, formed of closely spaced back-lit mahogany beams which echoed the vertical wall planking. The deep Cubist lounge chairs reinforced the theme and 16 abstract wall tapestries (by Corpora, Cagli, Capogrossi, Turcato, Santomaso and Bernini) completed the remarkable décor. For cruise service, the First-Class lounges could be connected to the Cabin-Class ballroom and main lounge adjacent; these had similar furnishings with a large composition by Severini on the forward bulkhead and another, by Corpora, on the aft one. In contrast, the spaces designed by Zoncada – such as the First-Class entrance hall – were almost minimal with back-lit ceilings, glossy wall veneers and polished vulcanised rubber flooring. There, Mazzacurati created a silver embossed replica of the famous self-portrait by Leonardo, housed at the National Library of Turin. In addition, Zoncada arranged the stairwells in all three classes with abstract murals and plate-glass balustrades, and drew up the First- and Cabin-Class dining saloons. Pulitzer, meanwhile, furnished the 52 deluxe cabins.[8]

On 18 June 1960 the *Leonardo da Vinci* left Genoa to make a brief Mediterranean shakedown cruise and, on 30 June, started its maiden voyage to New York, on which service it served regularly for 16 years, interrupted only by occasional cruises to the Caribbean and elsewhere.

Italy's promotion of the *Leonardo da Vinci* as a future nuclear-powered liner was largely swagger, but it reflected a belief in ongoing technological momentum. Looking back at engineering developments during the last half-century from a 1950s viewpoint, anything, it then seemed, might be possible. Besides which, nuclear-powered military vessels were already a reality and merchantmen were on the drawing boards. The first,

and, as it turned out, one of only a handful of nuclear-powered merchant ships, the American passenger-cargo liner *Savannah* was designed by George G. Sharp Inc.'s Lorentz Hansen. In profile, the vessel was inevitably 'futuristic' – a streamlined, white 'shape of things to come' with the superstructure located aft and 'atomic' graphic designs on the topsides. The *Savannah*'s real wonder was below deck, however, viewed in the public rooms by closed-circuit television: a Babcock & Wilcox nuclear reactor. But its glories, from a design and style perspective, were the interiors.

Designed by Jack Heaney and Associates, long associated with Sharp, the *Savannah*'s accommodation required to serve more complex functions than those normally associated with 'combi' vessels, as she was also a floating showcase for American art, industry and science. Admittedly, some of the artwork was rather didactic in its theme – for example *Atomic Freedom*, 'a strong piece of abstract sculpture in steel and concrete', in the library. The dining room was striking, focused around Pierre Bourdelle's all-white sculptured mural *Fission*, located behind the Captain's table, and Jean Woodham's tall metal sculpture in the stairwell. At the entrance was a gold-plated model of the original *Savannah*, the American vessel that had been the first to cross the Atlantic using steam power. All of the cutlery, china and napery was specially designed. In the lounge, surrounded by windows on three sides, were two remarkable coffee tables, sliced from wood from the Petrified National Monument in Arizona on special loan from the National Park Service. Decking reflected the most diverse range of materials and motifs – from the unique use of non-skid ceramic tile in the enclosed promenade deck to a carpet, wrought in two different heights of pile in concentric ovals, in the lounge, which was also fitted with a brass-framed white translucent vinyl dance floor.

The *Savannah*, after the initial world-girding 'show the flag' cruises, beginning in August 1962, settled down briefly on the New York–Mediterranean run, managed by American Export Lines, but, by August the following year, the ship had ceased to carry passengers. On 10 January 1972, the *Savannah* was laid up in its namesake port. By then, it had joined most of the United States' passenger fleet in early retirement.

Like most Western European nations, France's shipbuilding programme during the years immediately after World War II had concentrated primarily on producing smaller, dual-purpose passenger-cargo vessels that could be quickly and economically constructed and put into service using readily available materials and labour. Among the better-known of these were the *Flandre* and *Antilles*, the three-ship *Viet Nam* class, completed for the Far Eastern services of Messageries Maritimes in 1951–52 and the *Jean Mermoz*, delivered to the Compagnie de Navigation Fraissinet et Cyprien in 1956 for service between Marseilles and Pointe Noire in the Congo. From a technical standpoint, the most interesting French passenger ship to be built in this period was the Compagnie de Navigation Mixte's Marseilles–Casablanca 1952

*The lounge on the* Savannah *was centred upon a translucent white vinyl dance floor. To either side, floor-to-ceiling windows gave panoramic views across the promenade decks and out to sea.*

packet liner *El Djäzair*, the 'machinery aft' arrangement of which was the reference for later aft-engined liners, such as Shaw Savill's *Southern Cross* and *Northern Star*, Holland America's *Rotterdam* and P&O's *Canberra*.[9]

One final magnificent gesture towards creating a great ship to represent national pride and identity was made when the Compagnie Generale Transatlantique's (CGT) last express trans-Atlantic liner, the *France*, was ordered from Chantiers de l'Atlantique on 25 July 1956. Among the greatest concerns in designing and building such a ship was that of producing a worthy successor to the *Normandie* within the constraints of meeting new safety and fire regulations that would preclude the creation of the earlier ship's long axial vistas through large sections of its interiors. The great variety and richness of materials available to the *Normandie*'s designers had since been circumscribed to the use of non-combustible items – including aluminium and other metals, synthetics and plastic laminates, and a small selection of specially treated wood veneers.

In essence, CGT president Jean Marie's brief was that, as ship of state, the *France* should be the largest and fastest liner ever built. In reality, however, while the ship was certainly the longest yet seen, she would never outclass the then-still-undisclosed top speed of the *United States*. As with the *Normandie*, the vessel was to incorporate all of France's latest and most advanced shipbuilding and marine engineering technology, and be a showcase of the nation's best contemporary architecture, industrial design and visual arts, as well as offering the finest French service and cuisine.

The *France*'s hull was essentially a slab-sided variant of the *Normandie*'s Yourkevitch form, the fine lines of its bow and elongated form of the cruiser stern balanced against the massif of a dominant, gently aerodynamically formed superstructure. The earlier ship's whaleback and exaggeration of the forward sheer formed by an up-sweep of the line separating the black-and-white paint scheme were repeated,

*The magnificent* France *– the world's longest liner – is manoeuvred into its berth in Southampton by at least six tugs. The liner's winged funnels perhaps reflected the start of the influence of aeronautical design on liners at the time when the jet age was beginning.*

while the new ship's modernity was asserted by smoke deflection fins extending out from the tops of the aerofoil-shaped funnels. Ironically enough, their form was, of course, inspired by aircraft wings – a sure sign that the tectonic plates of design fashionability were shifting. Where previously, the 'ocean liner style' had been widely adapted on terra firma, now ships themselves were beginning to incorporate forms inspired by air – and even space – travel.[10]

The exceptionally widely spaced arrangement of the *France*'s funnels was a result of the machinery and auxiliary-power installations being completely divided between two entirely separate runs of watertight compartments, the forward one for the outer propellers and the aft one for the inner screws. Both installations comprised their own sets of four water-tube boilers and two sets of triple-reduction steam turbines, each driving a single propeller. The combined output of both engine plants yielded a sustained top service speed of 31 knots. During the *France*'s sea trials in early 1962, a maximum of over 34 knots was reached – well short of the *United States*' record. Perhaps the greatest commendation of the ship's outstanding technical design and engineering was that, while running on trials at 32 knots, there was no noticeable vibration found anywhere onboard, and noise levels – even in cabins located directly above the machinery spaces – were minimal.[11]

While the *Normandie* and the Cunard *Queens* were officially designated as Cabin Class to allow their owners the competitive flexibility to set passage fares outside the North Atlantic Passenger Conference's prescribed First-Class fare structure, the *France* complied with the conference's highest standards for First-Class service, clearly setting the liner in an elitist role of offering a truly luxury alternative to other ships and to the prestige of fast air travel in the early years of the jet age. In keeping with the ship's high standard of luxury and service, Tourist Class was called Rive

*One of the bedrooms in the First-Class Normandie suite on the* France*: as with the liner's great predecessors in the CGT fleet, a variety of fashionable Parisian decorators were selected to create the public room and cabin interiors. While extremely elegant, the results of their efforts possessed neither the grand ornamentation of the* Normandie, *nor the Modernism of l'Esprit Nouveau.*

*Above (top): Illuminated coloured panels against a dark background create a special atmosphere around the bar in the France's Tourist-Class cabaret.*

*Above (bottom): The Tourist-Class dining saloon was a double-level space, designed by Marc Simon.*

*Above (right): The lofty First-Class Fumoir by André Arbus occupied the aft section of the promenade and boat decks. The centre section – including the dance floor – was raised, partly to give a better view to those seated inboard and partly to enable a heightened deck head in the First-Class lounge below.*

Gauche, identifying it more with the hip cachet of Paris's Latin Quarter, rather than merely as being the lesser class.

Operating on a coordinated schedule with the American superliner *United States* – and thus competing directly against Britain's Cunard – either of the two ships would sail from Le Havre and Southampton each Friday, arriving in New York the following Wednesday morning, with the eastbound departure from New York being on Thursday evening, arriving the following Tuesday evening at Southampton and early the next morning in Le Havre. In essence, this allowed both lines to offer the alternative of a sea crossing to early jet setters as a relaxing long-weekend, rather than an eight-hour trans-Atlantic flight. Yet, the *France's* two-class structure and sandwiched layout was much more like the *Rotterdam* than the very traditional three-class standard of the *United States* or the Cunard *Queens*.

A complete run of public rooms was arranged on a similar plan for each of the two classes on two vertically adjacent decks, with the First-Class suite on Pont Veranda, as the principal promenade deck was called, and Tourist Class directly below on Pont Promenade. The dining saloons for both classes were three levels below the public decks, arranged on a conventional liner plan, with Tourist aft and First Class forward.

An exceptionally wide range of public spaces was provided, with 17 rooms in First Class and 12 for Tourist. These were laid out around a centreline arrangement of funnel uptakes, engine casings, stairways and other vertical services more reminiscent of the *Ile de France* than of the *Normandie*'s axial plan. However, given that the exhaust uptakes were so widely spaced, as on the *Rotterdam*, the midships areas had a very open atmosphere. Keeping pace with current living trends of the age, the Fumoir – or smoking rooms – of each class were secondary in their significance only to the dining saloons. Fitted out with large American-style sit-up bars, these were the main centres of informal social activity, serving also as cafés and club lounges.

The First-Class Fumoir was situated aft, incorporating also an open-plan terrace-lounge overlooking the open afterdecks, with the midships-located Grand Salon being of a more formal atmosphere, primarily intended to serve as an evening venue and ballroom. Below, on the promenade deck, locations of corresponding Tourist-Class rooms were reversed, with the Fumoir amidships and the Grand Salon aft. This allowed for an upward extension of the Tourist-Class Grand Salon's ceiling above its dance floor, ingeniously creating a raised central floor area in the First-Class Fumoir above, and providing a greater sense of diversity when the public rooms of both classes were combined for cruising.

Forward, as on the *Rotterdam*, there was a double-height theatre/cinema. This was one of several 'crossover' spaces, designed for use by both classes, where passengers in each would at least glimpse the domain of the other. The universally accessible men's and ladies' hairdressing salons, infants' crèche and children's playroom, along with the teenagers' soda fountain and gaming arcade, introduced as new features to cater to a growing population of young 'baby boomers', were located forward of the First-Class rooms on Pont Veranda. This – and the shopping arcade – provided at least one spot onboard where shipboard lovers and interlopers between the two classes could quite legitimately mingle into the early hours of the morning.[12]

Jean Marie and his colleagues at CGT consulted the Société des Artistes Décorateurs (Association for the Decorative Arts) on the design, artistic direction and choice of designers and artists for the ship's completion, as his predecessor, John Dal Piaz, had done at the time of *Normandie*'s early planning. Those chosen to coordinate the new *France*'s interior design and decoration included the architect Guillaume Gillet, the artist and painter Roger Champlain-Midi and the art critic Pierre

*As with previous French liners, the First-Class dining salon was the most important public room on the* France. *Named the Chambord and designed by Darbois Gaudin, passengers entered via a grand descent into a vast chamber with a shallow dome surrounded by slightly tilted brass panels. The spectacular effect was rather similar in concept to the contemporary General Assembly at the United Nations in New York.*

DECK
PLAN
OF
S.S.
SHALOM
THE TRANSATLANTIC LUXURY LINER
ZIM

*Above (left): All of the publicity material for Zim Lines' Shalom was given a Modernist graphic treatment, reflecting the progressive identity of the liner itself, as shown by the cover of this fold-out deck plan.*

*Above (right): The Shalom is seen here dressed overall shortly after entering service on Zim's Haifa–New York route. As with several contemporaries, machinery was aft located and therefore twin stacks were fitted towards the stern.*

Mazars, along with an additional architect, M. Royon, appointed by CGT to coordinate their work with the shipyard's technical department. Among these, Guillaume Gillet (1912–87) was, at the time, also working on the Eglise Notre Dame in the town of Royan at the mouth of the River Gironde and the French Pavilion for the 1958 Brussels World's Fair. The significance of his commission for the French Pavilion in Brussels somewhat paralleled Rhulmann's involvement with the 1925 Exposition Internationale des Arts Décoratifs et Industriels Modernes shortly before he was appointed to a similar role in the *Ile de France*'s planning. Although the Brussels World's Fair was less of a purely design-orientated event, it, nonetheless, served to showcase much of what was considered to be the latest in contemporary design and living trends in the 1950s and 60s.

As with the *Normandie*, however, the need to employ established designers, appointed from the academy, to represent the nation, meant that the *France*'s decoration – while undoubtedly magnificent in scale, luxurious in quality, chic in style, sometimes quirky in manner, and, overall, very French – was also a little passé. Had it been built a decade before, it would surely have made a far greater impact on the post-war design world as a whole.

Special consideration was given to lighting and the successful combination of incandescent and fluorescent sources. Research was done on the balancing of fluorescent lighting for use in public areas, such as the lounges and dining rooms, to show the true palette of the decoration and artwork, and to avoid some tendencies of early cold-cathode illumination to distort the hues of ladies' makeup and the visual palette of various foods presented in the dining rooms.[13]

Whatever might have been sacrificed in terms of the *Normandie*'s legendary richness was amply compensated for by the use of modern materials and the fine craftsmanship that went into the *France*'s outfitting and decoration. Among the more notable individual rooms aboard the *France* was the First-Class Salle à Manger, with its futuristic-looking shallow circular dome. Passengers entered the room through frameless plate-glass doors to make the final stage of their *grande descente*, down a flight of wide red-carpeted stairs under the dome's star-lit ceiling. Around the dome, tilted brass panelling warmly reflected the light and movement below – but also echoed any noise into a cacophonous background din. The overall form of the space was actually very similar to that of the United Nations' General Assembly chamber in New York. The room's Tourist-Class counterpart was arranged on a spacious mezzanine plan, with its upper level at the main deck, where it was flanked on the port side by an outer row of cabins and, to starboard, by the children's dining room.

Perhaps most reminiscent of the *Normandie*, was the First-Class Fumoir. This room was effectively of double height, extending up into an enclosed space aft of

the boat-deck cabin accommodation. Its side walls had the same type of double-height windows as *l'Atlantique* and the *Normandie* had featured in their main public rooms, with French doors opening onto the enclosed promenade and their upper halves revealing an unobstructed view skywards at boat deck level. With elegant and comfortable seating arranged on both the First-Class Fumoir's promenade deck level and its raised central podium, where there was also a small bandstand in one corner and a centrally located dance floor, this room could accommodate a variety of different activities at any given time. André Arbus's decorative scheme was elegantly minimal, but the entire space was vividly brought to life by a single vibrant tapestry on the forward bulkhead by Jean Picart le Doux called *Les Phases du Temps* (the phases of time).[14]

Among the *France*'s most memorable Tourist-Class public rooms was the Fumoir, amidships on the promenade deck, decorated by Micheline Willimetz in warm saturated colours and with an animated atmosphere for this class's generally younger clientele to enjoy. A large mural by Sicard, depicting a night scene of revellers in Paris, provided the room's main artistic focus, and was an appropriate backdrop for couples to dance away romantic evenings at sea. With its L-shaped sit-up bar beneath a contemporary close-beamed canopy, informal asymmetrical seating plan with room dividers arranged as decorative panels, this room was truly a hub of the ship's Rive Gauche ambience.

The enclosed Tourist-Class swimming pool, gymnasium and bar, located aft on the upper deck, was covered by a Perspex dome with glass doors accessing an open deck at the ship's stern. Although there was no provision for the dome to be opened, the whole pool and bar area's flexible indoor/outdoor character was instrumental in setting the trend for other covered pool lidos with retractable glass roofs to appear later in the mid-1960s on the Soviet *Ivan Franko* class liners, and aboard the Home Lines cruise ship *Oceanic*. With facilities such as this, the *France*'s Rive Gauche passengers could enjoy the exclusive use of some of the ship's more remarkably advanced features.

In answer to the question then on many peoples minds as to why such a ship had been built at a time when there were so many new developments in commercial aviation and other modes of transport, C.M. Squarey, a noted travel critic of the day, pointed out that CGT firmly believed there would always be enough people with the time and money to be attracted to a modern ship of the *France*'s comfort, elegance and high standards of service. Though he rightly suspected that the vessel would probably never turn a profit for its owners, he believed that the subsidy of her operation by the French Government would be money well spent in promoting all that the nation offered to the world as a whole.[15] Yet, the *France* only served CGT

*The* Shalom*'s oval-shaped First-Class Circle Lounge contained groupings of Arne Jacobsen Egg and Swan chairs, set against full-length curtains and tapestry panels by Jacob Wechsler.*

with great distinction for 12 years, during which time she departed from her express North Atlantic schedules during the winter months in 1972 to make a spectacular round-the-world cruise that set a high standard for other ships to emulate, including Cunard's then-new *Queen Elizabeth 2*. In 1974, however, the newly elected government of Valery Giscard d'Estaing curtailed the *France*'s operating subsidies, with the liner consequently being withdrawn from service in September and laid up at Le Havre for four years before being finally purchased by the Lauritz Kloster Rederei of Oslo and converted for Caribbean cruising as the *Norway*.

Following the *France*'s triumphant entry into service, Chantiers de l'Atlantique was commissioned to construct a new flagship for Israel's Zim Line. Unlike France, whose national flagships were required to combine modern design with opulent reflections of a haute couture tradition, originating in Versailles, Israel was less hide-bound by establishment forces of conservatism. Indeed, the *Shalom*, like the American *Savannah*, would prove to be one of the most avant-garde passenger ships ever seen.

By the time the *Shalom* was ordered in 1962, Zim's favoured architect, Al Mansfeld, had taken on a recent immigrant from South Africa, Ben Kaplan, as a senior assistant. With a smattering of French acquired from a colleague, Kaplan and his family moved to France and settled in St. Nazaire to supervise the *Shalom* project. Kaplan was a graduate of the University of the Witwatersrand, whose architectural school was one of the pioneer Modernist schools in the world, totally committed since 1932 to the philosophy of the International Style:

*One of the Shalom's First-Class cabins: while furnishings were standard throughout, each cabin had its own mix-and-match colour scheme*

Graduates of this school were subjected to a regimen dominated by the principles and mystique of the masters of the Modernist Movement. Three aspects are particularly relevant here: from Le Corbusier's *Vers Une Architecture* we learned of the influence of ship design on the aesthetics of modern architecture; from Gropius we understood the relationship of architecture and industry; and Mies taught us that 'God was in the details'. I do not know if Le Corbusier's romance with maritime architecture was a subconscious factor in Kaplan's decision to undertake this unique project, but from his day-to-day work diary (which I have examined) his sympathetic attention to the interface of architecture and industrial design, and the care given to the smallest architectural detail, amply demonstrate that he had absorbed the school's prevailing ethos.[16]

The *Shalom* was an impressive ship, from every point of view. Approximately 638ft (195m) long, and measuring 24,500 tons, she had nearly three times the capacity of Zim's previous flagship, the *Theodor Herzl*, and could also carry more than twice the number of passengers (1,100) plus a crew of 450. Designed as a large luxury liner, linking the ports of Haifa, Marseilles, Naples, Malaga and New York, she was powered by two CEM Parsons-type geared turbines, providing a service speed of 21 knots. When cruising, passengers were reduced to 650, and the crew increased to over 500.[17]

Passenger accommodation spanned eight decks and, as with the *Rotterdam* and *France*, two classes were provided. Indeed, the *Shalom* combined the former's machinery-aft layout with the latter's circulation pattern around two main stairways,

*The* Shalom's *synagogue was particularly notable for its many installed artworks. To the left, the curtain concealing the ark was designed by Bezafel Schatz.*

*The* Shalom's *stairways were immaculately detailed and, thanks to concealed lighting, they appeared to float in front of Op Art murals by Yaacov Agam.*

located fore and aft. In addition to the functional centrality of the stairways, they were given an extraordinary visual emphasis: the main stairway, with its light 'floating' treads, was a celebration of movement and continuity of space. 'This impression,' wrote Mansfeld, 'is strongly supported by the 30ft (9m) high mural of Yaacov Agam, who took the principle of vertical and lateral movements of people on the stairs, to create a three-dimensional composition whose colours and shapes change according to the viewer's position in space'.[18]

As the name *Shalom* suggested, the vessel was themed around ideals of peace and international goodwill – aims entirely in keeping with the spirit of the Modern Movement.

Twenty-nine First-Class suites and staterooms were located on the upper deck – the 'Olive Branch Promenade' – while, on the deck below, there were the 44 interchangeable cabins. Irrespective of class, the majority of cabins had portholes and en-suite bathrooms; upper-deck cabins even had television sets – a real novelty. The cabin colour schemes were bold, with a preference for bright, but subtle, mutations of basic shades. A moulded chair upholstered in turquoise was contrasted with a couch in deep pink; a yellow chair stood next to a bed with a turquoise cover. The intent was to create an ambience of Mediterranean modernity, lightness and brightness.

The public rooms were generously proportioned, although they were, of course, restricted in the vertical dimension by the constraints of the deck heights. As with the *France*, there were essentially three categories of spaces: those for the First and Tourist Classes, and those for universal usage, which included a large theatre/cinema amidships on the promenade deck, seating some 270 patrons, with a monochromatic colour scheme of black, grey and white, contrasting with the yellow and orange upholstery of the seats. Along the side walls, at eye level, were photo murals by the graphic artist Harry Frank, depicting the history of the theatre in Israel. Opening off the foyer, adjacent, were a barber's shop, beauty parlour, and children's dining room and playroom, designed with a light whimsical touch by the English artist George Him.

Balancing the children's area, but on the port side, was a winter garden. There were detailed exchanges between Mansfeld, Gad, Kaplan, and Zvi Miller (a respected landscape architect) ranging from the specification of the modular chairs to the onboard planting. Public spaces common to all passengers also included the shopping centre and the Noah's Ark Nightclub, located below on the 'Rainbow Deck' and decorated with wittily drawn animals by the Rumanian-born Parisian surrealist Victor Brauner. The synagogue and a small interdenominational chapel (a first for a Zim ship) were one deck lower. As in all synagogues, the focus was the ark, containing the Torah scrolls. The *parochet* – or curtain concealing the ark – was decorated in embroidery and appliqué by Bezalel Schatz in 'hot' orange-browns, while the adjoining wall (by Louise Schatz) was inscribed in decorative Hebrew letters with Maimonides's 'Prayer of the Sea'.[19] The chapel, designed by Motte, a French artist-architect, was a lush gold and its ceiling consisted of open gold and white cylinders of varying dimensions. Finally, on the lowest passenger deck was a recreation facility for all passengers comprising an indoor swimming pool, steam baths, massage rooms and yet another bar.

The open-air swimming pool on the 'Lido Deck' was available to First-Class passengers only, while the main First-Class public spaces were grouped on the Rainbow Deck, comprising the Circle Lounge, the Library and the Peace Pipe Room. These were accessed by a stair, leading from the First-Class entrance hall and cabins. The Circle Lounge derived its name both from its oval shape and from the theme of its internal layout: the circular tables with their softly rounded Arne Jacobsen chairs, the circular light fittings shining through the ribbed metallic ceiling, and the round dance floor. Decorative tapestries by Jacob Wechsler, extending from floor to ceiling, echoed the circular theme with their stylised depictions of the orbs of the sun and moon. A sweep of windows extended across the full width of the ship, looking forward towards the prow. In the Carmel Restaurant, located below, the décor was the work of two artists. The Carmel theme was set by the sculptor Dov Feigin, with a long plaster relief suggesting the topography and subdued tones of the Carmel ranges, contrasting with a strongly patterned and coloured abstract tapestry by Avigdor Arikha. The First-Class dining room was served by a galley common to both classes.

The Tourist-Class dining room, the Sharon Restaurant, seating 450, was approached from the main entrance hall. There were enamel decorations in strong vibrant colours by Aharon Kahana, and long stained-glass panels by Jean David. These panels were back-lit, to simulate an external light source and to give an added

*The Shalom's main public room decks are colour coded into red (First Class) and blue (Second Class) with purple spaces available to both classes. First-Class suites fill the forward half of the upper Olive Branch Deck, with the cinema auditorium amidships and the Tourist-Class winter garden astern to port and children's play facilities to starboard. On Rainbow Deck, below, the Circle Lounge is forward with the library and Peace Pipe Room (smoking room) adjacent to starboard and the Noah's Ark nightclub to port. Amidships is the Tourist-Class Havah Nagilah Hall and The Tavern is aft, facing the lido deck.*

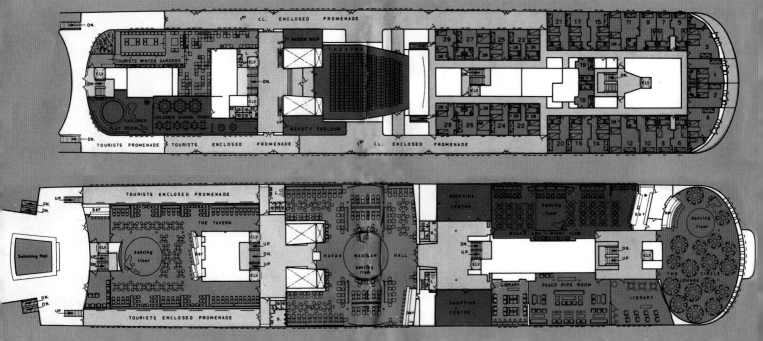

sense of space to a large, low room which, being near the waterline, had no natural illumination. Ascending two floors to the Rainbow Deck, one reached two large tourist lounges, each with its own bar and dance floor. The Hava Nagilah Hall contained two murals by the Mexican artist Rufino Tamayo, inspired by impressions he had acquired on a visit to Israel of the arid Negev Desert (in rich earthy reds, browns and gold) and the verdant Sharon plain (in soft greens). The Tavern opened up on either side to the enclosed port and starboard promenades and, towards the stern, there was a second open-air swimming pool, this time for Tourist-Class passengers. The renowned American artist Ben Shahn was responsible for the principal decorative elements in the Tavern, consisting of a tapestry and two giant mosaics.

Never before had such an unrelentingly Modernist approach been attempted on a ship. The *Shalom* was, however, very well received both by architectural critics and by the all-important New York travel trade. This was a beautiful ship, thoroughly in tune with its era. Alas, early mechanical troubles and a collision with a tanker in the Hudson River spoiled the *Shalom*'s reputation. Additionally, as this was Israel's flagship, the Chief Rabbinate insisted that the restaurants should, like all existing Zim liners, be exclusively kosher – a fact which arguably made the ship less popular with non-Jews and non-practicing Jews. When the *Shalom* went cruising, this policy was relaxed, but the ship continued to be perceived as a 'Jewish' ship, rather than an internationalist one, as the designers and Zim had also intended. In the context of the shipboard hospitality industry – as had been shown – a great deal of cultural flexibility was necessary to attract a wide audience. In the end, the jet age and the growing importance of El Al, Israel's national airline, brought a premature end to the *Shalom*'s career as a trans-Atlantic liner. Sold in 1967 to German interests, the liner became a successful cruise ship and, after consecutive rebuilds, finally was consigned for scrap in 2001. By then, practically every fragment of the original design had been eradicated and, as a final irony, the empty hulk sank off the South African coast while under tow.

As Britain already had a successful – if slightly dowdy – trans-Atlantic liner fleet, headed up by Cunard's enviable *Queen Mary* and *Queen Elizabeth*, so far as new

*Below (left): A view looking outboard between court cabins on the* Oriana: *this arrangement enabled inboard rooms to enjoy some daylight.*

*Below (right): A night-time view of the* Oriana *at Sydney's Circular Quay in the early 1960s. The liner's 'piled up' superstructure and hull massing created an aura of great power and speed.*

and innovative tonnage was concerned, attention was focused instead on express routes via Suez to Australia. Without conference agreements to dictate the provision of various categories of accommodation and attracting large numbers of youthful emigrants, the Southampton–Sydney route never had been more popular.

Among the most significant events in the post-war British liner era were the signing of contracts to build two large express deep sea liners, one each for Orient Line and P&O, on a joint service to Australia, New Zealand and onwards to the Pacific Rim, as well as Cunard's announcement of plans to replace the ageing *Queens* with a single new liner of around 80,000 tons.

Orient Line and P&O both found themselves responding to the trading conditions of a rapidly changing world, with the 1947 creation of India and Pakistan as separate Dominions and independence being also accorded the following year to Sri Lanka (Ceylon) and Myanmar (Burma). In consequence, the roles of both lines in providing the necessary government, military and postal services to these countries were curtailed. While the demand for emigrant accommodation to Australia seemed boundless, Orient and P&O found themselves facing competition from newly formed European lines, providing low-cost travel to these and many other destinations around the world using converted older tonnage.

P&O and Orient Lines decided to meet these challenges on the basis of a collaborative effort with much larger and faster ships, capable of shortening the voyage times between Britain and Australia or New Zealand by a full two weeks. The greater size of the ships themselves would provide significantly increased passenger capacities, as well as the economy-of-scale effect of increased comfort and service over their competitors' tonnage. Each of the two lines would build one ship of around 40,000 tons, with two-class accommodation for 2,000 passengers and a service speed of 27.5 knots. The great significance of this venture was that, when ordered in 1956, these were to be the world's largest new passenger ships built since Cunard's *Queens*, and that the subsequent fusion of the two owning companies would form the world's largest single liner shipping company.

The new vessels were designed and built almost completely independently from

*The* Oriana's *First-Class Princess Lounge, designed by Misha Black and featuring mural panels by John Piper, which appeared to float beneath the room's boldly modelled ceiling.*

one another, each line making its own choice of architectural design, outfitting and equipment within an overall agreement on the standards and style of service to be jointly offered. Both were of advanced structural and technical design, with welded aluminium superstructures and lifeboats neatly recessed within their sides, rather than occupying a traditional 'upper decks' location. The *Oriana* introduced a number of advances in lightweight construction derived from the aircraft industry by Vickers Armstrong (Shipbuilding) Ltd., which had first been engaged as design consultants before the building contract was signed with them. Built by Harland & Wolff at Belfast, *Canberra* was designed with the machinery fully aft rather than amidships, following the example of the Shaw Savill liner *Southern Cross*, completed by the same yard in 1955.

The *Oriana* was arguably the more 'traditional' of the two ships, by virtue of its layout with the machinery amidships, bringing about a balanced superstructure profile, the decks terraced upwards equally from the bow and stern, with the funnel and navigating bridge in close proximity to each other at its summit. The internal layout concentrated the principal public rooms on the upper decks and, as Orient Line's first fully air-conditioned ship, the promenades flanking the *Oriana*'s veranda-deck public rooms were glassed-in, rather than open-sided. Sir Colin Anderson and Ford Geddes, a company director who shared Anderson's keen interest in ship design, decided that the *Oriana*'s size and prestige warranted the expertise of leading British designers. Thus, Misha Black's Design Research Unit (DRU) was commissioned to coordinate the design of the whole ship, as well as to work with Brian O'Rorke as consulting architect for the major First-Class public rooms and with R.D. Russell and Partners, who were responsible for the First-Class dining room and the majority of cabins. Ward & Austin were engaged to design some of the Tourist-Class public rooms, including the dining room and ballroom. Although most of the *Oriana*'s architectural and interior designers were brought into the process too late to have any significant influence over the structural arrangements of the passenger spaces, the overall effect was remarkably effective and the spaces designed by DRU showed the influence of Brian O'Rorke and his earlier work for Orient Line.[20]

The *Canberra* was of a more radical plan, with the machinery sufficiently far aft that its vertical casings and funnel uptakes were, for the most part, out of the way of the passenger spaces. The liner had a more dominant superstructure, the height of which extended over a greater part of the ship's overall length. Where cargo hatches were extended up part way through the *Oriana*'s superstructure to conventional

*Below (left): Clean surfaces and a boldly patterned bedspread feature in this First-Class cabin on the* Oriana, *designed by Misha Black of DRU.*

*Below (right): A dramatic aerial view of the* Canberra *at sea: the massing of the forward mast, bridge and officers' accommodation acting as a bold counterpoint to the aft-located funnels – much as on the earlier* Southern Cross *(see page 104).*

deck openings, the *Canberra*'s Number 2 and 3 forward holds were serviced by retractable 'lateral transporters', working through hatches in the ship's sides beneath the superstructure. This alternative freed up space for passenger accommodation and facilities as an integral hotel block throughout eight decks, with a vast, virtually uninterrupted, expanse of open-air recreation space above, between the officers' accommodation and navigating bridge housing and the funnels.

From the initial conceptions, showing an upper-decks arrangement of public rooms, the *Canberra*'s design progressed to a stratified approach, with the dining rooms lowest down amidships, the promenade deck public rooms relocated to coincide with the lower lifeboat-recess location at the base of the superstructure and a third suite of more flexible daytime/nighttime spaces uppermost on the 'Arena Deck'. The promenade-deck rooms, which also served as the lifeboat muster stations were, thus, conveniently situated at the accommodation's vertical midpoint, with two tiers of cabins above and below. Yet, despite the rationale of this plan and the reduced intrusion of machinery uptakes and cargo trunkways through the passenger hotel block, the *Canberra* followed a fairly conventional arrangement of stairways and other core services along the centreline, between two parallel circulation routes from bow to stern.[21]

Sir Colin Anderson's brother, Sir Donald, who was chairman of P&O, engaged McInnes Gardner and Partners along with Sir Hugh Casson, Neville Conder and Partners as the *Canberra*'s principal architects to work in close collaboration with the line's own technical department, headed by the naval architect John West. The work was divided between the two firms with McInnes Gardner being primarily responsible for technical and operational design and Casson's office creating the majority of First-Class spaces. The architects John Wright and Barbara Oakley were commissioned to handle the cabins and Tourist-Class public rooms respectively. Casson, whose recent work with Neville Conder then included buffet and restaurant cars for British Rail, a youth hostel in London's Holland Park and new university buildings at Cambridge, worked with John West on the *Canberra*'s highly effective exterior styling. When the liner made its debut in May 1961, there was almost unanimous agreement that it was a magnificent expression of crisp, clean-lined modern British design, both externally and internally.

Casson's most outstanding *Canberra* interiors were the First-Class Meridian Room, with its adjoining cocktail bar, ante-rooms and spiral staircase, along with the

*Above (left): The Crow's Nest Lounge on the* Canberra *was bright and spacious, offering commanding views over the liner's bow. Here, passengers recline on metal-framed Bertoia chairs.*

*Above (top): The* Canberra's *Pop-Inn was a teenage room with cartoon murals by David Hockney burned onto the wall panelling using a soldering iron. Perhaps fearing that youthful passengers might use cigarette lighters to extend this treatment elsewhere onboard, P&O had the murals removed after a single return voyage to Australia.*

*Above (bottom): The Cricketer's Tavern was a modern pub decorated with cricket memorabilia: it remained one of the* Canberra's *most enduring rooms.*

The Canberra's Tourist-Class Island Room
was an uncluttered and informal white space
– save for bright murals on the bulkhead.

*Previous pages:*

*Page 164 (top left): The* Canberra's *Bonito
Pool had a terraced surround, the curving
shape and colours of which were slightly
reminiscent of Berthold Lubetkin's Penguin
Pool at London Zoo.*

*Page 164 (top right): As befitted a liner
completed in the space age, the* Canberra's
*playroom was even equipped with a rocket for
young would-be astronauts to enjoy.*

*Page 164 (bottom): The* Canberra's *First-
Class Pacific Dining Room featured a lowered
centre section. The neat ceiling lighting
strips around the perimeter were particularly
effective in creating an intimate atmosphere
by night, when the curtains were drawn.*

*Page 165 (top): The view forward
from the* Canberra's *aft-most Tourist-
Class swimming pool, looking towards
the funnels and the glazed aft bulkhead
of the Alice Springs Lounge.*

*Page 165 (bottom): The Peacock Room was
a Tourist-Class lounge whose brilliant blue
ceiling and upholstery contrasted with wood
veneer panelling. The white floating ceiling
was removed early in the* Canberra's *career.*

Bonito Club ballroom and adjoining lido. Both of these were designed as integral open-plan spaces that readily adapted themselves to a variety of activities throughout the daytime and evening hours. They were highly sophisticated interiors, even by the standards of today's cruise ships. The Bonito Club, located among the upper strata of public rooms on 'Stadium Deck', was designed as a light and bright space to serve as an informal daytime lido café and lounge, becoming an elegant ballroom in the evening hours. The space ingeniously dissolved its indoor and outdoor activities by way of a glass wall that was hydraulically lowered to the floor, seamlessly bringing its large teakwood dance floor together with the lido, planked in the same wood. A series of terraces to either side and aft of the pool itself served to carry the connection onwards and upwards in several stages to the open-air deck above. Daytime food and beverage service was dispensed from an adjacent pantry, serving alternatively as a bar for evening dances and parties.[22]

The Meridian Room on promenade deck was designed as an open-plan space, encompassing also the intimate Century Bar, accessed through concealed doors. Also out of sight, yet still within earshot of the central space, were the writing room and library, arranged as a pair of anterooms further aft. Access to these from the Meridian Room was by way of sliding glass partitions, opening inwards from the outer walls overlooking the promenade. The arrangement created the remarkable visual illusion of infinite spaciousness – seemingly uncontained by internal boundaries – with its extremities melding into the areas beyond. Forward, a spiral staircase was undoubtedly one of the *Canberra's* most visually stunning interior features, it being a graceful helix in white marble and anodised aluminium inside a cylinder of dark oiled Indian laurelwood, rising from the Meridian Room through four decks to the Crow's Nest observation lounge. The only source of illumination was from fluorescent tubes concealed inside the aluminium-clad balustrades, reflecting light upwards from the white marble stair treads.[23]

John Wright's Tourist-Class public rooms essentially reflected the same design values and quality of outfitting although, by their nature, they tended to be less formal. Consideration was given to these spaces having to cater to the needs of far greater numbers of people, mostly younger, of whom a large proportion would be making their way to Australia on 'assisted passages' to make new lives for themselves and their families. Arguably, the *Canberra*'s most charming and enduring Tourist interior was the Cricketer's Tavern, designed on a sports theme, but without either being overly masculine or resorting to kitsch. The teenage Pop-Inn was another remarkable, but short-lived, space. This had Pop Art 'graffiti' murals by David Hockney, who used a hot soldering iron to burn them into the wall veneer. Perhaps fearing a ship-wide outbreak of similar 'vandalism', P&O had them removed shortly after the *Canberra* entered service.[24]

Cabins were an important design concern for both the *Canberra* and *Oriana* and these were planned to achieve a remarkably high capacity for First Class, as well as amply catering for the substantial emigrant trade. The approach adopted for both ships was remarkably similar, incorporating ideas from the P&O and Orient Line design teams. A 'court cabin' plan was adopted by the *Canberra*'s designers, inspired by the 'air light' system originally developed by the American naval architect George G. Sharp as early as 1927 and subsequently used on a limited scale in a number of US-flag ships, as well as the Italian Cosulich liner *Saturnia*. The *Canberra*'s court cabins were arranged in groups of four to eight on either side of a lateral access passage that widened progressively at each pair of rooms, creating a small internal court or veranda with windows in the ship's side. These admitted 'borrowed' daylight to the inner rooms through vertical ribbon windows facing the court where

*The* Canberra's *magnificent First-Class spiral staircase had brushed-metal balustrades with a continuous lighting trough set into their underside.*

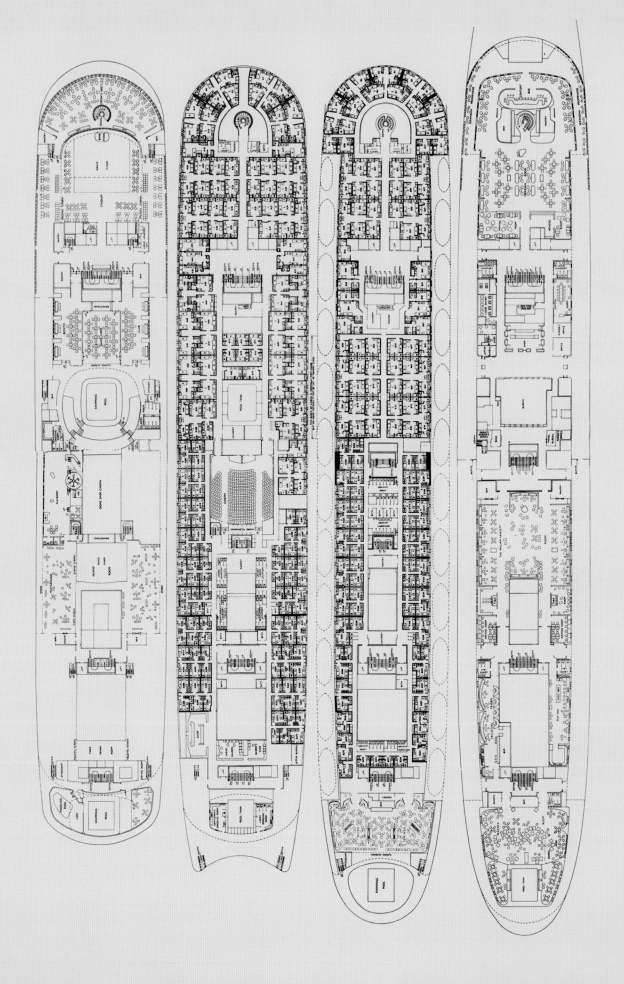

the passage widened. The court plan was also adopted on a less extensive scale aboard the *Oriana* for intermediate-grade First-Class accommodation where, rather than widening the court alley, a 'sawtooth' arrangement of the walls was adopted to admit daylight to the inner rooms.

Both ships were designed to carry large numbers of emigrant passengers in accommodation of a fairly basic standard. To increase the suitability of these cabins for other services including cruising, Orient Line's naval architect, Charles Morris, borrowed from railway sleeping car design to devise an ingenious convertible room. This could serve as either a four-berth cabin without facilities or a two-berth room with a shower and toilet compartment revealed when one pair of upper and lower berths was folded away. A cabin steward could easily make the change single-handedly by raising the upper bunk into the ceiling and folding the lower berth on end into the adjacent wall. A concealed partition with its own door slid into position, segregating the en-suite cubicle from the cabin proper, with its two remaining berths.[25]

Italy's state-owned Lloyd Triestino was a serious competitor to Britain's P&O and Orient Line in the Australia trade. Lloyd Triestino's finest liners were undoubtedly the superb *Galileo Galilei* and *Guglielmo Marconi*, delivered from the Cantieri Riuniti dell'Adriatico in 1963–64. Designed by Nicolò Costanzi, their hulls brought new profiles to the Italian fleet. They had unusual bow designs which were concave near the waterline, but convex higher up, giving a wine-glass profile when viewed head on and a distinct swan-neck shaped prow when seen from the side. Measuring 27,900 tons and 702ft (214m) in length, they had modern accommodation for as many as 1,647 passengers – but only 289 were First-Class berths, reflecting their predominantly emigrant clientele. The *Guglielmo Marconi*'s First-Class interiors were the work of Romano Boico, while Aldo Cervi, Vittorio Frandoli, Matteo Longoni and Umberto Nordio designed the Second-Class accommodation.[26] Spaces by Boico and Longoni, in particular, were characterised by their hard-edged angularity and by dark, rich textures for wall and ceiling finishes. Indeed, the fact that the ships had relatively low deck heights must have persuaded the architects to devise multi-layered ceilings, alternately with floating panels and lighting troughs to give an illusion of extra height and to prevent the larger Tourist-Class saloons from feeling oppressive. Gustavo Pulitzer Finali designed several major public rooms on the *Galileo Galilei*.[27]

Capable of a top speed of 27.5 knots, these ships also brought greatly improved standards to the predominantly low-fare Australian migrant trade. Replacing the

*Above (left): The forward-facing First-Class lounge on the* Guglielmo Marconi. *The liner's First-Class interiors were characterised by their striking angularity of form.*

*Above (top): This builder's trials photograph of the* Guglielmo Marconi *emphasises the liner's attractive lines. Note the swan-neck bow profile (concave near the waterline and slightly convex higher up), a feature typical of Italian liners designed by the naval architect Nicolò Costanzi in the 1960s.*

*Above (bottom): The ballroom on the* Guglielmo Marconi. *In many spaces, the liner had remarkable three-dimensional ceiling finishes and lighting treatments. As with all Italian liners, contemporary artworks formed an important part of the decorative schemes.*

*Opposite: A general arrangement drawing showing the* Canberra's *superstructure layout. Of particular note is the circular treatment of the forward section, similar to Delta Line's post-war passenger-cargo liners, illustrated on page 106.*

earlier 'Australia' class, they could make the passage from Genoa all the way to Sydney via Suez in just over three weeks. Both ships were later converted for cruising and each survived well into the 1990s – the *Guglielmo Marconi* being converted by Mariotti in Genoa into the *Costa Riviera*.

Apart from Lloyd Triestino, which was well-established, other Italian shipping entrepreneurs who found a lucrative niche in the migrant trades to Australia were the Lauro Line, the Sitmar Line and the Cogedar Line – all of which operated rebuilt second-hand tonnage. They also made the transition into the cruise business during the 1970s. Cogedar's *Flavia* was radically converted in 1961–62 from the Cunard passenger-freighter *Media* into a well-appointed, fully air-conditioned passenger liner with interiors by Matteo Longoni. Indeed, following this work, it would have been difficult to tell that the ship had been anything else.

In the mid-1960s, no less than four outstanding and innovative trans-Atlantic liners, amongst the last of their kind, were delivered from Italian shipyards. Indeed, these were arguably the ultimate expressions of the ocean liner, Italian style. One reason for such largesse well into the jet era was political, in that the Italian Government wanted to create employment in its shipyards and also for seafarers. Moreover, the veteran 1920s ex-Cosulich motor ships *Vulcania* and *Saturnia* remained in frontline trans-Atlantic service almost 40 years after their initial delivery, and were long over-due for retirement.

Their replacements were to prove arguably the most expensive, dramatic, dazzling white elephants in the history of passenger shipping. Ordered from the Sestri Ponente shipyard in Genoa and the Cantieri Riuniti dell'Adriatico at Monfalcone respectively, the *Michelangelo* and *Raffaello* were remarkable vessels. Technically, they were of the best, following on from the *Leonardo da Vinci*, but with many further improvements. Equally, they were noteworthy for being astonishingly backward-looking in conception at a time when other trans-Atlantic operators were diversifying with dual-purpose liner-cum-cruise ships (such as the Norwegian *Sagafjord* and the British *Queen Elizabeth 2*). In contrast, the new Italian vessels were intended purely for year-round trans-Atlantic service. Thus, to offer better storm protection, few cabins in the hull had portholes and so most were effectively inside rooms. Furthermore, there was a rigorously imposed three-class vertical segregation of the passenger facilities. The Third-Class was frankly spartan. It was adequate for express liner operations, but would not have been acceptable for long cruises.

*Below (top): The* Galileo Galilei*'s First-Class dining saloon: the ceiling and wall finishes are richly textured in contrasting ceramic and veneered finishes.*

*Below (bottom): The newly completed* Galileo Galilei *makes a fine sight at sea in this mid-1960s photograph.*

*Below (right): Leaving Genoa, the* Michelangelo *passes an inbound Tirrenia vessel in this mid-1960s scene. The liner's twin-lattice funnels were immediately recognisable, but served the very practical purpose of keeping smoke and soot clear of the after lido decks.*

Putting these obvious criticisms to one side, however, there is no doubt that, in terms of their external appearance and the design of their First-Class public rooms, the new flagships were amongst the most striking yet seen. Initial renderings suggested that the ships would appear as enlarged twin-funnel versions of the *Leonardo da Vinci*, but research carried out at the Turin Polytechnic on aerodynamics and smoke dispersal suggested that radical lattice-work funnel casings should be utilised, surmounted by plate-like smoke deflector fins to allow air to blow beneath and so prevent downdrafts sucking soot and gases onto the extensive lido areas, amidships and aft of the funnels.[28]

Furthermore, the hull lines were straight, except for the bows which had considerable sheer. Apart from giving an aggressively muscular character to the vessels, this also made them rather stiff and unyielding in stormy weather. Thus, although impressively stable, they allegedly suffered stresses and strains in high waves. Indeed, during one particularly severe storm in the spring of 1966, the *Michelangelo* was seriously damaged by an exceptional wave which ripped off most of her bow bulwark and punched a 30ft x 60ft (9m x 18m) hole in the forward superstructure. Two passengers and one crew member were killed as a result. Thereafter, extra steel reinforcement was built into both ships.[29]

As with the *Leonardo da Vinci*, an architectural competition was held to design the interiors, with submissions by invitation only. On the *Michelangelo*, Vincenzo Monaco and Amedeo Luccichenti planned an extensive complex of First-Class rooms in collaboration with Nino Zoncada. Unlike previous Italian liners, very little woodwork was used; instead, aluminium ceilings were contrasted with colourful wall finishes, abstract artworks and typically Italian velour- or leather-clad Cassina armchairs on pedestals. The most remarkable interiors on the *Michelangelo*, which was decoratively the more hard-edged of the two sisters, were the First-Class ballroom and the cocktail bar. The former had a double-height central section above the dance floor with three enormous Lucite chandeliers. The Fiorenza Lounge, adjacent, featured a tapestry by Giuseppe Capogrossi. The cocktail bar had a dark blue open lattice ceiling with rather sinister black leather lounge chairs and tan padded leather wall coverings.[30]

Gustavo Pulitzer Finali designed the First-Class dining rooms and hallways, making interesting use of three-dimensional finishes with built-in glass chandeliers to create interest in what were relatively low-ceilinged spaces. Giulio Minoletti designed the group of Tourist-Class public areas, having planned similar accommodation on the

*Below (left): The* Michelangelo*'s First-Class Mediterraneo Cocktail Bar by Monaco and Luccichenti featured an irregularly shaped bar counter snaking around two sides and rather sinister black leather chairs.*

*Below (right): The* Michelangelo*'s First-Class swimming pool was located ahead of the funnels. Taking a more southerly route from Genoa to New York, the liner had three pools, one to serve each class.*

*Above (left): The* Michelangelo*'s First-Class Florence Ballroom by Zoncada, working with Monaco and Luccichenti, was dominated by three large Lucite chandeliers and tapestry panels designed by Tranquillo Marangoni in collaboration with Zoncada.*

*Above (right): The spacious First-Class Miami Veranda featured the polished rubber flooring and armchairs on splayed metal legs so typical of Italian liners of the 1960s.*

*Leonardo da Vinci.* The principal outdoor spaces were the work of Matteo Longoni, who created the lido areas for the three classes in his distinctively angular style with free-form mosaic surrounds to the swimming pools, diving platforms and adjacent cocktail bars. The Italian Riviera truly went to sea on these ships.[31]

In contrast with the *Michelangelo*, the sistership *Raffaello* was rather softer in manner with curvilinear forms predominating and more homely comforts. The main lounges were assigned to the group that included the Rome-based architects Attilio and Emilio La Padula, who had worked on the *Andrea Doria*. In the Cupola Ballroom, a space dominated by chandeliers in circular aluminium frames, a dense pattern of aluminium grilles covered the walls and, around the bar, extensive use was made of abstract tapestry panels to focus attention. The same architects also created the principal Tourist-Class areas in similar style to the First Class. Michele and Giancarlo Busiri Vici, also based in Rome, acquired their first and only experience in marine outfitting on the *Raffaello*, designing the First- and Tourist-Class hallways, stairwells and the dining saloons of all classes. The white ribbed ceilings, formed of interconnecting circular mushrooms, grew from trumpet-shaped columns – giving a remarkably fresh and spacious effect. Trieste-based architects – Aldo Cervi, Vittorio Frandoli, Umberto Nordio, Gigetta Tamaro, Luciano Semerani – designed the principal Third-Class spaces.[32]

Overall, despite their dramatic appearance, the *Michelangelo* and the *Raffaello* were of dubious merit; their most luxurious First-Class interiors were grand and glitzy in the great ocean liner tradition – an era that was dying by the time they appeared on the scene. Their lesser interiors were often banal – did Italian national identity in ocean liners matter any longer? Despite their expense, Italian architecture and interior design magazines failed to mention anything about the ships' interiors at all.

Moreover, the oil crisis of the early 1970s made sailing *a tutta forza* at 25 knots plus increasingly uneconomic. In 1975 the inevitable happened; the *Michelangelo* and the *Raffaello* were withdrawn, stripped of their artworks and laid up. Norwegian Caribbean Line turned them down, convinced that their lack of outside cabins and convoluted three-class accommodation precluded them from ever becoming economic propositions as cruise ships. Instead, they were sold in 1976 to the Imperial Iranian Navy for use as barracks ships in Bandar Abbas and Bushire respectively. The *Raffaello* was destroyed by aerial bombardment during the Iran-Iraq war, and the latterly decrepit *Michelangelo* was sold to Pakistan for scrap in 1991.[33]

The *Leonardo da Vinci* had been taken out of service in 1977 also due to unacceptable operating costs and, after being laid up for a period, was transferred to the fleet of Italia Crociere Internazionali SpA (ICI). This was a company financed by public and private money, created to employ Finmare ships in the cruising sector. So, the ship re-crossed the Atlantic and was used for a period for short voyages to the Bahamas, from Miami and from New York. The results were not encouraging and new losses were incurred by ICI, forcing them to lay up the ship in the gulf of La Spezia in 1978. Here, the neglected vessel was gutted by a fire started on 3 July 1980, and sank in shallow water. Salvaged in 1981, the wreck was sent to the breakers in May 1982.[34]

While the Italian Line could, at least for a time, enjoy largesse with the benefit of generous state subsidy, privately owned shipping lines required to think more pragmatically. Home Lines was one of the most innovative and a truly international operation; initially Greek, Swedish and Italian owned, but flying the Panamanian flag, its head office was in Switzerland, but everything else – from the architecture to the staff and cuisine – was Italian. Backed by the Swedish American Line, the Italian Cosulich family and the Greek Eugen Eugenides, the company had emerged in the aftermath of World War II in the migrant and tourist trades to North and South

*An elevation and general arrangement drawing of the* Michelangelo's *upper decks, showing the liner's straight-lined mid-body and also the rather complex series of vertical divisions into three classes. Consequently, the liner was not easily operated as a one-class cruise ship.*

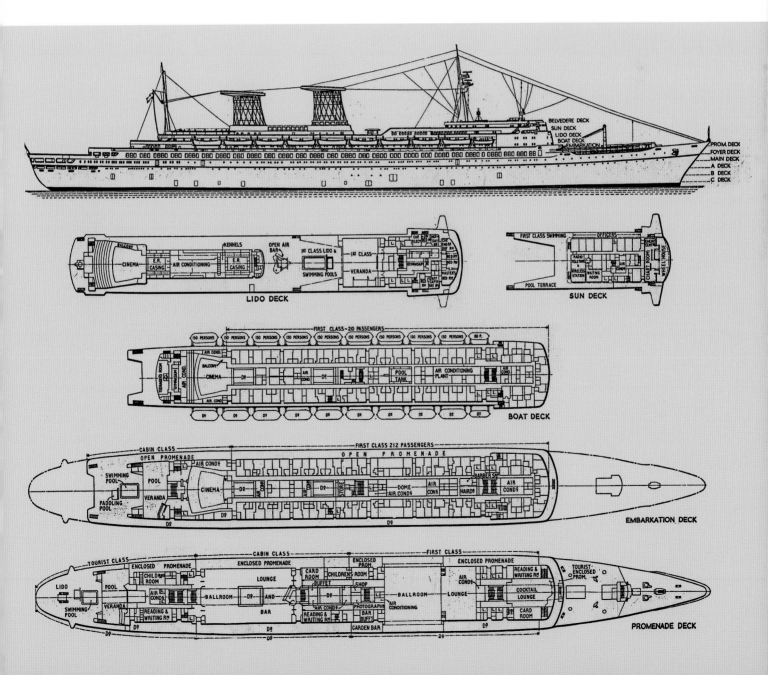

America with a motley collection of former-Scandinavian vessels, mainly dating from the 1910s and 20s. Added to these were two former American Matson liners, the *Atlantic* (ex *Matsonia*), acquired in 1948, and the *Homeric* (ex *Mariposa*), purchased in 1953. The two were extensively modernised by Home Lines and placed on its trans-Atlantic routes from Italy to the United States and Canada.[35]

With optimism – but also an eye on the future – Home Lines ordered its first major new building from the famous Cantieri Riuniti dell'Adriatico shipyard at Trieste for delivery in 1965. The *Oceanic* was also intended for trans-Atlantic operation between Genoa and Montreal but, by the time she was delivered, that trade was in decline and so the ship was placed on year-round cruising from New York. Fortunately, Home Lines and its architects had shown greater foresight in designing the *Oceanic* than the Italian Line had with its most recent liners, and it proved an ideal cruise ship. Indeed, it was claimed in publicity material that this was the first liner purpose-built with cruising in mind. That was not strictly true, but the ship's entire layout was most innovative and it was the first to introduce many of the features found on cruise vessels entering service even today.

Thanks to a notably efficient hull form devised by Nicolò Costanzi, the *Oceanic*'s three boilers in a single machinery space, driving sets of geared turbines, were much more economic than the power plants of the Italian Line rivals. Indeed, the hull was a creation of majesty and of beauty. As with the earlier *Guglielmo Marconi* and *Galileo Galilei*, the bow was shaped like a swan's neck with a bulb below the waterline. Amidships, the sides gently sloped outwards towards the waterline to enhance stability and, aft, the sheer of the stern was almost as pronounced as that of the bow. Although spoon-shaped above the waterline, a transom below increased the effectiveness of water flow over the propellers. This design was used by Costanzi on subsequent vessels – and was revived by the British naval architect Stephen Payne in his designing of the stern for the giant 2004 Cunard flagship, the *Queen Mary 2*. Payne has observed that, in terms of speed and fuel economy, the *Oceanic*'s hull was one of the most effective ever built for a passenger ship.[36]

The hull was surmounted by a long, low superstructure in receding layers with the lifeboats nested in recesses above the promenade deck and below the ship's most remarkable feature – the full width lido area, which filled the greater part of the upper deck amidships. This was protected by glazed screens on either side and from above

The launch of the Raffaello at the Cantieri Riuniti dell'Adriatico shipyard near Trieste on 24 March 1963.

by a retractable glazed magradome roof, making it usable all year round. The lido itself contained two oval-shaped bathing pools in free-form mosaic surrounds with shallow water in which to relax. The decking was laid in a 'crazy paving' pattern, like the terrace of a contemporary hotel on the Italian Riviera; with tables under colourful parasols and groups of loungers. It was a real 'sun trap' and the prototype for the lidos of many subsequent cruise ships. The bridge and officers' accommodation were piled up forward with the funnel aft. Both in arrangement and appearance, the ship was clearly inspired by the 1961 British liner *Canberra*, completed shortly before the *Oceanic* was designed. Aft, the sun decks were arranged similarly to those of the pre-war French Liner *Normandie* with a series of receding curved tiers.[37]

The *Oceanic*'s interiors were largely the work of Nino Zoncada with other famous Italian architects – such as Ponti and Pulitzer – designing suites and individual public rooms. Incidentally, the ship's most exclusive cabins, abaft the bridge, had their own private verandas. This was not an innovation as the *Vulcania* and *Saturnia* had featured these, but it was to be another feature of many subsequent cruise ships. Unlike the Italian Line vessels, the *Oceanic* was planned as a two-class liner but, when operating as a single-class cruise ship, it was nearly impossible to spot where the divisions lay.

The *Oceanic* was more internationalist than most, both in ownership and in terms of Zoncada's chosen theme for the interiors. This was the era of the United Nations, the construction of the World Trade Center (representing international Modernism at the service of global commerce) and of the nascent European Commission. Consequently, the aim was to give the *Oceanic*'s American passengers a grand tour of European culture from the moment they stepped onboard – albeit one with a heavily Italian accent. The nominally First-Class public rooms were located forward of the lido, comprising the Eden Roc cocktail bar and Escoffier dining room. The Montmartre Club, the ship's late-night venue for music and dancing, was located aft, overlooking the stern and the ship's wake. Adjacent was a teenage discotheque of very original design, called the Fun-o-rama. Throughout, the main passenger stairwells were on either beam, which opened up unobstructed vistas from one space to another through plate-glass partitions. These stairwells were adorned with metal and ceramic bas-reliefs, depicting famous European monuments and characters. White laminate panelling, polished rubber flooring, matt brushed-aluminium railings

Home Lines' splendid Oceanic is seen in the Hudson River in New York in the early 1970s. As with Canberra, the liner had machinery aft and nested lifeboats to open up the full width of the topmost superstructure decks for recreational purposes.

and plate-glass balustrades made for a cool and stylish environment which the Oceanic's passengers probably considered to be the last word in European design sophistication.

The principal public rooms were located on the promenade deck and comprised two large ballrooms – the Italian Hall and the Aegean Room (by Pulitzer) – forward and amidships, with the Skäl Bar and Europe Observation Lounge aft. The fore and aft spaces were oval-shaped, following the curving and slanted forms of the superstructure and these forms were visually reinforced by cove-lit ceilings, arranged in concentric rings and focusing attention on the dance floors. Bright velour-clad furniture, abstract artworks and festoon blinds completed the effect – perhaps these spaces were the ultimate expressions of Zoncada's Italian shipboard aesthetic in that they connected the forms and structural elements of naval architecture to the passengers' activities and to the glamorous social world of liner travel.

Filling the hull two decks below was the main dining saloon – one of the largest single span spaces on any ship, its vast rectangular ceiling dome punching through to the deck above. It was a memorably impressive space – all the more so as the ceramicist Emanuele Luzzati encrusted the walls and the ceiling dome with abstract tiles and decorative panels. The tables in the middle of the room were circular and arranged in groups of three around lighting standards with three shaded globes on arms to light each group individually.

New Yorkers took the Oceanic to their hearts and, over the next 16 years, the vessel developed a peerless reputation for its luxury, relative affordability and, above all, for the warmth and charm of the Italian officers and crew. Indeed, by the latter 1970s, it was the only large liner sailing regularly from the city, all year round. In 1981, the Oceanic was sold to Florida's Premier Cruises and, since 2001, it has operated in the Mediterranean for the Spanish firm Pullmantur. Nowadays, it is the last of the great Italian liners to remain in operation – although little remains of the original interior design.

Thereafter, a miniature diesel-driven version of the Oceanic, named the Italia, was ordered from the Cantieri Navale Felszegi at Muggia, near Trieste, by a group of business entrepreneurs. Unfortunately, both the owner and the yard went bankrupt during construction and so the entire project was taken over by the major creditor – the Banca Nazionale del Lavoro, which completed the vessel through a subsidiary company in 1967, then chartered it out to other cruise operators. Measuring only 12,219 tons (compared with the Oceanic's 39,200 tons), the Italia was intended to carry 452 passengers – about the load of a wide-bodied jet aircraft. Fly cruising was seen to be the future – but the *Italia* was Pulitzer's swansong project and he died in 1967, shortly before the liner was delivered, after more than 40 years of producing consistently remarkable shipboard designs.[38]

The design of the 1966 Costa Line flagship *Eugenio C.* owed much to the *Oceanic*, it being the work of the same team of naval architects and designers, and constructed in the same shipyard. As with the *Oceanic* and the *Italia*, the *Eugenio C.* was to prove an enduring success. This new vessel for Costa Line's express service from Genoa to South America was somewhat smaller than the *Oceanic*, measuring 30,567 tons. It was, however, every bit as aesthetically pleasing and effective – three boilers and two sets of steam turbines generating 60,500 horsepower and enabling it to sail at 27 knots with ease. Indeed, the *Eugenio C.* was the fastest, largest and most glamorous liner on the South Atlantic. Costanzi and Zoncada collaborated on the design – even working together on the styling of the exterior profile which was rather more curvaceous than the *Oceanic* and with twin funnels towards the stern. As with the *Michelangelo* and *Raffaello*, these were the result of further research into smoke dispersal at the Turin Polytechnic and the idea was

*The* Oceanic's *sheltered lido deck amidships contained two splash pools, the abstract surrounds of which had shallow water in which to paddle. A retractable glazed magradome roof (here pictured in the open position) allowed the space to be used all year round – important on a cruise liner sailing regularly from New York.*

EUGENIO C

*Above (left): The* Eugenio C., *like its older fleet mate, the* Federico C., *had three outdoor pools. Here, we see the Second-Class lido area, aft of the liner's twin funnels.*

*Above (right): The* Eugenio C. *steams towards the camera in this dramatic 1960s photograph. Unlike the straight-lined* Oceanic, *this liner had considerable sheer. Note too the pronounced tumblehome (inward slope of the hull topsides) amidships and how the funnels slope outward.*

*Previous pages:*

*Page 178 (top): The Fun-o-rama teen room on the* Oceanic *had terraced flooring with cushions on which to lounge.*

*Page 178 (bottom): The* Oceanic's *lido area with the magradome roof in the closed position.*

*Page 179 (top): The view aft from the* Oceanic's *port bridge wing: note the cabins with private verandas and glazed partition screens in the foreground. Today, the latest generation of cruise ships have a majority of 'staterooms' with verandas – but the* Oceanic *was among the first to boast this feature.*

*Page 179 (bottom): Designed by Nino Zoncada, the* Oceanic's *main dining saloon was encrusted with ceramic panels by Emanuele Luzzati.*

that exhaust could be routed though one stack or the other to ensure smoke blew downwind of the ship.[39]

As Zoncada had exclusive control of the interior design, the *Eugenio C.* also was more coherent than its Italian Line contemporaries, whose passenger spaces had tended to be the work of many hands. Most of the public rooms were located on the lounge deck, interconnected within each of the three classes through glazed partitions. Each saloon took its name and decorative theme from a precious or semi-precious stone and, as with previous Zoncada designs, the work of modern Italian artists was prominently displayed – a panel by Massimo Campigli in the oval-shaped First-Class Ambra Lounge, tapestries by Emanuele Luzzati in the Rubino Lounge and bas-relief sculptures by Marcello Mascherini in the Turchese and Opale Lounges, further aft. One deck below, the dining saloons were far less ostentatious than on the *Oceanic*. Three relatively modest but elegant spaces were located forward, to starboard and aft of a single large galley to port. All were single-height with cove-lit pegboard ceilings and with structural columns encased in brushed aluminium. The First-Class 'Flauto Magico' restaurant was particularly fine and showed how Zoncada could achieve striking effects even in rectangular, low-ceilinged shipboard spaces through the judicious choice of colours and the thoughtful placement of furniture and lighting.[40]

On 31 August 1966, the *Eugenio C.* set sail from Genoa on its first liner voyage, thereafter crossing from Lisbon to Rio de Janeiro in only six and a half days at an average speed of 27.5 knots – a speed record which still stands. The ship continued south to Montevideo and Buenos Aires, before returning to Genoa. During the maiden voyage, some 15,000 visitors trooped up its gangways to marvel at the elegance and modernity of the interiors and, thereafter, the ship became the favoured mode of transport of politicians, businessmen, diplomats and the high clergy of the Roman Catholic church when they sailed between Southern Europe and South America.

Although an increasing amount of its time was spent cruising, rather than crossing the South Atlantic, the *Eugenio C.* remained in liner service until relatively recently, making its final voyages in 1982, the last one cancelled due to the outbreak of the Falklands War. Thereafter, it became a popular cruise ship until 1996, when it was laid up in Genoa. Sold to the German Bremer Vulkan shipyard in part payment for a new vessel, named *Costa Victoria*, the ageing *Eugenio C.* eventually passed to a succession of cruise operators, but with little success. Quite simply, the ship was worn out and was subsequently sold for scrap.

In 1960s Scandinavia, meanwhile, the effective blend of discrete design innovation and commercial pragmatism which had characterised previous generations of passenger ships was continued. By this point, Scandinavian Modernist design had

reached an international audience – thanks not only to furniture exports and to such attention-grabbing jet-age icons as Arne Jacobsen's SAS Royal Hotel in Copenhagen, but also to innovative schools, town halls and housing – which reflected progressive social policies.[41]

As car traffic grew rapidly on DFDS's North Sea routes, the time-consuming crane-loading of vehicles into the holds of the existing passenger ships *Kronprins Frederik* and *Kronprinsesse Ingrid* was no longer satisfactory, especially as the Danish Government was avidly promoting tourism in Britain. Consequently, DFDS ordered a new North Sea passenger liner with drive-through car capacity from the Helsingør Shipyard for delivery in 1964. This was the 8,221-ton *England*, the largest and most elegantly appointed vessel of its type on the North Sea.

In 1960, DFDS had appointed an Englishman as its new chief superintendent engineer – Brian Corner-Walker. He was ex-Royal Navy and, as World War II ended for him with Denmark's liberation, he decided to stay in Copenhagen and to study naval architecture there. At DFDS, he was responsible for the design of the new passenger vessels of the 1960s and 70s, initially working under J.A. Kørbing. He recalls that:

> Chairman Kørbing realised that growth in car traffic was becoming a significant trend and that new ships would be required. He was initially suspicious of car ferries as he thought that they might not be sufficiently robust to cope with North Sea storms. Instead, he wanted a solid passenger liner which happened to carry cars as well. Comfort was a priority and I was asked to make the *England* as smooth-sailing as technology would allow. The ship evolved as a large, graceful motor yacht with very fine hull lines and she did indeed prove to be a most outstanding performer, even in the worst North Sea weather.[42]

The *England*'s sleek hull design was developed from that of the Portugese-owned liner *Funchal*, completed at Helsingør the previous year. Two 14,000-horsepower Burmeister and Wain (B&W) diesels gave a speed of 21 knots with reserve power to catch up in case of delays – very important in the treacherous North Sea.[43]

Internally, the *England*'s relatively large dimensions enabled a spacious interior to be developed. Forward on the saloon deck was the First-Class smoking room, the interior form of which followed the curved and slanted shape of the superstructure. It was panelled in teak and, like all the passenger spaces, was fully air-conditioned – with ribbed ceilings specially designed to blow in cool air and extract stale air all over

*The* Eugenio C.'s *main saloon deck contained a succession of lounge spaces separated by plate-glass partitions. These took their names and colour schemes from semi-precious stones. The oval-shaped First-Class Ambra Lounge overlooked the bow and, aft of the forward vestibule, were the Rubino and Opale lounges. The Turchese Lounge was aft of amidships.*

– to keep the ship fresh and evenly heated. As on the earlier *Prinsesse Margrethe*, the furniture and light fittings were bespoke designs by Kay Kørbing. To the rear of the First-Class section was the First-Class dining saloon, with a decorative panel in yellow by Arne L. Hansen. In between was a hallway with floor-to-ceiling plate-glass bulkheads and doors without frames to give an uninterrupted vista from one space to the next. On the port side, there was a copper panelled cocktail bar adjoining the smoking room and, to starboard, a writing room. The First- and Second-Class areas were separated by the galley, which served both restaurants – incidentally the one in Second Class was very similar to its First-Class counterpart. Its central feature was a relief panel depicting the sun's rays over the sea by Rolf Middelboe. Overlooking the stern and the sun deck was the Second-Class smoking room, which was light and airy thanks to floor-to-ceiling windows in the rear bulkhead. Spacious, undeniably luxurious and fully stabilised, the *England* brought a new level of quality to short-sea passenger ship design and effectively made Kay Kørbing's reputation in Scandinavia and beyond as a highly talented architect of ship interiors.[44]

Building on the renown of the *England*, Kørbing next contributed to a most prestigious commission – a new flagship for the Norwegian America Line's trans-Atlantic service from Copenhagen, Oslo and Bergen to New York. Responding to the jet era, in 1960 its directorate instructed their technical department to draw up specifications for a passenger liner to serve both trans-Atlantic and cruising purposes. As with recent Norwegian America Line predecessors, the *Oslofjord* and the *Bergensfjord*, the new ship was to be a twin-screw motor vessel with an all-welded aluminium superstructure. Norwegian America Line's own chief naval architect, Kaare Haug, was in charge of the overall design.[45] In September 1962, a contract for the construction of the ship was signed with the French shipbuilders, Société des Forges et Chantiers de la Méditerranée at La Seyne, for delivery in 1965. The keel was laid in May 1963 and, later that year, it was announced that the name for the new ship was to be *Sagafjord*.

The interior design of the *Sagafjord* was to represent a radical change in direction for Norwegian America. In line with the upsurge in Norwegian national sentiment following Norway's liberation from Germany, the interiors of the company's initial post-war ships had been in the national romantic style, designed largely by Arnstein

*Below (top): An aerial view of DFDS' 1964-delivered passenger- and car-carrying vessel* England *motoring through the North Sea off Harwich. In many respects, the design was developed from that of the earlier* Prinsesse Margrethe, *built by the same shipyard.*

*Below (bottom): The sitting area of a First-Class suite on the* England: *even this relatively small overnight vessel offered the luxury of private space for those willing to pay.*

*Below (right): Models pose at the cocktail bar in the* England's *First-Class smoking saloon in this 1964 DFDS publicity photograph. In reality, overnight ferry travel probably never was quite as stylish as these smartly dressed drinkers suggest.*

Arneberg (the architect of Oslo City Hall). In contrast, to make the *Sagafjord* more appealing to the wealthy, cosmopolitan clientele Norwegian America's directors hoped to attract for luxury cruises, they assembled a team of progressive, mainly Scandinavian, architects and designers under the coordination of Fritjof S. Platou, whose firm was based in Oslo. The most spacious room on the ship was the Tourist-Class ballroom, designed by Finn Nilsson. With its high ceiling and a floor area covering 8,000ft$^2$ (745m$^2$), a bright red colour scheme and subdued lighting, it was spacious, yet instantly welcoming. From this room, glass doors led out onto the lido deck and open-air swimming pool which had an illuminated fountain at night. The Saga Dining Room seated 468 and was designed by Platou and Njål Eide. Its central section was two decks high and, descending a splendid staircase leading down from the deck above, passengers made a grand entrance through doors in a double-height fully glazed bulkhead. Behind the staircase, there was a bas-relief panel of Viking longboats by the Norwegian artist, Carl B. Gunnarson.[46]

Kay Kørbing was put in charge of the design of the First-Class accommodation, at the forward end of the Veranda Deck. The circular Garden Lounge, located forward, was built on split levels around a sunken circular dance floor and ingeniously combined the daytime role of a quiet, airy sitting room with that of an intimate nightclub. This was achieved by means of four vertically slatted matt gold metal screens, which gave the space a cosy and warm-toned inner area and a bright and airy perimeter. The ceiling

*The* England's *spacious First-Class smoking saloon, the shape of which reflected the sweep of the ship's forward superstructure. The special ceiling design enabled stale air to be extracted all over, keeping the space fresh and evenly heated.*

*Norwegian America Line's magnificent Sagafjord lies in Oslo Harbour early in her career in the mid-1960s.*

*Opposite: The curving stairway in the Sagafjord's First-Class hall appeared to float in front of a curving panel clad in strips of teak and panels of onyx. Kay Kørbing's design remained intact throughout the liner's lengthy career.*

above the central section featured lighting coves with a colour-change system for use at night when there was lounge dancing. Elsewhere, many of the same fittings were used as on the *England*. The First-Class hallway, immediately behind, was an impressive atrium with a dramatic under-lit open tread staircase plunging down the full height of the ship and appearing to float in front of a gently curving wall, panelled in strips of teak and onyx marble. Moving further aft, the library, writing room and North Cape Bar were on either beam. The latter was well lit through large windows by day, but full-length curtains ensured that it was dark and sociable by night.

The *Sagafjord* was eventually delivered in September 1965, some six months behind schedule. Undoubtedly one of the most harmonious-looking ocean liners ever built, it was renowned for its flowing lines and remarkable consistency of forms and details. Behind the long, flared bow, the superstructure was piled up in receding tiers with swept back bridge wings and an imposing tapering funnel, the profile of which matched the sweeping lines of the aft sun decks. The *Sagafjord* sailed on its maiden trans-Atlantic voyage from Oslo on 2 October 1965 and, on 10 November, left New York on its first cruise to the West Indies. This liner soon established itself as one of the finest and most popular cruise ships afloat and spent an increasing part of the time in this role. Such was the *Sagafjord*'s popularity that a similar fleetmate, named the *Vistafjord*, was delivered in 1973.

In the mid-1960s, meanwhile, the Danish DFDS company was approaching its centenary and celebrating in style with an unprecedented expansion and a new building programme, requiring no less than five new passenger and car liners, each one significantly larger than the ship it was to replace. The most competitive construction bid was from an unusual source, however – the Italian shipyard of Cantieri Navali del Tirreno e Riuniti at Riva Trigoso near Genoa. This family-owned firm built ships literally on the beach and launched them in almost complete condition. The first of the series, intended for North Sea service, was launched as the *Winston Churchill* in May 1967. The new ship's hull form was designed to be loaded with cars through the bow and stern, whereas the otherwise similar *England* loaded from the side.

*Above (left): The First-Class Garden Lounge on the* Sagafjord, *designed by Kay Kørbing, was a circular space, arranged around a sunken dance floor.*

*Above (right): The sitting area in one of the* Sagafjord's *deluxe suites, designed by Kay Kørbing. The patterned curtain behind the sofa separated this from the bedroom space.*

There were lifting bow and stern visors designed to continue the shape of the hull so that, when they were closed, no one would have known that the ship was a car ferry. The hull also contained an extra deck so that the car deck could be double-height to enable the carriage of lorries and buses. Apart from that, the *Winston Churchill*'s passenger accommodation was essentially similar in layout and decoration to that of the *England*, albeit using darker wood veneers – such as Italian rosewood and African wengé – and brighter upholstery colours.[47]

While the finishing touches were being added to the *Winston Churchill*, two new car ferries for the Copenhagen–Oslo route – the second *Kong Olav V* and *Prinsesse Margrethe* – were also under construction for delivery in 1968. These too had interiors by Kay Kørbing, who split up their First- and Second-Class accommodations into a number of intimate rooms with glass partitions. The centrepieces of their First-Class nightclubs were their brass-panelled circular bar counters and dance floors. In the stairwells, immediately aft, there were colourful murals by Per Arnoldi. As the Oslo service took 16 hours, these ships had extensive restaurants, bars and shops.[48] In contrast, the Copenhagen–Aalborg route, for which the final pair of new DFDS ships, named the *Aalborghus* and *Trekroner*, was constructed, was a short overnight hop linking the north of Jutland with the Danish capital. It was very popular in the 1960s as passengers could board the ships late in the evening and arrive the next day early in the morning for a full day's business in the city. Thus, these vessels had few public rooms – but many cabins and reclining seats.

As, one by one, the great trans-Atlantic and colonial liners – however Modernist in appearance, planning or technology – were withdrawn, unable to compete with jet airliners, it appeared that the future of passenger sea travel would be with car ferries, such as these.

The short-sea roll-on/roll-off ferry already had a long history, dating back, in fact, to the early railway age. Starting in February 1850, the Edinburgh, Perth and Dundee Railway had introduced a succession of steam-powered paddle vessels to traverse the River Forth between Granton, near Edinburgh, and Burntisland, carrying railway vehicles northward (the Forth Railway Bridge had yet to be constructed).

The designer of these craft was the brilliant marine engineer and shipbuilder Robert Napier and the shoreworks and loading ramps were devised by Sir Thomas Bouch, who was later blamed for the collapse of the Tay Bridge, further north on the same line.[49]

Denmark and Sweden followed Britain's lead and, by the turn of the century, the sea belts of Northern Europe were well connected by fleets of steam-powered, paddle-driven train ferries. By the inter-war era, a new generation of screw steamers and motor ships had been introduced and, during the 1930s, the first car ferries emerged. Thereafter, car ownership grew as the European economy expanded in fits and starts, held back by war and by post-war rationing. In Denmark, car ferry design development was particularly rapid and this directly reflected increasing demand. In 1946, at the end of World War II, there were 200,000 licensed cars but, by 1959, this figure had increased to 370,000 and the ratio of cars per member of the population had decreased from 1:23 to 1:13. Over the same period, there had also been a steep increase in the number of lorries and so the Danish Ministry of Transport's Road Directorate had published a long-term plan to improve and increase the country's road network. At the same time, there was greater wealth and disposable income to be spent on holidays and short trips.[50]

Since the 1930s, the Danish State Railway (DSB) – and, indeed, British Railways in the UK – had only grudgingly acknowledged the need for car ferries, but had built many fine train ferries and passenger-only vessels to sail on rail-connected routes. This reticence to encourage car use was understandable – but the new reality could not be ignored and DSB, in particular, developed arguably the world's most innovative, capacious and efficient car ferries in the latter 1950s and throughout the 1960s. DSB had a very singular design policy; it believed that its own expertise was the best and that there was no need to look elsewhere for inspiration.

In 1952, DSB took delivery of the *Broen* from Frederikshavn Værft and Flydedock A/S, their first post-war car ferry, capable of transporting 1,000 passengers and 60 cars, to serve on the principal Great Belt route between Nyborg and Korsør. This linked Sjælland (where the capital, Copenhagen, is located) with Fyn, home to the 'second city', Odense. There then followed a whole series of car and train ferries, jointly designed by DSB's Technical Department and the drawing office at the

*Below (left): The aft-facing Second-Class smoking saloon on the* Winston Churchill *featured an entirely glazed rear bulkhead, overlooking the stern.*

*Below (top): The Danish State Railways car and train ferry* Broen *brought a new streamlined profile to the fleet, partly inspired by the* Kronprins Olav *(page 75) and by the American* Princess Anne *(page 80).*

*Below (bottom): The larger* Kong Frederik IX, *delivered shortly after the Broen, further developed the aesthetic and set the standard for Danish railway-owned ferry tonnage delivered during the ensuing decade.*

Helsingør Shipyard, where most were built. For the next 10 years, DSB took delivery of a new ferry on pretty much an annual basis as the Danish economy expanded rapidly and people became more mobile.

The next DSB ferry, the 4,084-ton *Kong Frederik IX* was a combined train-and-car carrier, built to operate from Gedser in Denmark across the Southern Baltic to Grossenbrode in Germany. As with nearly all of the DSB fleet, it was a twin screw vessel, powered by twin B&W diesels. The train deck had three tracks, but could equally accommodate 82 cars. Throughout, a very high standard of outfitting was achieved with fine wood veneers and modern furniture, making for a distinctly elegant onboard environment. Indeed, as befitted a vessel named after the king, it was, in ambience, a miniaturised liner of the era, but designed for a crossing of not much more than one hour's duration with quick turnarounds at each end.[51]

As Danish domestic car traffic across the Great Belt increased from the mid-1950s onwards, DSB decided to open dedicated ports at Halsskov and Knudshoved, each adjacent to the main train ferry ports of Nyborg and Korsør. With this in mind, a new car ferry, the *Halsskov*, was ordered from Helsingør for delivery in 1956. This was the first 'double decker' ferry on the Great Belt, able to load and unload simultaneously on two levels and capable of carrying 200 cars, or more than twice as many as the single-decked *Kong Frederik IX*, while accommodating nearly as many passengers (1,000 versus 1,200).[52] Two further multi-purpose car and train ferries, named the *Knudshoved* and the *Sprogø*, the latter named after an island in the Great Belt, followed the *Halsskov* into service in 1961–62; both were built at Helsingør and were clearly developed from the *Halsskov*'s planning and layout. Later, DSB ordered a further, significantly larger, car ferry for the route. When first introduced in 1963, the 4,836-ton *Arveprins Knud* was the world's biggest triple-decker car ferry and capable of transporting 1,500 passengers and 341 cars each on crossing.[53]

As the West German 'economic miracle' gathered pace and its economy boomed in the 1960s, both rail and road traffic also greatly increased across the Baltic. In response to this, DSB decided to commission a new flagship for the Rødby–Puttgarten route, again to be built at Helsingør. This was to be not only the world's largest train ferry hitherto constructed, but also a significant car carrier with a vehicle deck capable of accommodating 211 cars above a commodious three-track train deck. One might have assumed that such a craft would not have been an object of beauty but, in fact, the new 6,532-ton *Danmark* was arguably the handsomest DSB ferry yet seen. At 472ft (144m) in length, the vessel made an impressive sight – particularly when viewed side-on. As with the CGT trans-Atlantic liners *Normandie*

and *France*, it had a whale-back bow with the DSB black hull painted on with a false sheer line to give the impression of a graceful sweep from prow to stern. The superstructure was well proportioned with the majority of passenger facilities on a single main deck, consisting of restaurants forward and a fast-food cafeteria aft. A large smoking saloon was also located forward on the boat deck above. Altogether, the *Danmark* was a prestigious flagship for the DSB fleet. Indeed, at the time of its introduction in 1968, the ferry was one of Denmark's biggest passenger vessels and only outsized by DFDS's Harwich–Esbjerg ships *England* and *Winston Churchill*.

British Railways, whose fleet dominated coastal waters around the UK, was less venturesome when it came to ferry design. There was a good reason for this conservatism. In 1953, a terrible tragedy had occurred when the railway-owned Stranraer–Larne ferry *Princess Victoria* foundered in the Irish Sea after storm waves stove in the stern door, causing the car deck to flood with an almost instant loss of stability. However, Britain's rail industry, nationalised only in 1948 by the post-war Labour Government, was facing severe problems by the 1960s as it struggled to keep up with road and air travel, managing as best it could with outdated infrastructure, rising costs and a dowdy image. While there was no political will to invest in new high-speed lines, as had happened to great acclaim in Japan, costs could be slashed through closures and redundancies and the railway's image could simultaneously be modernised by professional industrial designers. A new chairman, Dr Richard Beeching, was appointed in 1963 with a brief to oversee these changes. Beeching was hired from Imperial Chemical Industries (ICI) to bring a more business-orientated approach to the public sector rail industry. At the same time, a new Modernist corporate identity was introduced, the result of quasi-scientific legibility testing by Jock Kinnear of DRU, and a new livery, based on a Corbusian colour palette of blue, yellow, off-white and red, was introduced. Most successful was Kinnear's new British Rail logo – a bold, white 'double arrow', both sufficiently abstract, yet elegantly proportioned, to signify a new railway age.[54]

The new railway image was impeccable in terms of Modernist theory; in a nationalised business with a clear top-down management structure, it could be imposed uniformly on every aspect of the railway's operation – including its ships. Yet, there was no escaping the fact that it consisted only of paint and transfers to be applied mostly to existing – and sometimes elderly – vehicles, buildings and vessels. Moreover, it would be introduced against a backdrop of cuts and closures, thus throwing gradual modernisation and sudden, very obvious decline together in a poignant dialectic.

*Above (left): A Danish State Railways brochure for train- and car-ferry services across the Southern Baltic to West Germany. On this route, the ferries carried trains and commercial vehicles in their hulls with cars loaded on a separate deck in the superstructure above.*

*Above (right): Danish State Railways' flagship ferry was the* Danmark *– a large train-, car- and passenger-carrier linking Denmark and West Germany. Notwithstanding the vessel's complex operational requirements, a notably attractive design solution was achieved, aided by the application of a sweeping false sheer line, much as on the French trans-Atlantic liners* Normandie *and* France.

The application of the British Rail corporate identity to railway shipping was, arguably, the most successful aspect of the entire operation. As the steamers and ferries were repainted on an annual basis, it allowed a quick impact to be made. The monastral blue hulls, white superstructures, grey masts and bright red funnels looked particularly smart on the most modern ferries, whereas older steamers looked rather uncomfortable in such Modernist garb.

British Rail's ferry design was the responsibility of its own 'in house' Naval Architecture Department, headed by Tony Rogan. Working with the interior designer Neville Ward of Ward & Austin, many outstanding ferries were produced – especially during the latter 1960s and early 1970s. Reflecting safety concerns and railway traditions, the majority of these were highly compartmentalised two-class vessels with little of the open planning found on their Scandinavian counterparts.[55]

Development was rapid during the 1960s; the *Avalon*, of 1963, built on the Clyde by Alexander Stephen of Linthouse, was a passenger-only turbine steamer for the Harwich–Hook-of-Holland route. The vessel was highly praised for its excellent appointments but, in every other respect, was hopelessly old fashioned. Towards the end of the decade, the *St. George* of 1968, Tyne-built by Swan Hunter for the same route, was a diesel car ferry. The multi-purpose train and car carrier *Vortigern* followed from Swan Hunter in 1969 to serve on the Dover Strait and, during the first half of the 1970s, a whole succession of robust, yet attractive, ferries joined the British Rail fleet. By then, its shipping division was marketed under the snappy title of Sealink, emblazoned in white Helvetica on the blue topsides of the ships. The *Horsa*, *Hengist* and *Senlac*, which, as with the *Vortigern*, were named after Medieval warriors, were built at Brest in France for the Folkeston–Boulogne and Newhaven–Dieppe routes. These very popular and successful ships had bright, easily maintained interiors. Their First-Class stairwells, forward, were adorned with glassfibre bas relief panels by Franta Belsky. Second Class was more basic, with high-backed seats around tables and luggage racks above, much like in railway carriages – but at least there was indoor seating for all passengers in an air-conditioned environment. That innovation alone was a great leap forward on British short-sea routes.[56]

As well as building its own ferries, Sealink also chartered and purchased several ferries from Scandinavian private sector operators, most notably Sweden's Stena Line. Stena was one of several upstart Danish, Swedish and Norwegian ferry firms to have emerged during the 1960s to challenge the hegemony of the railway shipping

*Below (left): The bow of the British Railways steamer* Avalon, *dressed overall at the beginning of what would prove to be a short career operating between Harwich and the Hook of Holland.*

*Below (right): At dusk, passengers congregate at the gangway of the* Avalon. *Rail-connected overnight continental ferry services such as these allowed passengers to sleep while they sailed.*

fleets and other established (and complacent) incumbents on various short-sea routes within Scandinavia. What nearly all of these firms had in common was that they favoured the Copenhagen-based consultant naval architects Knud E. Hansen A/S to design their ships. Indeed, since the latter 1930s, Knud E. Hansen's firm had come to dominate the market so far as ferry design was concerned. Sadly, in 1960, Hansen's life came to a tragic end when he fell overboard and drowned while sailing his yacht, just as his business was reaching its zenith. Fortunately, he had employed several expert designers who continued his work. The most significant of these were Svend Aage Bertelsen, Tage Wandborg, Dag Rogne and Poul Erik Rasmussen. Between them, they designed dozens of very innovative – and remarkably beautiful – ferries for a variety of Scandinavian owners.[57]

So far as innovative hull, superstructure and interior design was concerned, Wandborg, in particular, became a leading light in the company and, as we shall see, he oversaw the design of a succession of outstanding ferries and cruise ships throughout the 1960s and 70s. A passionate and effusive gentleman, he worked closely with his colleagues to transform the passenger ship in Scandinavia and beyond by developing new design and construction techniques – such as prefabricated interiors – to improve quality while cutting costs. Knud E. Hansen A/S ferry designs were shallow-drafted, easily manoeuvrable and economic, yet also aesthetically pleasing. Externally, they were characterised by a forward-weighted, 'teardrop' form, as first utilised by Raymond Loewy during the 1930s. Wandborg, who styled the ferries' superstructures, described this wilful, thrusting form as his 'hungry look'. Often, an observation lounge – located in a dummy streamlined funnel device slightly forward of amidships – accentuated the effect and this was often painted in the shipping company's livery. In terms of technical design and layout, Knud E. Hansen A/S favoured the use of four relatively small medium-speed diesels, coupled in pairs to the propeller shafts, in order to reduce the vertical height of the engine room and to free up space for a larger, clear-span vehicle deck, directly above. This also meant that a ferry could continue in service even after an engine breakdown as there was sufficient redundancy built in to maintain a reasonable speed on three, or even two, motors. Routing the exhausts and access stairs through side casings also helped to achieve a rational layout and, in the passenger accommodation, open planning was favoured to achieve a large capacity within compact overall dimensions. Many examples of this type of ferry entered service on short Scandinavian crossings in the 1960s. In addition, they were often characterised by bright liveries and bold graphic design on the hull topsides.[58]

*The old and new order in Southampton docks in 1966: the* Reina Del Mar, Queen Mary *and other famous British liners lie strike-bound in the background while, in front, the new ferry* Sunward *is berthed stern-in at the linkspan. Shortly, the* Sunward *moved to Miami, becoming the pioneer cruise ship of Norwegian Caribbean Lines.*

The success of these ships was notable given that, by the mid-1960s, the passenger shipping industry as a whole was in turmoil. While ferries of the type devised by Knud E. Hansen A/S were displacing the traditional passenger ships on short-sea routes, on the trans-Atlantic and other 'deep sea' trades, the jet airliner was having an equally profound effect. As we have already seen, though, many newly built passenger liners of the 1960s were designed as dual role liner-cum-cruise ships as cruising was seen as a potentially lucrative alternative source of income. However, such exclusive ships as Norwegian America Line's *Sagafjord* were aimed at the wealthy and leisured – certainly not at the mass market.

It was Knud E. Hansen A/S who, thanks largely to Wandborg, developed the first purpose-built mass-market cruise ships, based upon their earlier car ferry design precedents. The 8,666-ton *Sunward*, delivered in 1966 from the Bergens Mekaniske Verksteder, was a key ship in this development, it being essentially an enlarged version of the company's typical car ferry design. This ship had been ordered by Knut Kloster of the Lauritz Kloster Rederi of Oslo. In the early 1960s, Kloster believed that he had spotted a gap in the market for a ferry service from Southampton to Lisbon and Gibraltar to carry British holiday-makers and their cars south to the sun.[59]

Unfortunately for Kloster, however, British government restrictions on currency for foreign travel and growing diplomatic tension with Spain over Gibraltar made Kloster's service a failure. Meanwhile, in Miami, an entrepreneur called Ted Arison had chartered two Israeli-owned ferries, the *Nili* and the *Bilu*, to operate short cruises to Nassau in the Bahamas and Montego Bay in Jamaica. When their owner went bankrupt, the United States authorities seized the pair, leaving Arison with plenty of potential passengers but no ship. When he found that the *Sunward* was available, he contacted Kloster and the two firms joined forces to launch the Norwegian Caribbean Line. Carrying both passengers and trailer traffic from Miami to Nassau in

the Bahamas, the ship was an immediate success and a second was quickly ordered, this time from the Weser shipyard at Bremerhaven. Also designed by Wandborg, it represented a further development of the *Sunward*'s design. The building process was somewhat unusual as the ship was constructed in two halves, which were joined together in dry dock, and the complete assembly was finished in only 12 months. The 12,940-ton *Starward* was delivered in the autumn of 1968 while a further vessel, the *Skyward*, arrived from Weser in 1969.

These larger ships could each carry around 740 passengers. They were distinctive-looking with an all-white colour scheme, featuring blue accents, and streamlined funnels, located towards the stern. Forward, there was a sheltered lido area with a three-storey glazed sun lounge above the bridge. The arrangement was very successful and gave the ships a large area of sheltered deck space for sunbathing. The car ferry origins of the design showed in very cramped cabins in which the berths could be made into settees for daytime use (the staterooms on South Africa's famous Blue Train reputedly inspired their layout).[60]

Such was their success, however, that an additional pair of 16,600-ton liners, to be named the *Southward* and *Seaward*, was ordered from the Italian shipyard of Cantieri Navali del Tirreno e Riuniti at Riva Trigoso. These were to be Norwegian Caribbean Line's first fully fledged cruise liners and Wandborg worked closely with the Italian shipyard's technical staff to create a suitably innovative design. Wandborg recalls that:

> The shipyard had just completed five passenger liners for DFDS, designed by their technical staff and the architect Kay Kørbing… The DFDS ships were modern in the architectural, rather than in the technical sense. They used a lot of woodwork because Kay Kørbing liked that kind of finish and thought it

SHOPPING CENTRE

*The generation of onboard revenue through shops, bars, casinos and the sale of meals in the restaurants and cafeteria was an important aspect of the business model of commercially operated ferries from the 1960s onwards. Here, we see part of the shopping facilities on the Sunward.*

highly appropriate for ship interiors. Being perhaps more technically minded, I was anxious to use all of the latest synthetic materials in the new Norwegian Caribbean Line cruise ships as they were cheaper, faster to use and appeared to offer greater fire protection.[61]

Tage Wandborg's commentary reveals an ideological gulf between Kørbing's architectural Modernism (which followed the precedents of Kay Fisker and Ludwig Mies van der Rohe) and Wandborg's desire, as a naval architect, for technical modernity. Evidently, the two goals were not necessarily compatible. As for the design itself, Wandborg took inspiration from recent Italian liners:

As a young naval architect, my great hero was the Italian Nicolò Costanzi – a great innovator who not only revolutionised hull design and hydrodynamics through rigorous research, but also was an artist and a great aesthete. His most outstanding ship, in my opinion, was the *Oceanic* of 1965. This was a remarkable design with a big, powerful hull upon which there sat a low, streamlined superstructure. There was a wrap-around promenade at main deck level with the lifeboats recessed above this. With machinery located aft, this layout meant that the top of the superstructure could be entirely given over to sun deck space with several swimming pools and glazed screens on either side, making a spacious sheltered sun trap. It was the ideal model from which to develop a modern cruise ship.[62]

When Wandborg arrived at the shipyard, he found that Knut Kloster had already requested two ships of the same design as the earlier *Starward* and *Skyward*. Wandborg persuaded him that it was possible to do much better, but there was very little time until construction was due to begin. He recalled that 'the new ships were actually drawn on large sheets of paper on the floor of my hotel room, facing onto the beautiful Ligurian coast. My patio door was opened and the warm sunshine and sea air filled the space. It was the most inspiring setting one could imagine in which to design ships.'[63]

As with the *Oceanic*, the lifeboats were stowed at main deck level to give a full-width uncluttered lido area on top, sheltered by sweeping glass screens. The tapering line of these was continued in the shape of the after decks – making a bold, yet harmonious, composition. The *Southward* entered service in December 1971, but the *Seaward* project was abandoned when industrial unrest at the shipyard increased her price by more than 50 per cent. Instead, the unfinished hull was sold to P&O and completed as the *Spirit of London*.

*The* Sunward's *success as a Caribbean cruise ship gave rise to a succession of purpose-built vessels to carry cruise passengers from Miami. Here, the* Skyward, *Norwegian Caribbean's third cruise ship, arrives in Miami.*

Ferries, hybrid cruise-ferries and even fully fledged purpose-built cruise ships began to appear in ever larger numbers in the latter 1960s. From being perceived to be merely a perfunctory means of sea transport from A to B, or an idle pleasure enjoyed only by the very wealthy, these vessels were marketed to the masses with low fares and the lure of plentiful inexpensive food, relatively cheap drinks at the bar and tax-free shopping. 'Smorgasbord' buffet dining and self-service cafeterias provided new kinds of unstuffy shipboard catering, allowing for a high throughput of passengers. Live dance bands and DJs were another attraction – making even a crossing lasting no more than a few hours into a veritable 'mini cruise'. Above all, casinos and tax-free shops generated substantial profits, further offsetting the already moderate ticket prices by increasing onboard revenues.

It was in the Baltic, between Sweden and Finland, that such cruise ferries became most popular and a succession of state-of-the-art vessels entered service during the 1960s. There, the Finnish Wärtsilä shipyards in Helsinki and Turku made the most significant contribution to car-ferry and, later on, to cruise-ship design. At a time when long-established British yards – which traditionally had built much of the world's passenger fleet – were struggling for survival, the Finnish upstart began its long association with passenger-vessel design and construction. This happened notwithstanding an exceptionally harsh climate with temperatures often lower than -20° Celsius during the winter.

Wärtsilä's first car ferries were the *Skandia* and *Nordia* for Silja Line's route from Norrtälje, a town to the north-east of Stockholm to Mariehamn and Turku in Finland. Delivered in 1961–62, they were motor ships, powered by two nine-cylinder Wärtsilä-Sulzer diesels driving twin controllable-pitch propellers, the blades of which could be swivelled to adjust the speed. The *Skandia* and the *Nordia* loaded vehicles through both bow and stern doors and each carried no less than 175 cars, or 100 cars and 20 lorries, in addition to a passenger complement of 1,200. With grey hulls and white superstructures, they appeared crisp and purposeful-looking, albeit with rather bluff hull lines. Their 'funnels' were unusual features as they actually housed observation lounges with reclining seats (engine exhaust was vented instead through their rear masts).[64]

*Norwegian Caribbean Line's* Southward *had a similar hull form to the recent* Starward *and* Skyward, *but borrowed the idea of nested lifeboats and a full-width lido deck from the* Oceanic. *The vessel had a very distinctive and attractively resolved silhouette, as shown in this view taken in Miami.*

A third Wärtsilä delivery was the *Ilmatar*, completed in 1964 for the Finland Steamship Company's Stockholm–Helsinki service. Of sleek external appearance and with elegant interiors, designed by the Finnish architect Jonas Cedercreutz, it operated a passenger-orientated service of a type fast becoming anachronistic with the rapid development of networks of car-ferry routes. Wärtsilä learned quickly, however and, less than two years later, it delivered the first of a series of five very large and well-appointed ferries, named the *Finnhansa*, the *Finnpartner*, the *Prins Hamlet*, the *Finlandia* and the *Bohème*. All of these 'first generation' Wärtsilä passenger ships were sturdily constructed to ice-breaking specifications.

The *Finhansa* and the *Finnpartner* were introduced in 1966 by Oy Finnlines – a part of the Enso Gutzeit industrial conglomerate – a firm specialising primarily in the paper and wood export trades and with a large fleet of cargo vessels. Enso Gutzeit was also a renowned patron of Modernist design, it being a regular client of the internationally regarded Finnish Modernist architect Alvar Aalto, whose office designed the interiors of some Finnlines passenger-cargo vessels.[65] The *Finlandia*, with interiors by Cedercreutz, was delivered in 1967, this time to the Finland Steamship Company, and was very much an improved version of the earlier pair – indeed, the ship was regarded as the Finnish national flagship and was widely acclaimed for the beauty and modernity of its exterior and for the elegance of the passenger accommodation. The *Bohème*, completed in 1968, had been intended for North Sea ferry service between Harwich and Hamburg but, between ordering and taking delivery, its owner, Sweden's Wallenius Lines, had a change of heart and it actually entered service as a cruise ship from Miami.

In the mid-1960s, ferries on the central Baltic routes remained comparatively basic in terms of size and the facilities on offer. Certainly, the *Skandia* and the *Nordia*, compared favourably with anything sailing in British waters at that time but, on the Baltic, the most outstanding ships were used on the lengthy route from Helsinki to Travemünde in West Germany.

The first vessel for central Baltic traffic that was large enough to be compared on an equal footing with the Helsinki–Travemünde ships was the *Fennia*, built in Sweden by the Öresundvärvet in Landskrona and delivered in 1966 to Silja Line. Every day, it sailed between Stockholm, Mariehamn and Turku and quickly made a very positive impression on account of its futuristic profile and crisp, modern interiors. Externally, the ship somewhat resembled Holland America Line's 1959-built *Rotterdam* with a dove-grey hull and twin exhaust stacks, located two thirds aft. In order to balance

*Above (left): During the 1960s, Finland emerged as a major builder of ferries and cruise ships. Initially, Finnish ferries crossing the Baltic Sea to West Germany showcased the know-how of Helsinki's naval architects and interior designers – as shown by the restaurant of the 1967-built* Finlandia.

*Above (top): The* Finlandia *was typical of larger ferries built for longer Baltic and Scandinavian routes in the second half of the 1960s.*

*Above (bottom): The forward-facing smoking saloon on the* Finlandia: *throughout, the interior design was by Jonas Cedercreutz.*

*The dining saloon on the Fennia, the largest and best appointed ferry for cross-Baltic service yet constructed. The architect Bengt Lundsten intended that the ferry's interiors' muted colours should act as a stylish backdrop to passengers' activities.*

the profile, an ovoid-shaped observation lounge was located amidships, atop the superstructure.[66]

Being intended both for night and day crossings in the fairly sheltered waters of the archipelago, the hull was quite beamy with a pronounced knuckle joint at car-deck height and a commodious superstructure. Cabins and saloons, containing large numbers of reclining seats, were provided on the main deck of the superstructure with a smoking lounge, restaurants and a cafeteria located on the deck above. The accommodation was designed by the renowned Finnish architect Bengt Lundsten and was superbly appointed with Eero Saarinen 'Tulip' and Arne Jacobsen 'Swan' and 'Ant' chairs in leather, set against unadorned expanses of rich wood-veneered panelling. Lundsten believed that a ship's interior should act as an elegant backdrop to the passengers, whose clothes and movement provided colour.[67] This approach was very different from that of subsequent Baltic ferry interior designers, who invariably preferred glitz and bold ornamentation to understatement. Below the car deck, there were further cabins, a cinema, a swimming pool and a sauna bath and, on the topmost deck, there was a cocktail bar with a 360-degree panoramic view across the beautiful archipelago scenery. The *Fennia* set the standard for subsequent ferries to emulate and the vessel went on to enjoy a long and highly successful career on a number of Baltic routes.

While these – and many other similarly innovative and well-appointed ferries – had been entering service, Britain's Cunard had been fretting about the future of its increasingly outmoded trans-Atlantic liner fleet. When Kloster's Knud E. Hansen A/S-designed *Sunward* had first appeared in Southampton in 1966, it had berthed adjacent to the strike-bound *Queen Mary*, providing one of the most remarkable design contrasts between the venerable Cunard liner and the futuristic-looking new car ferry. Cunard was pushed in the direction of Modernism due, in part, to pressure from the architecture and design press. Hugh Casson, who was editor in chief of *The Architectural Review*, reported glowingly about the new car ferries – particularly Ward & Austin's transformative work for British Rail's shipping division.[68]

Consequently, Cunard's planned successor to the *Queen Mary* and *Queen Elizabeth* was about to change from being a near-direct replacement North Atlantic liner of around 80,000 tons in to a more agile ship of between 50,000 or 60,000 tons with as much capability for worldwide cruising as for express service between Southampton and New York. By this time, Cunard's chairman, Sir John Brocklebank had invited James Gardner to Cunard's headquarters at Pier Head in Liverpool to lend the benefit of his experience – from such projects as the Vickers Viscount airliner interiors for British European Airways and Britain's pavilion for the 1958 Brussels World's Fair – to the styling of the new liner. Cunard's chief naval architect, Dan Wallace, and his team were faced with the colossal problem of trying to design a huge, extensively enclosed, air-conditioned ship without it ending up resembling a floating apartment block. Apart from being considerably taller than the *United States* or the new *France*, the planned Cunarder was being designed without the traditional curvilinear forms of fore and aft sheer, side-to-side deck camber or even a 'tumblehome' of her vast slab sides above the waterline. Yet, scarcely had James Gardner shaped the exterior lines of Q3, as the proposed ship was code-named, than all plans to build it were scrapped.

In 1964, he was brought back into the design team for a second new ship, code-named Q4, but known as John Brown and Company yard number 736, and finally as the *Queen Elizabeth 2*. While Gardner was to handle the ship's exterior appearance, interior planning and decoration was largely in the hands of Lady Brocklebank, the chairman's wife.[69]

*Below (left): The forward-facing smoking saloon on the Fennia, equipped with large numbers of Arne Jacobsen Swan chairs, upholstered in brown and black leather – and even a white baby grand piano.*

*Below (top): When first delivered, the Fennia's silhouette and livery showed some similarity to the Rotterdam. Inboard, the ferry's attractions included an indoor swimming pool, sauna, tax-free supermarket and an observation lounge atop the superstructure, offering panoramic views in all directions.*

*Below (bottom): One of the well-appointed overnight cabins on the Fennia. Ferry cabins such as these were far more compact than their equivalents on liners, but passengers were only expected to sleep in them for a matter of hours, rather than living for days and weeks at sea.*

Lady Brocklebank was well qualified in her understanding of the travelling public's needs and preferences, and possessed a good understanding of the technical aspects of ship design and operation. Wisely, she also realised that the vast scale of this project and its significance in making an appropriate impression on modern British design worldwide was beyond her scope, and that top professional design expertise was needed. She had already started to assemble a team of progressive British designers – including Dennis Lennon and Jon Bannenberg, who eventually got to work on the project – but not before a number of political hurdles had been overcome. Unfortunately, the outward perception of Lady Brocklebank's involvement was unfairly viewed by the architectural and design establishment as merely fulfilling a traditional spousal role of choosing the colours, patterns and art pieces for the new ship as though she had been asked to decorate the family's country home. There was, in fact, great public controversy during 1965 over the new ship's design, with critical stories being run in the popular and trade press and questions even being asked in Parliament.

Within only a few months, this – and indeed the whole approach to the new ship's design – was changed, as Lady Brocklebank and others were dropped and James Gardner's responsibilities were extended as joint design coordinator. In the meantime, Sir John Brocklebank had resigned, owing to poor health, with British Overseas Airways Corporation's (BOAC) former managing director Sir Basil Smallpeice chosen as his successor. Smallpeice had played a key role in introducing BOAC's de Havilland Comet and Vickers-Armstrong VC10 jets, as well as early planning for the Boeing 747 jumbo and Concorde supersonic airliner. He was also familiar with Cunard's operations and financial standing through the BOAC-Cunard merger that had taken place in 1962 and was later wound up in 1966. Smallpeice's approach was to bring the line and its passenger services forward into the new world

*The* Queen Elizabeth 2 *lies at Ocean Terminal in Southampton at the start of what would prove to be a long and successful career. The liner's futuristic appearance was the result of careful styling by the industrial designer James Gardner.*

of international transport and travel that was, by this time, being shaped more by the airlines than the remaining steamship companies.[70]

Smallpeice met privately with James Gardner to discuss the formation of a new design team. When asked whom he thought should be appointed to coordinate the ship's interiors, Gardner recommended Dennis Lennon, whose recent work included interiors for the London's Cumberland Hotel, a housing estate in Camden, a chain of restaurants for J. Lyon & Co. and a modernisation of the Rome Opera House's auditorium and crush bar. Explaining this choice in his autobiography, Gardner observed that:

> Most designers I could think of would slip either 'Scandinavian' or 'Bauhaus' – and this wouldn't appeal to Cunard's American customers. If Lennon slipped I guessed it would be in the safer direction towards international Hilton (the best international Hilton). In practice he didn't slip at all, so we will never know.[71]

The Economist Intelligence Unit was consulted on the future possibilities of passenger shipping and cruising, and Sir Basil Smallpeice sought the Council of Industrial Design's assistance in the final choices of architects and designers who would be able to realise the concept of an up-to-date Cunard *Queen* liner as a modern ocean-going hotel, capable of both express North Atlantic transport and holiday cruising. Thanks to a six-month postponement of the ship's completion announced in 1966, an opportunity was created to realise more fully Smallpeice's wish to forego Cunard's sacrosanct three-class onboard social structure in favour of a more open arrangement, allowing all passengers to move freely about the ship from end to end. Consequently, the public spaces were rearranged to offer a broader range of facilities with the flexibility for those on one of the three

*The QE2's after decks were considerably wider than those of the France (see page 150 for comparison). Being built with a cruising role in mind, glazed shelter screens were provided and, again, James Gardner ensured that the whole ensemble appeared harmonious.*

upper decks to be segregated exclusively for premium-fare passengers only during Atlantic voyages.

Meanwhile, the full architectural design team was assembled with the addition of Michael Inchbald, who had designed the Tourist-Class public rooms aboard Union Castle's *Windsor Castle*, and Misha Black, whose firm, DRU, had handled the First-Class interiors for P&O's *Oriana* with Brian O'Rorke. Following the great success of his work on the *Canberra*, Sir Hugh Casson, who had established the Royal College of Art's interior design department, was given the opportunity for his students to give *QE2*'s youngest passengers the benefit of the college's famed lively and young-at-heart design approach in the children's and teenage areas. The prominent partnership of Crosby, Fletcher, Forbes was also commissioned to handle all aspects of graphic design and product identity from signage throughout the ship to brochures, deck plans, menu cards, ticket folders and cabaret playbills in an effort to establish the same sort of unified public identity as had been established for BOAC and British Rail through their own rigorously applied corporate design policies.

Meanwhile, the *QE2*'s technical design had emerged as an extremely sophisticated package in its own right, reflecting the advancement in weight-saving and space-usage efficiency of the modern airliner. Yet, in having to accommodate some 2,000 passengers in high standards of comfort and luxury, along with the space needed for a broader range of public rooms and deck spaces open to the sun, though sheltered from the wind, the new ship had to be proportionally narrower and taller. To improve operational flexibility, the draft also needed to be shallower, eliminating *QE2*'s dependency on the tides for access to Southampton and allowing the ship to dock alongside at a greater number of ports while cruising.

Following the *Oriana*'s example, *QE2*'s aluminium superstructure was designed to serve as an integral strengthening element of the entire ship, rather than merely imposing a deadweight load atop the hull. The uppermost strata of hull shell plating's thickness was reduced slightly to allow part of the bending and twisting forces of the ship's motion at sea to be taken up by the superstructure, the high-tensile alloy of which was pre-stressed to yield the elasticity needed to absorb and dampen, rather than amplify, these movements. This eliminated the need for the structurally complex expansion joints and the heavy strength decks used in conventional shipbuilding.[72]

The *QE2*'s compact and powerful machinery was contained within just three

*Below (left): James Gardner's original design sketch for the QE2's forward-slanted mast.*

*Below (right): The QE2's First-Class Columbia Restaurant was finished in dark brown leather panelling, copper-tinted ceiling finishes and apricot carpeting and curtains. The structure of the aluminium superstructure was expressed through a series of squared-off arches on either side, organising the seating into a series of niches.*

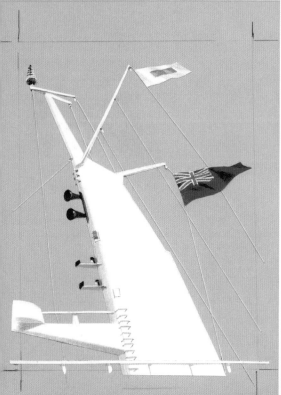

watertight compartments, extending only a quarter of its length, as opposed to the earlier *Queen Elizabeth*'s machinery and boiler compartments, which took up more than double the amount of fore-and-aft space. The space freed aboard the *QE2* could be allocated to various technical and service functions and ship's stores, releasing more of the decks for passenger recreation. Other auxiliary systems, such as the ventilation and air-conditioning plants, along with various hotel services and crew working spaces, were consolidated into integral 'service cores', extending along the centres of the upper hull decks.[73]

Passenger accommodation was located to either side of these, with rectangular hotel standard cabins. On the upper decks, enclosed promenades were revitalised as an integral part of the public domain, serving as the principal circulating arteries among the various lounges, dining rooms and other facilities and also providing access to the open decks aft. By also locating the dining rooms and galleys on the same upper decks as the lounges, the ceiling height could be reduced throughout the accommodation in the hull, with additional vertical space being saved by adopting the aircraft building technique of routing electrical and plumbing services through cutouts in structural I-beams without loss of strength. The overall effect of this was to gain an additional deck within the hull and, thus, greater exposure to the ship's sides to achieve a 75 per cent proportion of outside cabins with windows or portholes.[74]

*Above: Passengers relax on the QE2's tiered after decks. The liner's emphasis on outdoor recreation reflected changing social aspiration as, in the jet age, it was suddenly desirable to have a suntan. During the first half of the 20th century, in contrast, being tanned was thought unsophisticated.*

*Page 204 (above): The QE2 is completed in the fitting-out basin at John Brown's Clydebank shipyard: the aluminium alloy upper superstructure is still in undercoat and so this image gives a good indication of the extensive usage of this material.*

*Page 204 (below): Inboard, the QE2 was equally progressive. This view shows one end of the Queen's Lounge designed by Michael Inchbald, who made extensive use of glass-reinforced plastic mouldings to achieve a futuristic ambience.*

*Above (left): One of the QE2's First-Class cabins, designed by Stefan Buzas and Alan Irvine.*

*Above (right): The QE2's 736 Club on Boat Deck in full swing: designed by Stefan Buzas and Alan Irvine, it featured dark veneered panelling and illumination came from ships' navigation lights mounted on wall brackets.*

*Page 205 (above): The Queen's Lounge on the QE2, designed by Michael Inchbald, was notable for its back-lit lattice ceiling, trumpet-shaped columns and glass-fibre chairs.*

*Page 205 (below, left): The Coffee Shop and adjacent teenage room on the QE2 featured pop murals by a Royal College of Art student, Tim Sarson.*

*Page 205 (below, top right): The view aft, looking towards the QE2's tall, slender funnel. The aluminium alloy shelter screen in the foreground surrounded an outdoor area for deck games and acted as a counterpoint to the scoop shape at the base of the funnel.*

*Page 205 (below, bottom right): Waiters pose in the QE2's Britannia Restaurant. Every aspect of this vessel was carefully designed to create a coherent visual experience for the passengers – from the crew's uniforms to the bespoke tableware and furniture.*

The architectural design team faced the challenge of bringing the advanced structural design of the *QE2* forward from mere concept to iconic modern British ship of the 'Swinging 60s'. As Dennis Lennon observed during the project's early days, 'We realised we were not merely working for Cunard, for we were conscious of the fact that *QE2* would be taken as a national symbol, something which will show people everywhere what Britain can do in the way of design.'[75] Initially at least, Cunard appeared to have some difficulties adapting to the design team's Modernist approach, with so much outside influence on the design of *their* ship. Some designers complained of difficulties in getting the detailed specifications they needed and of restricted access to the ship to view the progress on the realisation of their work.[76]

James Gardner's exterior styling effectively turned a powerful and functionally intense piece of slab-sided marine hardware into a liner of great beauty and distinction. The funnel was one of *QE2*'s most distinctive external features. It combined a tall stovepipe, to carry the engine gases up high above the ship, with a cowling, through which return air from the ventilation and air-conditioning systems would be pushed upwards to help disperse the exhaust fumes away from the decks. A broad, low scoop at the whole structure's base took advantage of the airflow over the ship while underway to add an additional upwards push. Rather than showing the traditional Cunard funnel colours, this was visually balanced against the mast and painted a combination of black and white. Taking into consideration the replacement of multiple large steamer funnels with the altogether finer lines of his slender design, Gardner also replaced the traditional black hull paint scheme with a shade of dark charcoal grey to maintain a proper visual balance between the hull and superstructure masses to produce a less severe overall appearance. As the decks were completely flat amidships and turned slightly upwards towards the bow in a gradual slope, rather than a curved sheer line, the traditional appearance of sheer was superimposed in the paint scheme.

Gardner also took a fresh look at the arrangement of lifeboats, along with their davits and other handling gear, in an effort to achieve a more pleasing appearance. He succeeded in getting these arranged with the larger excursion launches amidships, the regular lifeboats fore and aft and the two small rescue craft near the bridge. He had the boat davits and other deck equipment, along with the inset of the boat-deck superstructure wall, painted in a medium khaki colour, rather than white. This effectively camouflaged the deck gear's appearance and created a pleasing visual illusion of the white boats and launches and the bright orange rescue boats floating free above the deck, particularly when viewed from a distance at sea.

Boarding by way of the midships hatches on 'Two Deck', passengers were immediately given a stimulating impression of the ship's being modern and remarkably different from every liner Cunard had previously operated (on *QE2*, the deck names were inverted – presumably to sound fashionably futuristic). The circular midships lobby, jointly designed by Dan Wallace and Dennis Lennon, was a complete departure from the institutional look of most ships' entrance halls. The concept of a round chamber with a single centre column, shaped to resemble an upward-facing trumpet horn, supporting a circular serrated fibreglass ceiling, was created by Wallace. The circular seating area around the column's base had upward-facing lighting fixtures to cast a soft shimmering glow onto the fibreglass 'umbrella' of the ceiling. The upholstery was in emerald green leather, the walls clad in dark blue leather, with the central column, banquettes, handrails and other details in stark white, giving the space almost a space-age quality – indeed, the liner was promoted as 'The Space Ship' and 'the most exciting thing to be launched since Apollo 1' in Cunard's publicity material.[77]

The Queen's Room, by Michael Inchbald, was designed to serve as the general

*The QE2's Double Room by Jon Bannenberg was a spacious lounge and ballroom, located at the after end of Upper and Boat decks.*

purpose First-Class main lounge in North Atlantic service and, otherwise, as a winter garden-style day lounge and alternative entertainment venue to the Double Room. It occupied an almost square space three-quarters aft, bounded vertically by the 9ft (2.8m) ceiling height of Quarter Deck. Inchbald created a sense of greater height here by using three indirectly illuminated white latticed ceiling sections, running fore and aft, with the four supporting columns also clad in white laminate and shaped into inverted trumpet horns, similar to the Two Deck lobby column. The forward and aft walls were decorated in a bold woodblock arrangement on a mirrored background to give a more open appearance while, to either side, where the interior promenade was routed through the room's outer extremities, concealed sliding glass panels with full-height drapes, allowed the lounge to be closed off into an altogether smaller and more intimate space. In a bid to improve the sight lines for entertainment and dancing, The Queen's Room was one of several spaces aboard *QE2* where the centre part of the floor was lowered slightly. Rather than surrounding this with a high railing, Inchbald chose to use low, white lacquered banquettes with plant troughs behind. Moveable furniture was designed with a similar white trumpet shape being used for the table pedestals and shell chairs, which were derived from Eero Saarinen's famous 1956 'Tulip' chair design. This room – with its cool white, gold and honey palette and fluid, aerodynamic lines – was the essence of thoroughly livable shipboard modernity and has, for the most part, remained as one of the *QE2*'s most admired and enduring interiors.

The Double Room was a vast multi-purpose space above the Queen's Room on the upper and boat decks that had emerged out of the change from three classes to a more open and flexible plan. The fusion of what was originally to have been the Cabin- and Tourist-Class lounges was simply achieved by cutting a large rectangular opening in the middle of the boat deck, creating a mezzanine plan space, claimed at the time to be the largest in any passenger ship then afloat. Jon Bannenberg wanted *QE2* to be a 'fantastically exciting ship' and felt that, rather than merely doing a cosmetic job of decorating an already defined space, his role was to design for people and their enjoyment of life in their surroundings.[78] He joined the room's two levels with a dramatic, semi-circular staircase in aluminium and steel, with deep red carpeting and plate-glass balustrades continued completely around the central well at the upper-level balustrade. Aluminium and steel were chosen largely for their light reflecting properties, complementing the side-to-side ribbed metallic ceilings and recessed fluorescent lighting, predominating on both levels. The palette of the upholstery and soft furnishings was in various hues of red and orange, giving the

*The layout of the QE2's main saloon decks made use of a perimeter circulation plan. Forward on Quarter Deck, a single large galley served all of the dining rooms with First-Class spaces filling the remainder of the deck. Above, Tourist-Class passengers enjoyed an unbroken run of public rooms on Upper Deck.*

QUEEN ELIZABETH 2

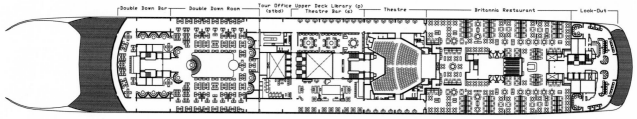

Upper Deck

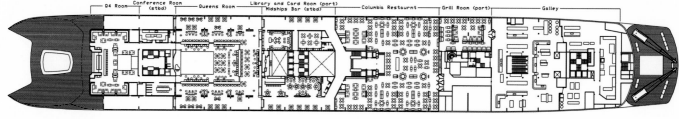

Quarter Deck

0  10  20  30  40  50 Metres

room a feeling of warmth and cosiness, despite its vastness. The staircase provided a focal point for the whole space. It was at the aft end, diametrically opposite a small circular bandstand, which was, in reality, inadequate for the coming cruise-ship age of cabaret and revue-style professional entertainment.

Other notable interiors included the Grill Room, designed as a latterday rendition of the Veranda Grill restaurants in the old *Queens*, located forward on the ship's port side adjacent to the First-Class Columbia Restaurant on Quarter Deck. Here, Dennis Lennon used rich maroon colours and statues representing the four elements, sculpted by artist Janine Jane, to set the right atmosphere for the enjoyment of the fine cuisine. The floor was raised slightly in progressive steps inwards from the room's outward side to maintain good sight lines for all of the 100 diners it could accommodate. The reality of shipboard design means that the formal and premium restaurants, which are usually most heavily patronised in the evening hours after dark, do not allow diners to benefit from their outlook to sea. The Grill Room's exclusivity was perhaps best asserted by its discrete access only from an intimate cocktail bar, located below on One Deck, and connected to the Grill Room by its own spiral staircase.

The cabins were mostly the work of Dennis Lennon and Partners and these reflected many of the practical ideas suggested by Lady Brocklebank during *Q3*'s early planning and, later, by Lady Tweedsmuir, the line's first female board member, who had been appointed in 1965. All rooms had their own en-suite bathrooms, with either showers or bathtubs, and at long last, the seaside 'rooming-house' practice of locating washbasins in the bedrooms was completely banished. Most berths were full-size hotel beds, with only a limited number of fold-away upper Pullman berths being fitted in cabins intended for family use, or other groups travelling together economically. The cabins had the warmth and luxury of being close-carpeted throughout. The less-expensive outer rooms featured a variety of interlocking 'L' and 'C'-shaped plans, providing space for a fore-and-aft arrangement of side-by-side beds, with narrower sitting alcoves at the ship's side or farther inboard. Inside rooms were, for the most part, arranged in centreline spaces between the main fore-and-aft passages.

At the time of her completion, *QE2*'s accommodations were criticised by some as being too old fashioned, with their more than 50 variations of cabin plan, and for lacking anything as radically new as the court-cabin arrangements of the *Canberra*

*Above (left): The British Rail Irish Sea ferry* St. Columba's *First-Class lounge by Ward Associates, containing Arne Jacobsen chairs and a bas-relief mural by the sculptor Franta Belsky.*

*Above (top): The* St. Columba *was a typical example of British Rail's 1970s ferry tonnage, sailing under the Sealink brand.*

*Above (bottom): The* St. Columba's *First-Class nightclub: built-in seating not only looked orderly, but stayed in place during Irish Sea storms.*

*A close-up image of Franta Belsky's* St. Columba *mural, depicting scenes from the life of Kentigern (St. Columba). Several members of British Rail's ferry fleet were decorated with notable artworks by, among others, Belsky and David Gentleman.*

and *Oriana*. The court arrangements and convertible accommodations of the P&O-Orient Line ships were, in fact, stop-gap solutions to providing greater comfort in larger numbers of compact cabins. *QE2*'s planning would later show itself to be the more progressive, looking ahead to the coming generations of large and luxurious cruise ships featuring a high preponderance of hotel-style cabins and suites arranged simply along the outer sides of parallel corridors, with service cores between, running along the centre line.

The *QE2* was a triumph of modern British architecture and design that succeeded in asserting a strong and appropriate sense of luxury and exclusivity, without being pretentious or condescending, and perhaps, most significantly, avoiding reference to the New Brutalism, associated with the Welfare State. Yet at the same time, British society as a whole was becoming less stratified, with more wealth distributed among a greater part of the population. Things of greater luxury were becoming available as the opportunities for discretionary consumer spending, travel, entertainment and other leisure pursuits increased and broadened. Television also brought a wider and more complex panorama of the world at large directly into the average family's living room – and the *QE2*'s design both anticipated and reflected this situation.

The type of modern luxury exemplified by the *QE2*'s design set new standards across the entire shipbuilding industry at a time when much new tonnage was being planned for holiday cruising and car-ferry services on short international routes throughout Europe and Scandinavia. Indeed, its influence immediately became apparent in such ships as the 1974-delivered Sealink ferry *St. Edmund*, the interiors of which were designed by Ward & Austin's successors, Ward Associates. This ship's public spaces, in particular, utilised many of the same materials and finishes that had gone into *QE2*'s luxury interiors. Perhaps most remarkably though, the central lounges were designed as a series of five circular spaces, each with a trumpet-shaped central column, attractive indirect perimeter cove lighting and a similar seating arrangement as used in the Double Room's periphery coves on *QE2*.[79]

Meanwhile, a trio of Finnish-built up-market cruise ships built for Norwegian-based Royal Viking Line showed a remarkable adaptation of *QE2*'s overall general arrangement to their 20,000-ton scale, as well as sporting lower and broader renditions of the new Cunard flagship's distinctive funnel. Among these, the *Royal Viking Sea*'s main lounge, designed by Norwegian architect Finn Nilsson, showed an uncanny resemblance to The Queen's Room's latticed ceiling.

While the 'Royal Viking' sisters were luxury cruise ships, marketed to a similar clientele as the *QE2*, the fact that British Rail Sealink ferries also began to copy the *QE2* aesthetic was potentially more problematic. On the one hand, Modernist ideology stressed the need for egalitarianism and a social approach to design in order to break down divisions between classes and races. On the other, Cunard had built the *QE2* to be a dollar-earner, offering a unique and exclusive experience.

Sealink's *St. Edmund* was followed in 1977 by the *St. Columba*, built to sail between Holyhead and Dun Laoghaire across the Irish Sea. Also with accommodation designed by Ward Associates, this vessel perhaps represented the apotheosis of the Modern Movement in British ferry design. Built by Aalborg Værft in Denmark, the *St. Columba* was a commodious and superbly appointed ship on which Neville Ward created some very memorable spaces. The First-Class lounge, for example, had green Arne Jacobsen furniture and a large Franta Belsky bas-relief, depicting Columba's voyage from Ireland. The nightclub was darkly toned with high-backed seating in niches and the teenage disco had walls laminated with designs from pop album covers.

The *QE2* undoubtedly set a high universal standard of sea-going comfort and elegance the influence of which spread far and wide. As for the *QE2* itself, the fact that lesser ships began to emulate its design, coupled with the passing fashionability of the 1960s styling, ironically caused Cunard gradually to refit it better to reflect the styles of 1930s predecessors. Nowadays, very little of *QE2*'s original Modernism remains and the liner is now largely an Art Deco 'retro' ship, evoking nostalgia for a lost 'golden era'. Back in the 1930s, even the grandest and most advanced of liners lacked *QE2*'s technical sophistication in terms of plumbing, air-conditioning, fire safety, hull design, stabilisation, navigational equipment and propulsion. Moreover, the majority of today's middle-class cruise passengers would not have been able to afford the relatively higher prices of First-Class transoceanic liner travel between the wars. Back then, the structure of society was very different from the present day and, ironically, it was the 1960s which arguably gave birth to today's more prosperous and egalitarian situation. Ironically, the *QE2*, in its original Modernist form best represented that fact.

*The entrance hallway on British Rail's* St. Edmund *featured five circular volumes with a glass-fibre trumpet column in the middle of each. The ferry's interior design by Ward Associates was inspired by the acclaim of similar spaces on the* QE2.

006: **RETRO AND THE MARINE POST-MODERN**

In 1932, Henry-Russell Hitchcock and Philip Johnson's The International Style imposed a phoney singularity on the various manifestations of exploratory thought and design which characterised the emerging Modern Movement in Europe. Modernism's highly diverse unleashing of creativity – reflected in the preceding chapters of this book – was reduced to a select few dozen examples of reductive 'white architecture' on terra firma. Once American high culture – represented by the Museum of Modern Art in New York, where The International Style exhibition was staged – had promoted the idea that the Modern Movement was somehow monochrome and minimalist, this constricted view of Modernism became orthodoxy.[1]

Later, in 1966, Robert Venturi employed arguably a similarly specious approach to imply that the apparent singularity of Modernism distinguished it from the plurality of every other design era in history. His book Complexity and Contradiction in Architecture argued that, in order to resonate with wide cross-sections of mainstream society, design should deploy a broad range of signs and symbols beyond Modernist abstract formalism.[2] Later still, Tom Wolfe's satire From Bauhaus to Our House, published in 1981, poked fun at the pretentiousness of European émigré architects – and, even more so, at their American admirers and copyists.[3]

Wolfe argued that, through the involvement of speculative developers, corruptible municipal authorities (and equally corruptible architects), the Modern Movement in America possibly had done more harm than good, blighting communities equally with poor quality social housing and with unsympathetic commercial development. Rather like the embarrassed sovereign in The Emperor's New Clothes, the Modern Movement in America was caught naked.

In Britain, a similar situation appears to have occurred. The highly coloured and diverse Festival-of-Britain aesthetic of the 1950s was superseded by the New Brutalism – a powerful and emotive form of architectural expression when designed by a talent such as Le Corbusier, Denys Lasdun or Ernö Goldfinger, but often visually disastrous in the hands of corrupt commercial interests. Moreover, Modernist buildings did not age gracefully in the wet and dirty British urban climate – meaning that, what had symbolised a fresh beginning for the post-war era very quickly looked shabby and undeserving of affection or admiration. From the 1960s onwards, Modernism on terra firma was criticised both for being insufficiently inclusive of established popular taste (a criticism with which both the German National Socialists and the Soviet Communist Party under Stalin would have agreed) and of dubious quality when actually manifested in built form.

*Below (left): The Carousel Lounge on the* Nordic Prince *was designed by the Finnish interior designer Vuokko Laakso in bold colours typical of the early 1970s. Inspired by the musical* Carousel, *the space arguably represents the beginning of themed interior decoration on modern cruise ships.*

*Below (right): A cabin on the 1968 Knud E. Hansen A/S-designed* Freeport, *which sailed from Miami to Nassau in the Bahamas, showing the compact cabin types fitted to 'first generation' purpose-built cruise ships for the American Caribbean market. The sofa could convert to a double bed and there was a third fold-down bunk mounted on the wall, with a shower and WC cubicle adjacent. Then as now, the idea was that passengers should spend as much time and money in the public rooms.*

Ironically, in Europe, the primacy of high culture as a civilising influence to which all should aspire was fatally undermined by the Holocaust and, thereafter, the expansion of higher education throughout the Western World in the post-war era had a new mandate; to create a dominant liberal elite to ensure that dictatorship would never happen again.

This new liberalism was reflected in debates and new scholarship about the history of design and visual culture. In these, the old canonical history – which sought to validate Modernism as the latest manifestation of high culture – was undermined by sociological and cultural studies approaches which related taste to issues of social and geographical positioning, rather than insisting that taste was a given, learned from those representing high culture and the establishment in a top-down manner. The primacy of the artist, designer or architect as 'creative genius' was negated and, instead, the experience of the consumer became central to the way in which visual culture was discussed. Consequently, for the first time, popular taste came to be taken seriously by a growing number of commentators – such as Venturi.

Furthermore, the Socialist ideals of conventional European Modernist discourse sat uncomfortably with American free market capitalism (even though, as we have seen, American Modernism in ocean liners occurred under conditions of strict governmental regulation). Besides, with the Cold War at its height in the early 1960s, it was necessary, from an American perspective, to incorporate commercial 'free market' design culture into the canon.

Thus, the concept of 'Post-Modernism' implies both a widening of the Modernist ideal of functionality and a multiplicity of theoretical departures from the established ideologies of the Modern Movement. For starters, Post-Modernism allowed a critical armature to re-assess commercial design, which, hitherto had been largely excluded from high cultural territory. To demonstrate new chains of causation, leading to the development of contemporary theme parks, resort hotels, malls and casinos – and, of course, mass-market cruise ships – commentators looked back to the emergence of the consumer society in 19th-century Paris.

It was in America, however, rather than Europe that the consumerist society came to dominate the popular culture of the latter 20th century – particularly in the Floridan theme parks of Disney World and in the gaming resorts of Reno, Atlantic City and, especially, Las Vegas. These locations – along with amusement parks, holiday centres

*The pioneering Royal Caribbean cruise ship* Song of Norway *(with the* Nordic Prince *to the rear) at Miami: the exaggerated bow rake, slanted forward superstructure, mast and funnel casing (with cocktail lounge) together create a modern and romantic corporate identity.*

215

*Above (left): The* Nordic Prince's *entrance hall by Mogens Hammer, featuring Mies van der Rohe Barcelona chairs and decorative panels of Viking longships by the Norwegian sculptor Ørnulf Bast.*

*Above (right): The steakhouse on the* Song of Norway, *adjacent to the main dining room and offering cruise passengers some choice of dining option (the lido buffet being a third possibility for those wishing to be informal). Cruise ships of this type were one-class only and with an emphasis on relaxation.*

and shopping malls – were the latest manifestations of a leisure and entertainment culture that, as it subsequently spread globally, remained partially Americanised in its stylistic nuances. From the mid-1950s onwards, however, critics and commentators began to address such environments in a more open-minded way, dubious though they remained in terms of what constituted 'good taste'. Just what was it about Las Vegas that made it so popular with the masses in a way that more restrained and uniform approaches arguably appeared to be incapable of emulating?

The answer was plurality. Thus, it was argued that in order to attract a wide diversity of consumers, each with their own conceptions of what constituted 'good taste', design in leisure and retail environments had to embody an equally wide range of cultural and stylistic references. After all, younger or older generations prefer a complexity of different (but often related) types of music, dancing, comedy, food, drink, clothes, furniture and so on. Post-Modern thinking, however, has embraced Modernist ideals and aesthetics as well; it was all a matter of finding an appropriate context for their usage. Thus, Modernism ceased to be viewed as being the ultimate expression of human achievement in the context of high culture, and became, instead, yet another possible design style which could be selected to differentiate one product or experience from another.

In the 1960s and 70s, the jet age effectively 'shrank' the world and brought its great diversity of cultures closer together – at least for some. 'Globalisation', the tag usually given to the political, industrial and military dimensions of this phenomenon, has brought about a vast expansion in the catering, hospitality and leisure industries worldwide. Nowadays, giant shopping malls and the chain hotels, resorts and casinos of Hilton, Radisson, Marriott and Holiday Inn more or less define popular conceptions of luxury. Of course, similar aesthetics are applied to the branding and to the interior design of commercially operated ferries and cruise ships.

Two constant features of Post-Modern space are, firstly, that it tends of be self-contained, and, secondly, that it is filled with conglomerations of wildly diverse imagery, usually far removed from its historical contexts. Such decoration exists solely to distract the viewer as a kind of theme-park spectacle. Commentators on Post-Modern space, such as John Urry, have adapted Foucault's notion of 'the gaze' to explain the manner in which users 'consume' these types of environment.[4] Unlike a historic or culturally significant environment, such as Trafalgar Square with its memorials to British heroes, which are intended to provoke strong and specific nationalistic associations in the collective memory, in Post-Modern space, the 'gaze' is all one way with little or no reciprocity and without specific cultural meaning being inferred. When promotional literature is produced to sell such environments to consumers, it is usual to find it described with vague, but suitably aspirational, terminology – 'classic', 'contemporary', 'traditional', 'modern' and 'luxurious' being the words most commonly used, sometimes in combination with one another. The idea is to be all things to all people – or, at least, to attract a broad cross-section of the middle classes. Just as in 19th-century Parisian department stores, the hermetic qualities of Post-Modern space are designed totally to immerse the consumer in the retail or leisure experience and to make them relax as they loose track of the passage of time.

The high-capacity Scandinavian car ferries and mass-market cruise ships designed by Knud E. Hansen A/S and the Wärtsilä shipyards represented a significant part of the passenger ship design output of the latter 1960s and early 1970s. Not surprisingly, the design concept of streamlined, 'modern' naval architecture containing a highly ornate 'retro' interior – albeit outfitted with the latest mod cons – became orthodoxy in cruise-ship design thereafter. Seen in such a context, passenger ships designed between the latter 1920s and 1960s – which attempted, one way or another, to reflect the ideals of aesthetic and technological unity associated with the Modern Movement – always were very much in the minority.

The three pioneering cruise ships for the Norwegian-owned, but Miami-based, Royal Caribbean Cruise Line perhaps first demonstrated Post-Modernism in the context of cruise-ship design. Realising the potential of the Caribbean as a cruise destination, an American hotel owner called Edwin Stephan, based in Wisconsin, had contacted three Norwegian shipowners – I.M. Skaugen A/S, Anders Wilhelmsen and the Gotaas-Larsen group – through the Fearnley & Eger ship brokerage in Oslo.

The shipping activities of these firms were widespread and diverse. For example, Skaugen was principally a cargo shipper which had begun its activities with sailing ships in the 19th century and had been briefly involved in the emigrant passenger trade after World War II. Wilhelmsen also operated cargo liners but was diversifying in the 1960s as an operator of roll-on/roll-off and container ships, as well as support services for the developing North Sea oil and gas industries. Gotaas-Larsen, primarily a tanker operator, had also been active in the emigrant trade and had, for some time, been represented in the Miami cruise business through its Eastern Steamship Lines operation. Royal Caribbean was formed in 1968 with the three Norwegian firms as partners. Gotaas-Larsen, with its expertise in cruise shipping, assumed overall responsibility for the development of the new fleet of three purpose-built vessels, exclusively for Caribbean cruising.

The initial design work was entrusted to Knud E. Hansen A/S, under the direction of Tage Wandborg. Technical design was by Martin Hallen, the Chief Naval Architect of I.M. Skaugen who worked in close cooperation with Knud E. Hansen A/S and with the Wärtsilä shipyard's drawing office in Finland, where the vessels were built. The interiors, however, were by the Danish designer Mogens Hammer and, most

*Below (left): The interior of the funnel-mounted Viking Crown Lounge cocktail bar on the Nordic Prince with a red Eero Aarnio glass-fibre Egg chair in the foreground.*

*Below (right): First generation purpose-built Caribbean cruise vessels of the latter 1960s and early 1970s had futuristic exterior profiles. This is the funnel with Viking Crown cocktail lounge attached on Royal Caribbean's Nordic Prince.*

distinctively, the external silhouettes were styled by the Norwegian architect Geir Grung, working alongside Tage Wandborg. Wandborg recalls that:

> Grung was a technically adventurous architect who was obsessed with glass. He was known to have designed a number of extraordinary glass villas around Oslo and his office had a plate-glass floor which I was at first afraid to stand on. To demonstrate how strong it actually was, he began jumping on it and this show of confidence immediately endeared him to me.[5]

Grung had also designed a number of villas for wealthy clients in upmarket suburbs of Oslo in the manner of Ludwig Mies van der Rohe's Farnsworth House and he was regarded as being an important Norwegian exponent of the Modern Movement.

The most striking and apparent innovation was the funnel design, which incorporated a circular cocktail bar, protruding high above the sun decks over the stern. This 'Viking Crown Lounge' was to become a Royal Caribbean trademark, included, in modified form, in all its subsequent ships. Along with all other structural elements, it was carefully 'sculpted' by Grung into a singular and cohesive composition.

The first of the Royal Caribbean fleet, the *Song of Norway*, was delivered by Wärtsilä in October, 1970. The *Nordic Prince* and *Sun Viking* followed, the latter distinguished from its otherwise identical sisters by the bow plating which, at Wandborg's suggestion, was carried up an extra deck, thus giving a more imposing forward profile. The 18,500-ton sisters could each carry 870 passengers on week-long circuits from Miami. They were unashamedly designed to appeal to Middle America, with bright and airy hotel-like interiors and large expanses of varnished teak sun decks. Spacious lido areas extended over the sides between the funnel and the mast. According to Wandborg:

> The design values of these cruise ships were totally different from the older liners and ferries. Externally, passengers expected to see sleek, white, even yacht-like silhouettes as the exteriors of cruise ships need to engender the kind of feel-good factor one gets when driving in a beautiful sports car or lounging on a big yacht. It is vital for a cruise line's success for passengers to perceive that its ship is the best looking in port. Inside, however, a completely different philosophy governs the design. Unlike liner or ferry travel, cruising is about relaxation, nostalgia and, possibly, over-indulgence. Thus, to be successful, cruise-ship interiors require to be filled with what might be called 'eye-candy' to at least distract or, ideally, to captivate and enchant the passengers.[6]

As with Knud E. Hansen A/S's 'second generation' car ferry designs, these ships were relatively shallow-drafted and flat bottomed with substantial bulbous bows, giving enhanced hydrodynamic efficiency and making them much more economically viable than earlier generations of passenger ships. As they were intended to operate mainly in calm conditions, a deep draft was felt to be unnecessary and, because they were not expected regularly to meet high waves, it was decided that a very pronounced 'clipper'-shaped bow profile would look impressive and would be attractive to passengers, perhaps reminding them of the romance of the days of sail.

In terms of internal planning, the cruise ships were somewhat different from Knud E. Hansen A/S's 'second generation' ferries of the same period. While the ferries tended to have their main public rooms fore and aft on the saloon deck with a starboard arcade to link all the spaces between together, the cruise ships had full-width public rooms with a rectangular-shaped perimeter circulation pattern, creating two aisles along the length of the saloon and cabin decks with two or three transverse lobbies containing the stairwells and lift shafts in between. Typically, the main public rooms and hallways had higher deck heads than on ferries, giving them a greater feeling of spaciousness but, as with the ferries, the interiors were often pre-fabricated and made much use of laminates, plastics, glass-fibre mouldings and enamelled aluminium.

On the Royal Caribbean ships, an unusual policy was used which saw public rooms named and themed after famous musicals (the 'Can Can Show Lounge', the 'King and I Restaurant' and so on). While themed interior decoration had been one of the distinguishing (and often criticised) characteristics of passenger ships since the latter 19th century, in the past, any themes tended to have their roots either in European 'high culture' (stately homes and palaces on terra firma) or in the vernacular (gemütlich 'beer kellers' on German trans-Atlantic liners, resembling scenes from Hansel and Gretel). On the new Royal Caribbean cruise ships, the chosen theme of musicals directly addressed mass culture in the forms of Broadway shows and Hollywood movies. Yet, Mogens Hammer's interior designs were also undeniably Scandinavian in their approach to these American phenomena – and Hammer also specified the inclusion of iconic Modernist furniture designs, such as groupings of Mies van der Rohe 'Barcelona' chairs in the ships' entrance hallways.

Whereas, in the latter 1920s, these chairs had been viewed in the original context of the Barcelona Pavilion as symbols of a possible – and anticipated – Modernist future, by the 1970s, they had become design classics – admired for what they represented in terms of modern architectural history and as desirable luxury goods, with their buttoned leather cushions and elegant chrome frames. Thus, in the Post-

*Above (top): The Finnish-built* Costa Atlantica *is one of a large series of very successful standard cruise ships built for Carnival Corporation's Carnival and Costa brands. While each ship is individually decorated internally, in terms of structure, they are practically identical and only the funnel design and livery distinguished Carnival vessels from those operated by Costa. Such standardisation leads to economy, meaning cheaper cruises and increased profits.*

*Above (bottom): The* Costa Atlantica's *giant atrium is richly ornamented and equipped with glass elevators. Designed by Joe Farcus, this top-lit space reflects the design of department-store interiors of the early 20th century, such as the Galleries Lafayette in Paris.*

*Above (right): The Bar Via Veneto on the* Costa Atlantica *reflects an Americanised view of Italy – but the idea of using a designer from the nation providing the bulk of a liner's passengers, rather than that in which it is registered, goes back to Cunard's 1936* Queen Mary.

Modern context of a cruise ship foyer, such chairs would have been viewed as curiosities, as talking points and as furniture of a kind distinct from what the mainly Middle American passengers were used to at home. In that sense, they became yet more sideshows in the shipboard theme park.

American passengers responded well to the informal atmosphere on these vessels. Entertainment was slick, with Las Vegas-style revues, discos and casinos, while the ambience was jovial, with steel bands playing on deck and waiters balancing trays of exotic cocktails on their heads. Increasing numbers of Europeans were also attracted by fly-cruise packages. Clearly, Royal Caribbean had found a winning formula. Such was the ships' popularity that, in 1978, the *Song of Norway* was returned to its builder to be 'stretched'. A new 90ft (27m) long midship section contained 400 additional cabin berths, new public rooms and enlarged sun decks. The *Nordic Prince* was similarly enlarged in 1980 but the *Sun Viking* remained unaltered throughout its Royal Caribbean career.

Subsequently, overtly 'themed' cruise-ship interiors were further developed by the Miami-based interior architect Joe Farcus in a whole flotilla of giant purpose-built 'fun ships' for Carnival, which grew continuously from the early 1970s onwards into the world's biggest cruise line. Carnival aimed to attract 'guests' who might never previously have thought that going on a cruise might be an affordable holiday option and this aim was realised successfully through the building of ever-larger purpose-built vessels to achieve better economies of scale and, in so doing, to make cruising even more affordable.

Joe Farcus came to be involved in cruise-ship interior design through his then-employer, the controversial Miami architect Morris Lapidus, who was in the early 1970s asked to redecorate an apartment owned by Carnival's founder, Ted Arison. Lapidus is most famous for having designed numerous flamboyant hotel resorts – including the Fontainebleu and Eden Roc at South Miami Beach – in a Post-Modern style that picked and mixed a variety of lavish historicist aesthetics and blended these with Modernism. Typically, Lapidus interiors featured grand atria with imposing staircases, Lucite chandeliers and contrasts between areas of dense neo-Baroque decoration and unadorned expanses. Farcus subsequently developed this approach – particularly the use of outlandish ornamentation – to create fantasy shipboard environments highly suited to short Caribbean party cruises.

Farcus had loved ships since childhood and, when in 1977 he heard that Arison was planning to buy the liner *SA Vaal* (formerly Union Castle's *Transvaal Castle*) for conversion to a cruise ship, he put in a personal bid for the contract. The ship became the *Festivale* and, thereafter, Farcus went on to design all Carnival's subsequent cruise liners until the launch of the *Carnival Dream* in 2009 – a total of 37 ships, the majority bigger than the largest trans-Atlantic liners of the inter-war era.

For Farcus, designing a ship entailed being intimately involved in the vessel's general arrangement planning from the earliest stages. Together with the shipyard and naval architect, he would discuss the overall configuration and shape his own interior design elements. A crucial aspect of ordering the passenger accommodation on such high-capacity mass-market cruise ships, with well over 2,500 passengers onboard, is the maximisation of shipboard revenue flows through what is known as 'adjacencies' – that is the careful placement of entertainment facilities in the most lucrative positions to extract the largest possible amount of money from passengers. (Unlike ocean liners of the past, today's mass-market cruise ships generate a great deal of revenue from passengers' onboard spend.)

Eventually Farcus employed two assistants, Lina Forsblom and Petteri Kummala, in the small studio across the courtyard in his Miami Beach house. He had noted their skills in planning meetings at Kvaerner Masa Yards, the Finnish builder of

*The Caffé Florian on the* Costa Atlantica *is a photo-real replica of the genuine Caffé Florian in Venice, achieved by photographing the decorative panels and printing these out on marine wall panelling.*

eight 'Fantasy'-class vessels for Carnival during the latter 1980s. Answering only to Ted Arison and his son, Micky, Farcus enjoyed enviable freedom to exercise his imagination. His cruise-ship interiors for Carnival were unlike anything previously seen afloat, rejoicing in clashing colours, eccentric shapes and complex neon (and, later, LED) lighting installations – all to engender a sense of fun and escapism. Every detail was created by the Farcus studio – from the ships' winged funnels, down to interior lighting fixtures and door handles. Chairs were bought at the Milan furniture fair each year, but usually covered with vivid fabrics chosen to blend 'high' design with a 'party cruise' aesthetic. Not surprisingly, Carnival's ships were instantly recognisable and, in a field in which good taste was often synonymous with safe design approaches, Farcus, like Morris Lapidus before him, was never afraid to flout conventional architectural manners.

From the outset, Carnival was highly profitable and, since the mid-1990s, it has used its accumulated wealth to buy out numerous long-established European lines, such as Holland America, Costa, P&O and Cunard.

At the start of the decade, Costa had commenced its own new building programme while still under Italian ownership, firstly by converting two container ships into cruise ships (the *Costa Marina* and *Costa Allegra*), then by building four brand new ships (the *Costa Classica*, *Costa Romantica*, *Costa Victoria* and a fourth unnamed vessel, which was delivered instead to NCL after its German builder went bankrupt). Both the naval and interior architecture were state-of-the-art and, as in the past, critically regarded contemporary Italian architects, such as the Genovese Pierluigi Cerri, Guido Canali from Parma and Studio DeJorio, also from Genoa, were employed. Little expense was spared and the finest materials, furnishings and art installations were specified with great expanses of mosaic and marble to give all of the ships a distinctly Italian coolness.[7] The only problem was that, when they cruised in the Caribbean during the winter season, their genuine contemporary Italian design did not square with Middle America's conceptions of how anything from Italy ought to appear. To them, the ships looked austere and nothing remotely like the ornate Venetian and Caesars Palace hotels and casinos in Las Vegas. Thus, when Costa was absorbed into the mighty Carnival empire in 1997, the new management decided that all subsequent new buildings should be entrusted instead to Farcus.

Since then, every Costa ship has, to some extent, resembled a vision of Italy

*Below (top): The* Costa Fortuna, *one of a class of 15 similar vessels, each measuring over 100,000 tons and all built in Italy by Fincantieri to designs by Carnival Corporate Shipbuilding. Costa own six of these, while nine are run under the Carnival brand. In terms of commercial success, they are among the most effective passenger ships ever constructed.*

*Below (bottom): One of several outdoor pools on the* Costa Fortuna, *enabling the liner's 3,400 passengers all to enjoy a swim and a place in the sun.*

*Below (right): The Degli Argentieri Restaurant on the* Costa Mediterranea *references the double-height dining saloons of past ocean liners – and their lavish decoration. The informal wavy lines of the balustrades and ceiling are typical of Joe Farcus's playful approach to cruise-ship interior design.*

imagined through American eyes – including photo-real frescoes and replicas of the Sistine Chapel and the Caffé Florian. Ships such as the *Costa Atlantica* and *Costa Fortuna* could not be more different in atmosphere and style from Costa's earlier new constructions – but both American and Italian guests love them – the former for their perceived Italian nuances and the latter for their American swagger.

Costa's chairman, Pier Luigi Foschi, works closely with Farcus on ideas for new cruise ships, sometimes himself suggesting 'passenger experiences' for Farcus to realise while, for his part, Farcus enjoys working closely with Italian engineers, artists and outfitters, whom he admires for their expertise and inventiveness. Most of the recent ships for both Carnival and Costa have been built in Italy, and Farcus would typically fly out to the yards every two months or so for an extended working visit. Even so, some Italians object to their country being represented in this way, especially given that Costa famously took the lead in commissioning and promoting the best of contemporary Italian design in the 1950s and 60s. Yet, cruise-ship interiors designed by Farcus have had such unprecedented commercial success in service that their owner can only be grateful. Indeed, his interiors are arguably merely a reflection of the fiercely competitive nature of the international cruise market which, in turn, is a powerful expression of the contemporary neo-liberal globalised economy.

While cruise ships embraced Post-Modernism, many ferries – particularly those operated by the public sector – continued to exemplify Modernist ideals and aesthetics. Indeed, during the 1980s, Modernism in ship design perhaps found its ultimate expression – aesthetically, technologically *and* ideologically – in the socialist context of Danish government-owned car and train ferries for the state railway company, DSB.

*Chandeliers, lilac neon and an illuminated dance floor are just some of the highlights of the* Costa Concordia's *Lisbona Disco*

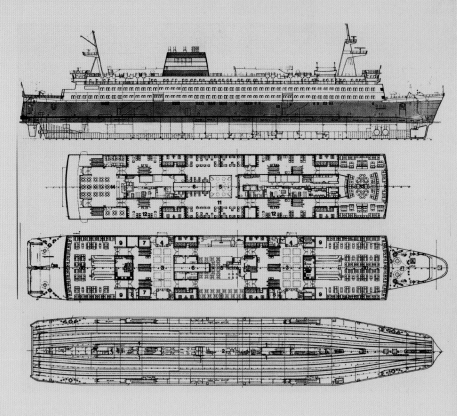

*Above (top): The ferry square on the Danish State Railways Great Belt train ferry* Dronning Ingrid *by Kay Kørbing represents the continuation of Modernism in ship interior design. The decorative panels on the funnel casing, in stripes of red, white and black, are by Arne L. Hansen.*

*Above (right): A general arrangement drawing of the three Great Belt train ferries: notice how, thanks to a symmetrical layout and circulation plan, facilities such as cafeteria serveries are duplicated on either side, meaning that one could be cleaned en route while the other was open to serve passengers.*

In a transport environment, Modernism was apparently most successful in situations where there was centralised control and top-down management to enable the rigorous application of a uniform design identity – as had been the case with London Transport under Frank Pick in the 1930s. Pick's careful attention to every aspect of design was later to inspire the highly successful British Rail corporate identity scheme of the 1960s. This, in turn, inspired DSB's management to follow suit in the 1970s by instituting its own centralised design policy. As with British Rail's much-admired scheme, devised by Jock Kinnear, the new DSB look would not only involve the repainting of the trains (using a patriotic livery of red, white and black), new station signs and graphics, but would also extend to the actual design of all new trains, stations and ferries. Jens Nielsen was appointed director of design at DSB and was responsible for this work. He initiated the process of recruiting architects to work as design consultants and, through his enthusiastic engagement in all aspects of transport design, he built up teams to modernise all aspects of DSB.[8]

At that time, DSB was Scandinavia's largest ferry operator with a big fleet of both train and car ferries, efficiently linking Denmark's many islands. By the mid-1970s, the route between Nyborg and Korsør across the Great Belt had come to be seen by DSB as the 'weak link' in Denmark's rail network, served as it was by a motley collection of relatively small ferries, some dating from the 1930s. At either end of the crossing, inter-city trains had to be split into several sections to fit onboard. Although DSB had perfected this to a fine art, it was still time-consuming and there was an overriding desire to cut journey times, especially between the principal cities of Copenhagen, Odense and Århus. The solution was to order three large train and passenger ferries, each twice as big as its largest predecessor at 11,500 tons. Each was to have four tracks on the train deck, with the possibility of loading two trains simultaneously through bow doors.

The architect and industrial designer Niels Kryger, who designed trains for DSB, prepared the initial design specification and general layout in conjunction with the naval architects Knud E. Hansen A/S and DSB's own technical department. At an early stage in the design process in 1977, Kay Kørbing was asked to take on a

leading role in the design of the passenger spaces on the new ships. This presented a new challenge:

> Unlike my previous ships, which led comparatively relaxed lives with long crossings and several hours at least in each port, these DSB train ferries were to operate on the most intensive of schedules – crossings of just under one hour with only 25 minutes to unload and load four trains with up to 2,000 passengers. All the passengers had to be got from their carriages up to the two main saloon decks to eat, drink and shop, and back down again before the ferry arrived, so that their trains could be offloaded immediately.[9]

Kryger proposed to make an impressive central focus in the middle of each of the ships – the 'ferry square', a two-storey space off which the shops and fast food bars were accessed. The main stair halls were forward and aft of this space. One was finished entirely in DSB red and the other in blue. To find their carriage again, passengers only had to remember a track number and the shade of the staircase.

For the Danish government, an exploitable side effect of the order for DSB was that it might be possible to stave off the closure of the struggling shipyards at Helsingør and Nakskov. The new ferries, to be named *Dronning Ingrid*, *Prins Joachim* and *Kronprins Frederik* were to be delivered in 1980–81, with the former building in Helsingør and the latter two at Nakskov.[10] With their straight lines and angular forms, these ships introduced a new look to the DSB fleet and their interiors reflected their exteriors in being appropriately solid and hard-wearing. To create a relaxing atmosphere, off-white laminate was used for wall coverings with dark brown brushed aluminium panelling in connective spaces. Smoke-tinted glass was used for doors and earthy hues for carpeting and upholstery. These neutral tones were accented by primary red and blue being applied to such details as door handles, staircase balustrades and artworks to colour code the ships' forward and aft areas. According to Kay Kørbing:

*Above (left): Another view of the* Dronning Ingrid's *ferry square, this time facing forward on the lower level and showing the snack bar. The provision of quick service to thousands of passengers was an important aspect of the design of these ships.*

*Above (right): The* Dronning Ingrid *and the two sister ships, the* Kronprins Frederik *and* Prins Joachim, *were characterised by their rectilinear profiles and rigorously orderly window arrangements. Trains were loaded and unloaded on two tracks via a lifting bow visor.*

One problem in designing interiors for such broad, regularly shaped ferries with relatively low deck heights compared with their width was that they were potentially vast unadorned expanses of ceiling, which could easily feel oppressive. We got over this problem very simply partly by highlighting the ship's main structural members as space dividers and partly by breaking up the ceilings with circular and rectangular cut-outs with concealed perimeter lighting to give a greater sense of height in the centres of the saloons. The bulkheads on each ship were decorated differently by artists who had worked with me on past projects.[11]

Thus, Ole Schwalbe produced a graphic motif on six enamel panels in the ferry square of the *Prins Joachim*. These motifs then re-appeared individually throughout the ship's passenger accommodation. The *Dronning Ingrid* had perhaps the most effective scheme of the three, displaying striking designs by Arne L. Hansen. The central ferry square featured two-deck-high panels, cladding the exhaust uptakes, wittily using the signal red, black and white stripes of the DSB funnel livery. The forward and aft stair halls were entirely lined with murals, depicting abstractions of the ship's lines plan. The third of the trio, *Kronprins Frederik*, introduced in April 1981, featured whimsical murals of sea creatures and fairytale characters by Helge Refn. Able to do the work of up to seven previous ships, the new trio were a great success on the Great Belt and, while they only marginally reduced the crossing time, their impressive range of passenger facilities at least made a welcome and relaxing break in long-distance train journeys.[12]

Next, DSB's management decided to replace its ageing car ferries on its northerly Kalundborg–Århus crossing, the longest DSB route taking around three hours. It was always something of a poor relation to the shorter Great Belt run and remained a passenger-orientated route until the introduction of the first of a pair of small drive-on ferries in 1960. The same ships were still operating over 20 years and an estimated 22 million passengers later. Design work began in 1982 and Kay Kørbing was again involved, working alongside Niels Kryger and the industrial designer Christian Bjørn.[13]

Passenger accommodation for 2,000 was spread over two decks and the central focus was an impressive atrium of a scale commensurate with the size of the ships;

this cut right through the main passenger decks and was topped by a series of rooflights to allow daylight to flood into the heart of the vessels. To allow maximum lighting and the best views, the public rooms were all located around the perimeter of the superstructure with the circulation spaces along the ships' centreline, effectively reversing the layout of the Nyborg-Korsør ships. The restaurants and seating halls were to be compact and even the main cafeteria, with over 300 seats, was split into several sections. This meant that during quieter periods, these spaces could be partially opened to prevent them from feeling empty and desolate. All passenger accommodation was finished in neutral shades of white, grey and blue with matt aluminium details. Such colour as there was came from vibrant abstract murals which liberally adorned the transverse bulkheads in the hallways, staircases and public rooms. The interiors were furnished with specially designed fittings and modern Danish classics, such as Arne Jacobsen's white bent plywood chairs, used in the cafeteria. Even upholstery and curtain textiles were specially designed and woven for the vessels.

Ordered from the Nakskov Shipyard, they were handed over in October 1985 and May 1986 as the *Peder Paars* and *Niels Klim*. Regrettably, they never attracted the hoped-for custom as they had too much passenger space, yet too little freight capacity for the route – a basic specification error on the part of DSB and the Danish Government. Political interventions also cut short their careers as the Government decided to build a bridge over the Great Belt, which, upon completion, would render much of the DSB fleet redundant. At the same time, DSB wanted to order a new ship for its short high-capacity Helsingør–Helsingborg route. The Government thought it could sell the *Niels Klim* and *Peder Paars* for a quick profit and give DSB some of the money back for the necessary new ship. Consequently, it ordered DSB to sell the modern sister ships in 1990.

The 20 minute-long Helsingør–Helsingborg crossing was DSB's shortest international route. The fact that it is also the quickest ferry link between Sweden and Denmark made it very popular and, during the 1970s, a succession of double-ended ferries was introduced there. As the Scandinavian countries became a single trade zone as part of EFTA, and more and more Swedes and Danes commuted to work using the route, DSB and its main competitor, Scandinavian Ferry Lines, decided to join forces and rationalise the situation by each ordering a single large, double-ended car, passenger and rail ferry, while retaining four of the older ships for rush-hour relief duties.

Notwithstanding its short length, Helsingør–Helsingborg is an attractively scenic crossing, giving fine views along the Danish and Swedish coasts up and down the Sound and towards majestic Kronborg Castle, by the entrance to Helsingør harbour. Therefore, the design of the new high-capacity ships was to feature large areas of glazing in the passenger areas. The naval architects Dwinger Marine Consult, in collaboration with DSB's technical department, worked out the technical design. Built by the Tangen Verft at Kragerø in Norway, the two sisters, named *Tycho Brahe* and *Aurora af Helsingborg*, were outwardly almost identical, except that the latter had full-width enclosed navigation bridges. Measuring 10,845 tons and able to carry 1,250 passengers and 240 cars each, they appeared purposeful and decisively modern – even sculptural – in comparison with so many other ferries of the period.

Each ship had the same straightforward internal layout, featuring a large central hallway with a cafeteria and a tax-free supermarket at either end on the main deck, and a restaurant, bar and fast-food kiosk with crew accommodation and a large sun deck above. On the north side of the hallway was a large double-height window to give passengers a panoramic view of Helsingør Castle and the attractive waterfront of Helsingborg. Yet, each owner had its own ideas about how the interiors should look and so the Swedes entrusted this work to Robert Tillberg, while, for the last time, DSB employed Kay Kørbing.

The resultant wildly contrasting approaches were at the extremes of Scandinavian ferry interior design. The *Aurora af Helsingborg* represented Tillberg's favoured manner, with much applied ornamentation, beamed ceilings, festoon blinds at the windows and other such Post-Modern decoration. In complete contrast, the Danish *Tycho Brahe*'s design placed emphasis on airy, comfortable spaces with high-quality, hard-wearing materials and specially commissioned abstract artworks.

Kay Kørbing retired from architecture upon the completion of *Tycho Brahe* in 1991. Subsequent state-owned Danish ferries, such as the recent *Prinsesse Benedikte* and *Prins Richard* on the Rødby–Puttgarten route, designed by Christian Bjørn and introduced in 1996, continued the Modernist tradition in Scandinavian ship design. As part of a major ideological shift since the 1980s, however, DSB's ferry division was privatised in 1997.

In the context of today's wholly commercial passenger shipping sector, it is questionable whether true Modernism ever could be arrived at and it is, furthermore, arguable that the Modernist ship was a phenomenon associated primarily with the state-subsidised ocean liners of the pre-jet age and with the public-sector ferry

*The cafeteria on the* Peder Paars *was split into a number of sections which could be opened sequentially as demand required. The space is furnished with chairs by Arne Jacobsen and Hans J. Wegner.*

*Above (left): The double-ended ferry* Tycho Brahe *was built to link Helsingør and Helsingborg – a 20-minute crossing between Denmark and Sweden. The vessel was arguably the ultimate development of Modernism in passenger-ship design before Denmark's remaining railway-owned ferry routes were privatised.*

*Above (right): The ferry square on the* Tycho Brahe *featured a grey marble floor and an open-tread spiral staircase linking the various levels of passenger accommodation. Bright decorative panels by Erik Mortensen depicted the signs of the zodiac and reflected Tycho Brahe's life as an astronomer. The approach was atypical of ferry- and cruise-ship interior design in the 1990s.*

*Opposite: On the* Tycho Brahe, *the desire was to emphasise the nautical ambience and passing scenery through the installation of large windows. This ran contrary to the approach favoured on many overtly commercial ferry- and cruise-ship designs of the era, which instead had an inward focus. Here, we see part of the cafeteria which uses the same Kay Kørbing glass-fibre chairs as the 1957* Prinsesse Margrethe.

operations of British Rail's Sealink in the 1960s–70s and DSB in the 1950s–90s. Although new ships continue to be delivered which contain examples of 'vintage' Modernist design – an aesthetic popularly known today as 'mid-century modern' – this is explicable merely in terms of the cycle of taste and the fashion system, just like the revived Art Deco of the 1980s. Today, such past design aesthetics are viewed with the benefit of hindsight, whereas, back in Modernism's heroic period from the 1930s until the 1960s, they represented exciting glimpses of forthcoming design possibilities.

Being technologically charged, highly serviced, hermetic floating mega structures, large passenger vessels offered the possibility of representing a future Modernist world comprehensively and convincingly. Yet, as we have seen, the Modern Movement in ship design was influenced by a complexity of factors. Naval architecture had its own inherited traditions and methodologies, which often were poorly understood by architects, designers, theorists and critics working ashore. Ship owners, meanwhile, had their own commercial imperatives, while the most prestigious vessels additionally had to reflect the cultural and political objectives of their countries of origin. Consequently, the vast majority of passenger ships shunned the avant-garde and, in reality, the progressive liners described in this book represented only a small percentage of the world's merchant fleet.

This situation notwithstanding, passenger-ship design undoubtedly provided a significant inspiration for Modernist architecture during the 1920s and 30s and, thereafter, Modernist design principles came to influence the planning and outfitting of subsequent generations of ships. The transfer of ideas between architects and naval architects, designers and ship designers was for mutual benefit and ships embodying Modernist principles often were notably successful and long-lived, achieving a widespread popular acclaim only rarely granted to prominent Modernist buildings on terra firma.

# NOTES

## INTRODUCTION

1　Le Corbusier, *Towards a New Architecture*, Rodker (London, 1931), p. 93.
2　Mardges Bacon, *Le Corbusier in America: Travels in the Land of the Timid*, MIT (Cambridge, Mass., 2001), pp. 32–33.
3　Nikolaus Pevsner, *Pioneers of the Modern Movement*, Faber & Faber (London, 1936), p. 128. This book has since been reprinted a number of times under the title *Pioneers of Modern Design*.
4　Sir Reginald Blomfield, *Modernismus*, Macmillan and Co. Ltd. (London, 1934), pp. 71–73.
5　Blomfield, *ibid*.
6　Pevsner, *op. cit.*, pp. 90–116. Art Nouveau was the first of a succession of fashionable modern decorative styles to find short-term international popularity. Between the First and Second World Wars, Jazz Moderne, Streamlined Moderne and a number of other Art Deco-derived modernistic styles found short-term success and were often fused together with elements of mainstream modernism. Pevsner infers that the more structurally adventurous end of the Art Nouveau spectrum was a precursor to the Expressionism of the 1920s and 30s.
7　George Orwell, 'Pleasure Spots' in *Collected Essays,* Vol. 4, Penguin (London, 1971), p. 48.

## CHAPTER 001

1　Kenneth Frampton, *Modern Architecture: A Critical History*, Thames and Hudson Ltd., (London, 1987), pp. 23–24.
2　Wolfgang Lauter, *Passagen, die bibliophilen taschenbücher Nr. 432*, Dortmund (1984), p. 102.
3　Arthur J. Davis, 'The Architecture of the Liner', *The Architectural Review*, April 1914, p. 109.
4　Klaus Jürgen Sembach and Birgit Schulte, *Henry Van De Velde*, Wienand Verlag (Cologne, 1992), p. 125.
5　Sembach and Schulte, *ibid*.
6　'The *Prince Baudouin* in Operation: Completion and Trials of the Fastest Diesel-engined Vessel in the World. A Ship Which Maintained Over 25 Knots on the North Sea and Holds the Blue Riband for Cross-Channel Service', *The Motor Ship*, September 1934, pp. 195–98.
7　Hermann Muthesius, 'Das Kunstgewerbe', *Die Weltwirtschaft* 1, 1906, pp. 315–25.
8　Eckhart Berckenhagen, 'La Decoration Intérieur des Bateaux aux Alentours de 1900', Le Bateaux Blanc, Centre Georges Pompidou, Paris, 1985.
9　Muthesius, *op. cit.*
10　Davis, *op. cit.*

## CHAPTER 002

1　*Magdalena Droste and the Bauhaus Archive, Bauhaus 1919–1933*, Taschen (Cologne, 1990), pp. 43–46.
2　Raymond Loewy, *Industrial Design*, Laurence King (London, 1979), pp. 74–76.
3　Foucart, Offrey, Robichom, Fillers, *Normandie: Queen of the Seas*, The Vendome Press (New York, 1985), p. 56.
4　'The Public Rooms of the *Normandie*: Some particulars of the great French Line turbo-electric liner', *Shipbuilding and Shipping Record*, June 1935, pp. 714–16.
5　N.R.P. Bonsor, *North Atlantic Seaway*, T. Stephenson & Sons Ltd. (Prescot, Lancashire, 1955), p. 214.
6　Arthur Chandler, 'Post War Paris', *World's Fair*, Volume VIII, Number 3, 1988; expanded and revised version, January 2000.
7　John Maxtone-Graham, *The Only Way to Cross*, Macmillan (New York, 1972), p. 248.
8　Algot Mattison, *The White Viking Fleet*, Tre Böcker (Göteborg, 1983), p. 7.
9　Fritz August Breuhaus De Groot, *Ozean-Express: Norddeutscher Lloyd Bremen/Turbine Schnelldampfer Bremen*, Verlag F. Bruckmann AG (Munich, 1929), pp. 106, 118, 134, 146–47, 174 and 184.
10　De Groot, *ibid.*, pp. 5–6.
11　Gordon Turner, *Empress of Britain: Canadian Pacific's Greatest Ship*, Boston Mills Press (Toronto, 1992), p. 31.
12　Philip Dawson, *The Liner: Retrospective and Renaissance*, Conway Maritime Press (London, 2005), p. 110.
13　Alan Powers, *Serge Chermayeff: Designer, Architect, Teacher*, RIBA Publications (London, 2001), provides a detailed description of Chermayeff's early career.
14　Julia Belchich PhD (History), 'Geniuses Aren't Born Often: In the wake of documents from Vladimir Yourkevitch's personal archives', Russian State Archives of Economics, Personal Files Department.
15　Baird Dennison, '534 And All That', *The Architects' Journal*, London, 25 January 1934, p. 156.
16　Maxtone-Graham, *op. cit.*, p. 293.
17　Neil Potter & Jack Frost, *The Mary: The Inevitable Ship*, George G. Harrap & Co. (London, 1961), p. 122.
18　Margaret Richardson, *66 Portland Place: The London Headquarters of the Royal Institute of British Architects*, RIBA Publications (London, 1984).
19　'Orion: The latest and largest of the Orient Line Fleet. Built and engined by Vickers-Armstrongs Ltd.', *Shipbuilding and Shipping Record*, August 1935, pp. 205–9.

20　Charles F. Morris, *Origins, Orient and Oriana*, McCartan & Root Publishers (New York, 1980), p. 83.
21　'Informality in Ship Furnishing', *Shipbuilding and Shipping Record*, December 1935, pp. 709–10.
22　William Tatton Brown, 'Architecture Afloat', *The Architectural Review*, London, October 1935, p. 134.
23　David L. Williams & Richard P. de Kerbrech, *Damned by Destiny*, Teredo Books Limited (Brighton, 1982), p. 172.
24　*Shipbuilding and Shipping Record*, 28 April 1938, pp. 559–60 and 19 May 1938, pp. 647–55 provide a comprehensive overview of the *Niew Amsterdam*'s design.
25　See Gilbert Herbert and Liliane Richter, *Through a Clouded Glass: Mendelsohn, Wijdeveld and the Jewish Connection*, Wasmuth (2008), for a detailed description of Wijdeveld's career.
26　Catalogue from an exhibition mounted in 2006 by the Netherlands Architecture Institute (NAI), 'Plan the Impossible: The world of architect Hendrik Wijdeveld'.
27　'The *Nieuw Amsterdam*: A floating palace of art', *The London Studio*, London, July 1938, p. 6.
28　*Ibid.*
29　Maxtone-Graham, *op. cit.*, p. 166.
30　C. M. Squarey, *The Patient Talks*, Thos. Cook & Son (Tonbridge, 1955), p. 53.
31　Squarey, *ibid.*, p. 60.
32　*Magazine of Art*, July 1938, p. 422.
33　Kay Fisker, 'Skibsaptering', *Arkitekten*, 1949, pp. 106–11.
34　Poul Kjærgaard, 'Kay Fisker Til Søs', *Architectura: Arkitekturhistorisk Årskrift*, No. 15, Copenhagen, 1993, pp. 155–56.
35　The Passenger ship *Hammershus*: Third Motor Vessel for the Bornholm Steamship Company', *The Motorship*, August 1936, pp. 180–82.
36　*BornholmsTrafikken 1866–1991*, p. 18.
37　Kjærgaard, *op. cit.*, pp. 165–66.
38　Kjærgaard, *ibid.*, pp. 158–60.
39　Kjærgaard, *ibid.*, pp. 167–68.
40　P. E. Hemke and G. B. Garson, 'Streamlining Superstructures of Ships', *Marine Engineering*, November 1936, p. 688.
41　*Marine Engineering*, August 1936, p. 434.
42　Steven J. Russel, *Kalakala: Magnificent Vision Recaptured*, Puget Sound Press (Seattle, 2002) and M.S. Kline and G.A. Bayless, *A Legend of Puget Sound Ferryboats*, Bayless Books (Seattle, 1983) provide detailed accounts of the history of the *Kalakala*.
43　Loewy, *op. cit.*, p. 95.
44　Loewy, *ibid.*, pp. 94–95.
45　Loewy, *ibid.*, p. 97.
46　Norman Bel Geddes (1893–1958) started as a theatrical set designer, and in 1930 turned to industrial design. In addition to his streamlined ship proposal, he designed the interiors of Pan American Airways' airliners, radios, furniture and the Futurama Building at the 1939–40 New York World's Fair.
47　*New York Times*, 23 April 1939.
48　Loewy, *op. cit.*, p. 104.
49　A similar problem occurred in office blocks with glazed curtain wall facades – such as the Seagram and Lever buildings in New York's Park Avenue. To maintain their visual purity, it was necessary to insist that all tenents install the same type of blinds, which could only be closed to two fixed points – half-shut or fully shut.

## CHAPTER 003

1　Luisa Quartermaine, 'Slouching towards Rome: Mussolini's imperial vision', T. J. Cornell and Kathryn Lomas (eds.) *Urban Society in Roman Italy*, UCL Press (London, 1995), p. 204.
2　Donato Riccesi, *Gustavo Pulitzer Finali: Il Disegno della Nave*, Marsilio Editori (Venice, 1985), p. 68.
3　'The 24,000-ton liner *Saturnia*: The largest and fastest motorship: Speed of 21.3 knots attained with machinery output of 23,000 bhp', *The Motor Ship*, Vol. 8, October 1927, pp. 239–48; 'The 20-knot liner Victoria in service', The Motor Ship, Vol. 34, July 1953, pp. 156–57.
4　Riccesi, *op. cit.*, pp. 34–35.
5　Riccesi, *ibid.*, p. 72.
6　Maurizio Eliseo and Paolo Piccione, *Transatlantici: The History of the Great Italian liners on the Atlantic*, Tormena (Genoa, 2001), pp. 92–111, 274.
7　*Six Wonderful Days: Un invito al viaggio sulle grandi navi Italiane*, Tormena Editore (Italy, 2002), p. 15.
8　Eliseo and Piccione, *op. cit.*, pp. 246–47.
9　Eliseo and Piccione, *ibid.*, p. 268.
10　Paolo Piccione, *Nino Zoncada: Interni Navali 1931–1971*, GMT Edizione (Genoa, 2007), p. 31.
11　'The 21-knot Norwegian M.S. *Vega*: Fastest and Largest North Sea Passenger Ship', *The Motorship*, February 1938, p. 412.
12　'Passenger Accommodation in the *Vega*, *The Motorship*, March 1938, pp. 476–77.
13　'The *Vega* in Service: A 21 -knot 7,500-ton North Sea Passenger and Cargo Ship', *The Motorship*, June 1938, pp. 82–85. See also *Shipbuilding and Shipping Record*, 26 May 1938, pp. 680–87 for a detailed description of the *Vega* upon delivery.
14　'A Transatlantic Liner: The Proposed Swedish American Line Motor Vessel', *The Motorship*, October 1936, p. 227. See also 'A 28,000-ton Transatlantic Liner: Triple-screw 19-knot Ship for the Swedish American Line', *The Motorship*, December 1936, p. 307.

15 E. Th. Christiansson, 'Exterior Design of Passenger Liners', *Shipbuilding and Shipping Record*, 5 November 1953, p. 617–18.

16 *The Shipbuilder and Marine Engine Builder*, London, May 1940, pp. 206–7. See also *Shipbuilding and Shipping Record*, London, 2 June 1938, p. 722.

17 Bruce Peter, *Passenger Liners Scandinavian Style*, Carmania (London, 2003), pp. 85–99.

18 Riccesi, *op. cit.*, pp190-194.

19 Bramstedt, E. K., *Goebbels and National Socialist Propaganda*, Cresset Publishing (London, 1965).

20 *Shipbuilding and Shipping Record*, 17 March 1938, pp. 323, 335; and 21 April 1938, p. 524.

21 'Passenger Liners For German Workmen: 25,000-ton Ships, One with Diesel-electric Machinery, Designed for Economical Cruising', *The Motorship*, March 1937, p. 460.

22 R. Keine, *Schiffbau, Schifffahrt und Hafenbau*, Vol. 40, 1939, pp. 206–16.

23 '25,000-ton German Motor-Cruising Liners', *The Motorship*, April 1937, p. 26. See also 'A Cruising Liner For Workmen: The 24,000-ton 15 -knot Geared Diesel M.S. *Wilhelm Gustloff*. The First of a Series of New Liners', *The Motorship*, April 1938, p. 24.

24 Keine, *op. cit.*

## CHAPTER 004

1 *Marine Engineering*, November 1945, p. 162

2 *Ibid.*, February 1946, p. 120 Three other immediate post-war liners also championed aluminium in their construction and for good reasons, they were heavily modified versions of the "Victory" standard wartime freighters, for the Alcoa Steamship Co., an affiliate of the famous aluminium company. Alcoa Cavalier (8,481 tons) was launched at Oregon Shipbuilding on 25 September 1946 followed by Alcoa Clipper three days later and Alcoa Corsair on 2 October. Their two uppermost decks and funnel were built of 55 tons of aluminium and like the Del Norte trio, they were entirely air-conditioned. Sharp created the interior architecture but left the decorative elements to Lurelle Guild Associates which made extensive use of 'the latest plastics, structural glass and modern materials' to increase the sense of space in public rooms of modest proportions and with low ceilings.

3 Henry Dreyfuss (1904–69) started his industrial design firm in 1929. Among his instantly recognisable designs are the Hoover upright vacuum cleaner, the U.S. Bell rotary telephones and the Honeywell thermostat. He also designed the U.S. Pavilion at the 1939 New York World's Fair.

4 C. M. Squarey, *The Patient Talks*, Thos. Cook & Son (London, 1955), p. 89.

5 *Marine Engineering*, March 1951, p. 87.

6 John Malcolm Brinnen, *The Sway of the Grand Saloon*, Delacarte Press, New York, 1971, p. 526.

7 Frank O. Braynard, *The Big Ship: The Story of the SS United States*, The Mariners Museum Newport News (1981), p. 77.

8 Gregory J. Norris, 'The Once and Forever Champion: SS *United States*', Steamboat Bill (Spring 1980), p. 7.

9 Philip Dawson, *The Liner: Retrospective and Renaissance*, Conway Maritime Press (London, 2005), p. 161.

10 Frank O. Braynard, *By Their Works Ye Shall Know Them: The Life and Ships of William Francis Gibbs 1886–1967*, Gibbs & Cox (New York, 1968).

11 Maurizio Eliseo and Paolo Piccione, *Transatlantici: The History of the Great Italian liners on the Atlantic, Tormena* (Genoa, 2001), pp. 146–7.

12 Donato Riccesi, *Gustavo Pulitzer Finali: Il Disegno della Nave*, Marsilio Editori (Venice, 1985), p. 192. In the overall architecture of a ship, *opera morta* ('dead construction') refers to everything above the waterline, *opera viva* ('live construction') to that below.

13 Paolo Piccione, *Cruising into Art: Art onboard Italian Liners*, Costa Crociere (Genoa, 2002), pp. 30–31.

14 Giò Ponti, 'Alcuni interni dell'*Andrea Doria*', *Domus* 281, April 1953 pp. 17–24.

15 For an illustrated history of the shipyard, see Ian Johnston, *Beardmore Built: The Rise and Fall of a Clydeside Shipyard*, Clydebank District Libraries & Museums Department (Clydebank, 1993).

16 The legal implications of this act of plagiarism remained unresolved for over 75 years.

17 Eliseo and Piccione, *op. cit.*, pp. 246–47.

18 Eliseo and Piccione, *ibid.*, p. 247.

19 'The 21-knot liner *Giulio Cesare*: First of two ships with double-acting Fiat machinery of 25,000 bhp using boiler oil', *The Motor Ship*, Vol. 31, February 1951, p. 355; 'The completion of the *Giulio Cesare*: An Italian liner of 25,000 tons gross, propelled by 26,000 bhp machinery', *The Motor Ship*, Vol. 32, October 1951, p. 259; 'Largest post-war motor liner: The *Giulio Cesare*, an Italian vessel of 27,700 tons gross, propelled by double-acting Fiat machinery of 26,000 bhp', *The Motor Ship*, Vol. 33, January 1952, pp. 424–29.

20 Eliseo and Piccione, *op. cit.*, pp. 248–52.

21 'The *Andrea Doria*', *The Shipbuilder and Shipping Record*, Vol. 82, 13 August 1953, pp. 211–13.

22 Eliseo and Piccione, *op. cit.*, pp. 203–4.

23 Maurizio Eliseo and Paolo Piccione, *The Costa Liners*, Carmania (Greenwich, 1997), pp. 12–30.

24 Paolo Piccione, *Costa Crociere: Cinquant'anni di stile*, Silvana Editoriale and Costa Crociere (Genoa, 1998), pp. 47–67.

25 'Three 13,000-ton 18-knot passenger liners: The *Australia*, *Neptunia* and *Oceania* built for service between Italian and Australian ports. Twin-screw machinery of 14,000 bhp', *The Motor Ship*, Vol. 32, June 1951, pp. 98–99.

26 'The cargo and passenger liner *Africa* – a 191/2 knot 11,400-ton vessel for Genoa-Cape Town service', *The Motor Ship*, Vol. 31, March 1951, p. 381; 'The 20-knot *Victoria* in service', *The Motor Ship*, Vol. 34, July 1953, pp. 156–57.

27 'New Italian passenger liner *Ausonia*', *The Shipbuilder and Shipping Record*, Vol. 90, 17 October 1957, p. 523.

28 Gilbert Herbert, *Symbols of a New Land: Architects and the Design of the Passenger Ships of Zim*, The Architectural Heritage Research Foundation (Haifa, 2006).

29 For a full discussion of the nature of the architectural profession in the formative pre-state years, see Gilbert Herbert and Ita Heinze-Greenberg, 'The Anatomy of a Profession: Architects in Palestine during the British Mandate', *Architectura 2*, 1992, pp. 149–62. See also Gilbert Herbert, 'Bauhaus Architecture in the Land of Israel: is the concept of a modern, architect-designed vernacular a contradiction in terms?', *Architectura 2*, 1995, pp. 224–28.

30 For biographical details of Mansfeld see Anna Teut (ed.), *Al Mansfeld: an Architect in Israel*, Ernst & Sohn (Berlin, 1999).

31 For details of Weinraub's life and work see Richard Ingersoll, *Munio Gitai Weinraub: Bauhaus Architect in Eretz Israel*, Electa (Milan, 1994).

32 He later took the name of Munio Gitai.

33 Yeheskiel Gad: 'Architects comments on their work on S/S *Theodor Herzl*', undated typescript.

34 Anna Teut (ed.), *Al Mansfeld: an Architect in Israel*, Ernst & Sohn (Berlin, 1999), p. 50.

35 Selinger and Duek, 1995, p. 38.

36 *The Architectural Review*, September 1957, pp. 209–11.

37 Poul Kjærgaard, 'Kay Fisker Til Søs', *Architectura: Arkitekturhistorisk Årskrift*, No. 15, Copenhagen, 1993, pp. 171–74.

38 Interview with Kay Kørbing by Bruce Peter, September 1999.

39 *Ibid.*

40 *Ibid.*

41 'A 21 -knot Passenger Ship: The *Prinsesse Margrethe* built for the Oslo-Copenhagen Service. Machinery Aft and Funnel Amidships, *The Motorship*, September 1957, pp. 264–66.

42 Becky Conekin, 'Fun and Fantasy, Escape and Edification: The Battersea Pleasure Grounds' in Elain Harwood and Alan Powers (eds.), *Twentieth Century Architecture 5: Festival of Britain*, Twentieth Century Society (London, 2001), pp. 127–39.

43 W. A. Gibson Martin, 'Has the Festival of Britain any points of interest for the shipowner?', *The Motor Ship*, July 1951, p. 219. See Bevis Hillier and Escritt (eds.), *A Tonic to the Nation* and Alan Powers and Elain Harwood (eds.), *Twentieth Century Architecture 5: Festival of Britain*, Twentieth Century Society (London, 2001) for detailed descriptions of the Festival of Britain.

44 '*Saxonia*: New Cunard liner for St Lawrence Service', *Shipbuilding and Shipping Record*, September 1954, pp. 335–38.

45 See Clive Harvey, *The Saxonia Sisters*, Carmania (London, 2001), pp. 10–24.

46 Frank Jackson, 'The New Air Age: BOAC and design policy 1945–60', *Journal of Design History*, Oxford University Press (Oxford, Vol. 4, No. 3), 1991, pp. 167–85.

47 See Brian Haresnape, *British Rail 1948–1978: A Journey by Design*, Ian Allan (Shepperton, 1979) and Brain Haresnape, *Sealink*, Ian Allan (Shepperton, 1982) for detailed descriptions of the British Rail Modernisation Plan.

48 'The Passenger Ship: Backward or Forward', *The Architectural Review*, London, November 1960, p. 367.

## CHAPTER 005

1 N. R. P. Bonsor, *North Atlantic Seaway*, T. Stephenson & Sons Ltd. (Prescot, 1955), p. 301.

2 'Hutten voor passagiers', *Schip en Werf*, D.S.S. *Rotterdam* souvenir number, Rotterdam, September 1959, p. 30.

3 'The Secret Staircase', The New Flagship *Rotterdam*, Holland-America Line, guide booklet, Rotterdam, 1959, p. 3.

4 *Ibid.*, p. 9.

5 Paul Groenendijk, Piet Voolaard, *Guide to Modern Architecture in Rotterdam*, Uitgeverij 010 Publishers (Rotterdam, 1996).

6 *T/V Leonardo da Vinci*, Italia Compagnia Navigazione, Ansaldo Cantiere Navale and La Marina Mercant+ (Genoa, 1961), pp. 94–120.

7 *Ibid.*

8 *Ibid.*, pp. 268–320.

9 A. C. Hardy, 'Why Machinery Aft', *The Shipping World*, London, 7 March, 1951, p. 248–51.

10 'Trans-Atlantic Liner *France*: Luxury passenger liner for the French Line', *The Shipping World*, London, 7 February 1962, p. 171.

11 C. M. Squarey, 'Some thoughts about s.s. *France*', *Shipbuilding and Shipping Record*, London, 8 February 1962, p. 181.

12 Philip Dawson, *The Liner: Retrospective and Renaissance*, Conway Maritime Press (London 2005), p. 168.

13 Françoise Siriex & Philippe Conquer, 'Le Décoration du Paquebot *France*', *303 Arts, Recherches er Créations*, Nr. XXIV, Nantes, 1992, p. 41.

14 *Ibid.*, p. 48.

15 *Shipbuilding and Shipping Record*, 8 February, 1962, p. 181.

16 Gilbert Herbert, *Symbols of a New Land: Architects and the Design of the Passenger Ships of Zim*, The Architectural Heritage Research Foundation (Haifa, 2006).

17 'Shalom: French-built Israeli transatlantic liner', *Shipbuilding and Shipping Record*, April 1964, pp. 517–20.
18 Alfred Mansfeld, 's.s. *Shalom*: Integration of Art and Design', *Ariel*, XIII, 1966, p. 5.
19 Maimonides (Moses ben Maimon, Spanish-Jewish philosopher, 1135–1204) reputedly composed this prayer while on a stormy trip to the Holy Land.
20 Stephen Garrett, 'Amid Ships', *The Architectural Review*, London, September 1961, pp. 155–58.
21 Philip Dawson, *British Superliners of the Sixties: A design appreciation of the Oriana, Canberra and QE2*, Conway Maritime Press (London 1990), p. 84.
22 Dawson, *ibid.*, p. 65.
23 Dawson, *ibid.*
24 Philip Dawson, discussion with Sir Hugh Casson, London, September 1981.
25 George G. Sharp, 'Some Considerations in the Design of Modern Ships', paper read at the Society of naval Architects and Marine Engineers, New York, 1947.
26 'Triestino's liner *Guglielmo Marconi*', *The Shipbuilder and Shipping Record*, Vol. 102, 14 November 1963, p. 643.
27 'Italian passenger liner *Galileo Galilei* by our Italian correspondent', *The Shipbuilder and Shipping Record*, Vol. 101, 4 April 1963, pp. 447–49.
28 T/N *Michelangelo*, Italia Compagnia Navigazione, Ansaldo Cantiere Navale and La Marina Mercantile (Genoa, 1965), pp. 30–107.
29 Maurizio Eliseo and Paolo Piccione, *Transatlantici: The History of the Great Italian liners on the Atlantic*, Tormena (Genoa, 2001), p. 265.
30 T/N *Michelangelo*, *op. cit.*
31 *Ibid.*
32 Eliseo and Piccione, *op. cit.*, pp. 208–9.
33 Eliseo and Piccione, *Ibid.*, p. 268.
34 Eliseo and Piccione, *Ibid.*, pp. 267 and 270.
35 R. P. Bonsor, *North Atlantic Seaway*, T. Stephenson & Sons Ltd. (Prescot, 1955), p. 541.
36 Stephen Payne, 'Drawing up an efficient design', special supplement to *The Naval Architect*, Royal Institution of Naval Architects (London, 2004), p. 25.
37 '*Oceanic*: CRDA-built for Home Lines: The largest ever purely cruising vessel', *The Shipbuilder and Shipping Record*, Vol. 105, 8 April 1965, pp. 438–47.
38 Donato Riccesi, *Gustavo Pulitzer Finali: Il Disegno della Nave*, Marsilio Editori (Venice,1985), p. 217.
39 '*Eugenio C.*: C.R.D.A.'s fifth transatlantic liner delivery in three years', *The Shipbuilder and Shipping Record*, Vol. 108, 27 October 1966, pp. 571–73.
40 *Ibid.*
41 See Tobias Faber, *New Danish Architecture*, The Architectural Press (London, 1968) for an overview of these projects.
42 Interview with Brian Corner-Walker by Bruce Peter, 12 January 2000.
43 'Passenger Liner *Funchal*: Danish-built Ship with British Steam Turbines', *The Shipping World*, November 1963, pp. 379–81.
44 'The Danish-built and -owned *England*: an 8,221-ton North Sea passenger/ car ferry', *Shipbuilding and Shipping Record*, June 1964, pp. 778–81.
45 '*Sagafjord*: A New Norwegian America Liner', *Shipbuilding and Shipping Record*, October 1965 pp. 519–26.
46 '*Sagafjord*: A New Norwegian America Liner', *Shipbuilding and Shipping Record*, October 1965, pp. 519–26 and 555–57.
47 '*Winston Churchill*: Roll-on/Roll-off vehicle and passenger ferry for Denmark', *Shipbuilding and Shipping Record*, June 1967, pp. 901–4.
48 '*Kong Olav V*: The first of two passenger-vehicle ferries for service between Copenhagen and Oslo', *Shipbuilding and Shipping Record*, August 1968, pp. 159–96.
49 See John Rapley, *Thomas Bouch: The Builder of the Tay Bridge*, Tempus (Stroud, 2007), for an overview of Bouch's career.
50 *Denmark*, The Royal Danish Ministry of Foreign Affairs, 1961, p. 373.
51 'The Latest Danish Train Ferry', *The Motor Ship*, December 1954, pp. 364–66. See also 'The Danish Train Ferry *Kong Frederik IX* in Service', *The Motor Ship*, February 1955, p. 499.
52 'A Two Deck Motor Car Ferry', *The Motor Ship*, February 1955, pp. 498–99. See also 'The Danish Ferry *Halsskov*, *The Motor Ship*, August 1956, pp. 168–70.

53 'Danish Three Deck Ferry for 400 Cars', *The Motor Ship*, June 1963, p. 103. See also 'Europe's Biggest Car Ferry', *The Motor Ship*, November 1963, pp. 348–52.
54 Brian Haresnape, *British Rail 1948–1978: A Journey by Design*, Ian Allan (Shepperton, 1979), pp. 119–22.
55 See Don Ripley and Tony Rogan, *Designing Ships for Sealink*, Ferry Publications (Kilgetty, 1995) for a detailed description of British Rail's naval architecture in the 1950s–70s period.
56 Ripley and Rogan, *op. cit.*, pp. 44–46.
57 See Bruce *Peter, Knud E. Hansen A/S: Ship Design through seven Decades*, Forlaget Nautilus (Copenhagen, 2007), for a detailed study of the firm's passenger ship design output.
58 Peter, *ibid.*, pp. 51–54.
59 C. Barclay, '*Sunward*: Design Considerations', *Shipping World & Shipbuilder*, 19 January 1967, pp. 247–53.
60 Philip Dawson, *Cruise Ships: An Evolution in Design*, Conway Maritime Press (London, 2000), p. 81.
61 Interview with Tage Wandborg by Bruce Peter on 8 June 2002.
62 *Ibid.*
63 *Ibid.*
64 'Car and Passenger Ferry *Skandia*: New Vessel from Finnish Shipyard', *The Shipping World*, June 1961, p. 577.
65 These were the *Finnwood* and the *Finnpulp*. See Frederick Gutheim, *Alvar Aalto*, George Brasiller Inc. (New York, 1960), p. 29.
66 Anders Bergenek and Klas Brogren, *Passagerare till Sjöss: Den svenska färjesjöfartens historia*, Shippax Information (Halmstad, 2006), pp. 314–17.
67 Bergenek and Brogren, *ibid.*, p. 317.
68 'The Passenger Ship: Backward or Forward', *The Architectural Review*, London, November 1960, p. 366.
69 Neil Potter and Jack Frost, *Queen Elizabeth 2: The Authorised Story*, George G. Harrap and Co. Ltd. (London, Second Edition, 1969), pp. 124–25.
70 Potter and Frost, *ibid.*, p.49.
71 James Gardner, *Elephants in the Attic*, Orbis (London, 1983), p. 128.
72 Kenneth Agnew, 'Concept to Cunarder', *The Architectural Review*, London, June 1969, p. 418.
73 Kenneth Agnew, *ibid.*, p. 417.
74 D. N. Wallace, 'Queen Elizabeth 2: Some design considerations', *Shipping World and Shipbuilder*, London, January 1969, p. 87.
75 Potter and Frost, *op. cit.*, p. 129.
76 Potter and Frost, *ibid.*, p. 137.
77 Cunard Line inaugural season brochure for *Queen Elizabeth 2*.
78 Potter and Frost, *op. cit.*, p. 140.
79 Haresnape, *op. cit.*, p. 165.

## CHAPTER 006

1 Henry Russell Hitchcock and Philip Johnston, *The International Style*, Museum of Modern Art (New York, 1932).
2 Robert Venturi, *Complexity and Contradiction in Architecture*, Museum of Modern Art (New York, 1966).
3 Tom Wolfe, *From Bauhaus to Our House*, Vintage (London and New York, 1981).
4 See John Urry, *The Tourist Gaze: Leisure and Travel in Contemporary Societies*, Nottingham Trent University (Nottingham, 1990) for a detailed discussion of these issues.
5 Interview with Tage Wandborg by Bruce Peter on 8 June 2002.
6 *Ibid.*
7 Paolo Piccione, *Costa Crociere: Cinquant'anni di stile*, Silvana Editoriale (Genoa, 1998), pp. 126–49.
8 See Jens Nielsen, *DSB Design: Danish Railway Design*, Danish Design Council (Copenhagen, 1984) for a detailed description of this policy.
9 Interview with Kay Körbing by Bruce Peter on 19 June 2001.
10 'En markant færgeprofil', *DSB Bladet*, July 1980, pp. 12–14.
11 Interview with Kay Körbing by Bruce Peter on 19 June 2001.
12 'Nye DSB færger på Storebælt', *Arkitektur DK*, April 1981, pp. 52–61.
13 Poul Erik, 'Kalundborg-Århus færgerne', *Arkitektur DK*, March 1986, pp. 100–109.

# BIBLIOGRAPHY

## BOOKS

Benjamin, Walter, *The Arcades Project*, Harvard University Press (Cambridge, Mass.), 2002.

Blomfield, Sir Reginald, *Modernismus*, Macmillan and Co. Ltd. (London, 1934).

Bonsor, N.R.P., *North Atlantic Seaway*, T. Stephenson & Sons Ltd. (Prescot, Lancashire, 1955).

Bramstedt, E. K., *Goebbels and National Socialist Propaganda*, Cresset Publishing (London, 1965).

Braynard, Frank O., *By Their Works Ye Shall Know Them: The Life and Ships of William Francis Gibbs 1886–1967*, Gibbs & Cox (New York, 1968).

Braynard, Frank O., *The Big Ship: The story of the ss United States*, Mariner's Museum Newport News (Virginia, 1981).

Brêcon, Emanuel, Jacques-Àmile Ruhlmann: *The Designer's Archives: Book one: Furniture*, Flammarion (Paris, 2004).

Brêcon, Emanuel, Jacques-Àmile Ruhlmann: *The Designer's Archives: Book two: Interior Design*, Flammarion (Paris, 2004).

Brinnen, John Malcolm, *The Sway of the Grand Saloon*, Delacarte Press (New York, 1971).

Coleman, Peter, *Shopping Environments: Evolution, Planning and Design*, The Architectural Press (London, 2006).

Dawson, Philip, *British Superliners of the Sixties: A design appreciation of Oriana, Canberra and Queen Elizabeth 2*, Conway Maritime Press (London, 1990).

Dawson, Philip, *Cruise Ships: An Evolution in Design*, Conway Maritime Press (London 1999).

Dawson, Philip, *The Liner: Retrospective and Renaissance*, Conway Maritime Press (London, 2006).

Eliseo, Maurizio and Piccione, Paolo, *The Costa Liners*, Carmania Press (London, 1997).

Eliseo, Maurizio and Piccione, Paolo, *Transatlantici: The History of the Great Italian liners on the Atlantic*, Tormena Editore (Genoa, 2001).

Ericsson, Anne-Marie, *M/S Kungsholms Inredning: Mästerverk i svensk art deco*, Bokförlaget I Lund AB (Kristianstad, Sweden, 2005).

Foucart, Offrey, Robichom, Fillers, *Normandie: Queen of the Seas*, The Vendome Press (New York).

Frampton, Kenneth, *Modern Architecture: A critical history*, Thames and Hudson Ltd. (London, 1987).

Gardner, James, *Elephants in the Attic*, Orbis (London, 1983).

Gardner, James, *The ARTful Designer: Ideas off the Drawing Board*, Centurion (London, 1993).

Giedion, Sigfried, *Mechanization Takes Control*, W. W. Norton & Company (New York, 1948 and 1960).

Groenberg, Tag, *Designs on Modernity: Exhibiting the City*, Manchester University Press (Manchester, 2004).

Haresnape, Brian, *British Rail 1945-78: A Journey by Design*, Ian Allan Ltd. (London, 1979).

Haresnape, Brian, *Sealink*, Ian Allan Ltd. (London, 1982).

Harvey, Clive, *The Saxonia Sisters*, Carmania (London, 2001).

Harvey, Clive, *Queen Elizabeth*, Carmania (London, 2008).

Herbert, Gilbert, *Symbols of a New Land: Architects and the Design of the Passenger Ships of Zim*, The Architectural Heritage Research Foundation (Haifa, 2006).

Herbert, Gilbert and Richter, Liliane, *Through a Clouded Glass: Mendelsohn, Wijdeveld and the Jewish Connection*, Wasmuth (Tublingen, 2009).

Holland, Harry, *Travellers' Architecture*, George G. Harrap & Co. Ltd. (London, 1971).

Howarth, David and Stephen, *The Story of P&O*, Weidenfield and Nicolson (London, 1986, 1994).

Huldermann, Bernhard, Albert Ballinn, *BiblioBazaar* (Charleston, 2009).

Ingersoll, Richard and Weiraub, *Munio Gitai, Bauhaus Architect in Eretz Israel*, Electa (Milan, 2004).

Johnston, Ian, *Ships for a Nation: John Brown & Company, Clydebank 1847–1971*, West Dumbartonshire Libraries and Museums (2000).

Kludas, Arnold, *Die Großen Passagierschiffe der Welt Band V*, Band V, Gerhard Stalling Verlag (Hamburg, 1974).

Koltveit, Bård, *Amerikabâtene*, Norsk Sjøfartsmuseum (Oslo, 1984).

Lauter, Wolfgang, *Passagen, die bibliophilen taschenbücher* Nr. 432, Dortmund (1984).

Le Corbusier, *Towards a New Architecture*, Dover Publications Inc. (New York, 1986).

Loewy, Raymond, *Industrial Design*, Laurence King Publishing (London, 2000).

Manser, José, *Hugh Casson: A Biography*, Viking (London, 2000).

Maxtone-Graham, John, *The Only Way to Cross*, The Macmillan Company (New York, 1972).

Mulchrone, Vincent, *'The World's Finest Ship', Queen Elizabeth 2: Pride of British Industry*, Pitkin Pictorials (London, 1969).

Peter, Bruce and Dawson, Philip, *QE2: Britain's Greatest Liner*, Ferry Publications (Ramsey, 2008).

Peter, Bruce, *Baltic Ferries*, Ferry Publications (Ramsey, 2009).

Pevsner, Nikolaus, *Pioneers of the Modern Movement*, Faber & Faber (London, 1936).

Piccione, Paolo, *Costa Crociere: Cinquant'anni di stile*, Silvana Editoriale and Costa Crociere (Genoa, 1998).

Piccione, Paolo, *Gio Ponti: Le Navi : Il Progetto Degli Interni Navali, 1948–1953*, Idea Books (Viareggio, 2007).

Paolo Piccione, *Nino Zoncada: Interni navali, 1931–1971*, GMT (Genoa, 2007).

Potter, Neil and Frost, Jack, *Queen Elizabeth 2: The Official Story*, George G. Harrap & Co. Ltd. (London, 1969).

Potter, Neil and Frost, Jack, *The Mary: The Inevitable Ship*, George G. Harrap & Co. Ltd. (London 1961).

Quartermaine, Luisa, 'Slouching towards Rome: Mussolini's imperial vision', T. J. Cornell and Kathryn Lomas (eds.) *Urban Society in Roman Italy*, UCL Press (London, 1995).

Quartermaine, Peter, *Building on the Sea: Form and Meaning in Ship Architecture*, Academy Editions, 1996.

Quartermaine, Peter and Peter, Bruce, *Cruise: Identity, Design and Culture*, Laurence King (London, 2006) and Rizzoli (New York, 2006).

Rapley, John, *Thomas Bouch: The Builder of the Tay Bridge*, Tempus (Stroud, 2007).

Riccesi, Donato, *Gustavo Pulitzer Finali: Il Disegno della Nave*, Marsilio Editori (Venezia, 1985).

Robertson, Howard, *Modern Architectural Design*, The Architectural Press (London, 1955).

Selinger, G. and Duek, N. (eds.), *All Ways Zim: 50th Anniversary Album 1945–1995*, Zim Lines (Haifa, 1995).

Squarey, C. M., *The Patient Talks*, Thos. Cook & Son (Tonbridge, 1955).

Teut, Anna (ed.), *Al Mansfeld: an Architect in Israel*, Ernst & Sohn (Berlin, 1999).

Turner, Gordon, *Empress of Britain: Canadian Pacific's Greatest Ship*, Boston Mills Press/Stoddart Publishing Co. Ltd. (Toronto, 1992).

Vian, L. R., *Arts Décoratifs a Board des Paquebots Français 1880–1960*, Editions Fronmare (Paris, 1992).

Wealleans, Anne, *Designing Liners: A History of Interior Design Afloat*, Routledge (London, 2006).

Weeks, Willet, *The Man Who Made Paris: An Illustrated History of Georges-Eugene Haussmann*, London House (London, 1999).

Williams, David L. & de Kerbrech, Richard P., *Damned by Destiny*, Teredo Books Ltd. (Brighton, 1982).

*T/V Leonardo Da Vinci*, Italia Compagnia Navigazione, Ansaldo Cantiere Navale and La Marina Mercantile (Genoa, 1961).

*T/N Michelangelo*, Italia Compagnia Navigazione, Ansaldo Cantiere Navale and La Marina Mercantile (Genoa, 1965).

## JOURNALS

### The Architects' Journal
Baird Denison, '534 and All That', January 25, 1934, pp. 149–56.
's.s. *Rangitoto*: Interior design by Easton and Robertson', October, 1949, pp. 368–72.
'*QE2*: Design for future trends in world travel', April 1969, p. 985.

### The Architectural Review
Arthur J. Davis 'The Architecture of the Liner', April 1914, pp. 67–110.
William Tatton Brown, 'Architecture Afloat: The *Orion* sets a new course', October 1935, pp. 131–39.
Ian McCallum, 'Ship Interiors', February 1956, pp. 133–40.
'The Passenger Ship: Backward or forward', November 1960, p. 366.
Stephen Garrett, 'Amid Ships', September 1961, p. 155.
Sir Hugh Casson, 'A Ship is an Island', June 1969, pp. 399–400.
Kenneth Agnew 'Concept to Cunarder', June 1969, pp. 411–19.

### Ariel
Alfred Mansfeld, 's.s. *Shalom*: Integration of Art and Design', XIII: 1966, p. 5ff.

### Arts, recherches et creations
Françoise Siriex et Philippe Conquer, 'La Décoration du Paqebot France', 303, 1990, Nr. XXIV, p. 41.

### Design
QE2 Special Issue, April 1969.

### Domus
Giò Ponti, 'Alcuni interni dell'Andrea Doria', 281, April 1953 pp. 17–24.

### DSB Bladet
'En markant færgeprofil', July 1980, pp. 12–14.

### l'Illustration
'*Normandie*: Le nouveau paquebot de la Cie. Gle Transatlantique- Chef-d'oeuvre de la technique et de l'art Français,' Paris, June 1935 (special souvenir number)
'Le Paquebot "Pasteur"', September, 1939.

### Journal of Design History
Frank Jackson, 'The New Air Age: BOAC and Design Policy 1945–60', Vol. 4, No. 3, 1991 p. 167.

### The London Studio
'The *Nieuw Amsterdam*: A floating palace of art', Vol. XVI, No. 88, July 1928, pp. 3–17.

### Marine Engineering
P. E. Hemke and G.B. Garson, 'Streamlining Superstructures of Ships', November 1936, p. 688.

**The Motor Ship**

'The Pioneer Dover-Ostend Motor Ship: Launch of the *Prince Baudouin*. A 23 -knot Vessel with 17,000 s.h.p. Sulzer Machinery', October 1933, pp. 226–28.

'The *Prince Baudouin* in Operation: Completion and Trials of the Fastest Diesel-engined Vessel in the World. A Ship Which Maintained Over 25 Knots on the North Sea and Holds the Blue Riband for Cross-Channel Service', September 1934, pp. 196–99.

'The Passenger ship *Hammershus*: Third Motor Vessel for the Bornholm Steamship Company', August 1936, pp. 180–82.

'A Transatlantic Liner: The Proposed Swedish American Line Motor Vessel', October 1936, p. 227.

'A 28,000-ton Transatlantic Liner: Triple-screw 19-knot Ship for the Swedish American Line', December 1936, p. 307.

'Passenger Liners For German Workmen: 25,000-ton Ships, One with Diesel-electric Machinery, Designed for Economical Cruising', March 1937, p. 460.

'25,000-ton German Motor-Cruising Liners', April 1937, p. 26.

'The 21-knot Norwegian M.S. *Vega*: Fastest and Largest North Sea Passenger Ship', February 1938, p. 412.

'The Largest Scandinavian Liner: Special Features of the 27,000-ton Triple-screw Swedish American Line M.S. *Stockholm*', February 1938, p. 420.

'The Fastest Copenhagen-Oslo Passenger Ship', February 1938, p. 427.

'Passenger Accommodation in the *Vega*', March 1938, pp. 476–77.

'A Cruising Liner for Workmen: The 24,000-ton 15 -knot Geared Diesel M.S. *Wilhelm Gustloff*. The First of a Series of New Liners', April 1938, p. 24.

'The *Vega* in Service: A 21 -knot 7,500-ton North Sea Passenger and Cargo Ship', June 1938, pp. 82–85.

'The Motor Ship *Chinook*: Large Passenger Vessel with 4,800 b.h.p. Twin-screw Diesel-electric Machinery', September 1947, pp. 204–6.

'The 21-knot liner *Giulio Cesare*: First of two ships with double-acting Fiat machinery of 25,000 bhp using boiler oil', February 1951, p. 355.

'The cargo and passenger liner *Africa* – a 19 knot 11,400-ton vessel for Genoa-Cape Town service', March 1951, p. 381.

'Three 13,000-ton 18-knot passenger liners: The *Australia*, *Neptunia* and *Oceania* built for service between Italian and Australian ports. Twin-screw machinery of 14,000 b.h.p.', June 1951, pp. 98–99.

W. A. Gibson Martin, 'Has the Festival of Britain any points of interest for the shipowner?', July 1951, p. 159.

'The completion of the *Giulio Cesare*: An Italian liner of 25,000 tons gross, propelled by 26,000 b.h.p. machinery', Vol. 32, October 1951, p. 259.

'Largest post-war motor liner: The *Giulio Cesare*, an Italian vessel of 27,700 tons gross, propelled by double-acting Fiat machinery of 26,000 bhp', January 1952, pp. 424–29.

W. A. Gibson Martin, 'Ship Furnishing and Decoration: New Developments in American Productions', January 1952, pp. 392–93.

'The Latest Danish Train Ferry: M.S. *Kong Frederik IX*, Propelled by 9,200 i.h.p. Elsinore-B. and W. Machinery', December 1954, pp. 364–66.

'The 11,600-ton 19 -knot Passenger Ship *Victoria* For Service Between Italy, Pakistan, India and the Far East', March 1953, pp. 530–32.

'The 20-knot Liner *Victoria* in Service, July 1953, pp. 156–57.

'The Nuclear Propulsion of Ships: The Present Position in the Maritime Countries Relating to the Design and Construction of Naval and Mercantile Nuclear-propelled Vessels', January 1957, pp. 393–95.

'A 21 -knot Passenger Ship: The *Prinsesse Margrethe* built for the Oslo-Copenhagen Service. Machinery Aft and Funnel Amidships', September 1957, pp. 264–66.

'Danish Three-deck Ferry for 400 Cars', June 1963, p. 103.

'Europe's Biggest Car Ferry: The three-deck *Arveprins Knud* to carry 400 cars and 1,500 passengers enters Danish State Railways' Service between Zeeland and Funen. Twin-screw Elsinore-B. and W. Machinery of 11,200 bhp', November 1963, pp. 348–51.

'*England* – Largest Passenger Ship in the North Sea Service', July 1964, pp. 159–66.

Professor Dr-eng, Dr-Ing, E.h. J. S. Meurer, M.A.N, Augsburg, 'The Rise of the Diesel Engine – An Outline of Early Developments', April 1970, pp. 2–9.

J. Berring, 'Burmeister and Wain – Pioneers of Low-speed Marine Diesel Engines', April 1970, pp. 10–14.

**Schiffbau, Schiffahrt und Hafenbau**

Dipl.-Ing. R. Kiene, 'Das KdF Flaggschiff *Robert Ley*', Vol. 40, 1939, pp. 209–29.

**Schip en Werf**

'D.S.S. *Rotterdam*, Holland-Amerika Lijn', special edition, September 1959.

**The Shipbuilder and Marine Engine Builder**

'French Quadruple-screw Steamship *Pasteur*', May, 1940, pp. 209–12 and June 1940, pp. 256–60.

Canberra Souvenir Number, June 1961.

**Shipbuilding and Shipping Record**

'Quadruple-screw Passenger Steamship *l'Atlantique*', October 1931, pp. 429–38.

'*Orion*: The latest and largest of the Orient Line Fleet. Built and engined by Vickers-Armstrongs Ltd.', August 1935, pp. 205–9.

'Informality in Ship Furnishing', December 1935, pp. 709–10.

'The Public Rooms of the *Normandie*: Some particulars of the great French Line turbo-electric liner', June 1935, pp. 714–16.

'The *Nieuw Amsterdam*', May 1938, pp. 647–55.

'*United States*: A new American transatlantic liner', July 1952, pp. 77–83.

'The *Andrea Doria*', 13 August 1953, pp. 211–13.

E. Th. Christiansson, 'Exterior Design of Passenger Liners', November 5, 1953, pp. 617–18.

T. E. Alexander, 'Economy in Ship Decoration', July 1954, pp. 11–13.

'A Critical Review of Decoration During 1953', July 1954, pp. 50–53.

'*Saxonia*: New Cunard liner for St Lawrence Service', September 1954, pp. 335–38.

'*Cristoforo Colombo*: New Italian liner for transatlantic service', November 1954, pp. 663–66.

'New Italian passenger liner *Ausonia*', October 1957, p. 523.

C. M. Squarey, 'Some thoughts about ss *France*', February 1962, pp. 181–82.

'Italian passenger liner *Galileo Galilei* by our Italian correspondent', 4 April 1963, pp. 447–49.

'Triestino's liner *Guglielmo Marconi*', November 1963, p. 643.

'*Shalom*: French-built Israeli transatlantic liner', April 1964, pp. 517–20.

'The Danish-built and -owned *England*: an 8,221-ton North Sea passenger/car ferry, June 1964, pp 778–81.

'*Winston Churchill*: Roll-on/Roll-off vehicle and passenger ferry for Denmark, June 1967, pp. 901–4.

'*Kong Olav V*: The first of two passenger-vehicle ferries for service between Copenhagen and Oslo', August 1968, pp. 159–96.

'*Oceanic*: CRDA-built for Home Lines: The largest ever purely cruising vessel', April 1965, pp. 438–46.

'*Sagafjord*: A New Norwegian America Liner', October 1965 pp. 519–26 and 555–57.

'*Eugenio C*.: C.R.D.A.'s fifth transatlantic liner delivery in three years', 27 October 1966, pp. 571–73.

'*Queen Elizabeth 2*: A ship with a past . . . and a future', January 1969, pp. 145–64.

**The Shipping World**

'Trans-Atlantic Liner *France*', 7 February 1962, pp. 172–77.

'Passenger Liner *Funchal*: Danish-built Ship with British Steam Turbines, November 1963, pp. 379–81.

'Car and Passenger Ferry *Skandia*: New Vessel from Finnish Shipyard', June 1961, p. 577.

## NEWSPAPER ARTICLES

**The Guardian**

Jose Manser, 'Sir Hugh Casson: Festival of Britain architect who opened the Royal Academy of Arts to a wider public', August 17 1999.

Obituary for 'Franta Belsky: Czechoslovak-born sculptor who insisted his art was not for the elite but for the general public', 6 July 2000.

# AUTHOR BIOGRAPHIES

**Philip Dawson** is an author and journalist specialising in shipping, transport and design-related subjects. He was born in Brazil, and educated in England and Canada, thereafter having a diverse career in engineering, design and IT. Nominated for the Mountbatten Maritime Prize in 2006, his most recent book, *The Liner: Retrospective and Renaissance* (Conway, 2006), has won wide acclaim in popular marine literature. His earlier work *Cruise Ships: An Evolution in Design* (Conway, 1999) is widely regarded as a standard reference work in the ship-design field, and *Canberra: In the Wake of a Legend* (Conway, 1997) was a best seller as the official P&O-sponsored commemorative work on this ship. He is also a regular contributor to various industry publications, with commentary also appearing in other journals and periodicals including *The Architectural Review* and *Canadian Architect*. Recently elected as a Companion member of the Royal Institution of Naval Architects, Philip Dawson makes his home in Toronto, Canada.

**Bruce Peter** is an architecture and design historian working in the Glasgow School of Art's Department of Historical & Critical Studies, where he lectures on a broad range of subjects, relating mainly to twentieth-century design history and theory. He is a graduate of the Glasgow School of Art, the Royal College of Art and of the University of Glasgow. His research interests address the Modern Movement in architecture and design and its relationship with popular culture, mass leisure and transport environments. His recent publications include *Cruise: Identity, Design and Culture*, co-author Peter Quartermaine (Laurence King in the UK and Rizzoli worldwide, 2006), *Form Follows Fun: Modernism and Modernity in British Pleasure Architecture 1925–1940* (Routledge, 2007) *Knud E. Hansen A/S: Ship Design Through Seven Decades* (Forlaget Nautilus, 2007), *QE2: Britain's Greatest Liner*, co-authors Philip Dawson and Ian Johnston (Ferry Publications, 2008) and *Baltic Ferries* (Ferry Publications, 2009). Additionally, Bruce is a design journalist and critic, writing for publications in the UK, Denmark and Sweden. In 2007, he worked with Ian Johnston on the BBC TV documentary *QE2: The Last Great Liner* and in 2009 he acted as programme consultant for two BBC 4 *Timeshift* documentaries about liners and cruise ships.

**Gilbert Herbert** is Professor Emeritus at the Technion in Haifa and visiting professor at universities in South Africa, Australia, Israel, the USA and Brazil. Born in Johannesburg, he spent seven years in Adelaide, South Australia, finally moving with his family to Haifa in 1968. An architect and historian, he is the author of nine books on architectural history and the history of technology, and has made numerous contributions to journals, books and encyclopaedias worldwide, as well as assisting with exhibitions in Germany, Italy, Japan, France, the USA, South Africa and Israel. His wider interests include travel, painting, choral singing, poetry, politics and genealogy.

**Peter Kohler** is an historian and author specialising in passenger ship design and shipping history. A frequent contributor, since 1980, to such publications as *Ships Monthly*, *Sea Breezes* and *Steamboat Bill*, he has in addition written a number of books, including *Holland America Line, a 120th Anniversary Celebration in Postcards* (Ship Pictorial Publications, 1990), *Sea Safari, British India Line African Ships & Services* (P.M. Heaton, 1995) and *The Lido Fleet, Italian Line Passenger Ships & Services* (Seadragon Press, 1998). Peter has appeared on CNN, *Nightline*, *Good Morning America*, *Canada AM* and other news programmes as an authority on passenger ships as well as lectured at sea aboard liners and cruise ships. In addition to passenger shipping, he has a great interest in street railways and was Vice President of the National Capital Trolley Museum. Residing in Washington, DC, he is Travel Manager of Population Services International, a leading global health organisation with programs targeting malaria, child survival, HIV and reproductive health.

**Paolo Piccione** is an architect who designs ship interiors. He teaches naval and nautical industrial design in the Faculty of Architecture at the University of Genoa. His writings have appeared internationally in reviews and catalogues and he has published various books, including *The Costa Liners* (Carmania, 1997), *Costa Crociere: Cinquant'anni di stile* (Silvana Editoriale and Costa Crociere, 1998), *Transatlantici: History of the Great Italian Liners*, co-author Maurizio Eliseo (Tormena, 2001), *Cruising into Art: Art Onboard Italian Liners* (Tormena, 2002), *Nino Zoncada: Interni navali* (GMT, 2007) and *Giò Ponti Le Navi: Il progetto degli interni navali 1948–1953* (Idea Books, 2007). As part of Genoa: European City of Culture 2004, he assisted with the exhibition Transatlantici – Scenari e Sogni di Mare.

**Peter Quartermaine** is a Research Associate of the National Maritime Museum, Greenwich, an Associate of the Royal Institution of Naval Architects (RINA), and has served as a consultant to the Design Museum in London. He is the author of several books, including *Building on the Sea: Form and Meaning in Modern Ship Architecture* (Academy Editions, 1996), *Port Architecture: Shaping the Littoral* (Academy Editions, 1999), and a contributor on passenger travel to *A History of Seafaring in the Twentieth Century* (Conway, 2000). With Bruce Peter he wrote *Cruise: Identity, Design and Culture* (Laurence King and Rizzoli, 2006). A graduate in English and Philosophy with a doctorate in Australian arts, he now lectures worldwide aboard cruise ships on a variety of topics, including passenger ship design and construction. He is married, lives in Exeter, and has family in Italy and France.

# ACKNOWLEDGEMENTS

The authors wish to express their especial thanks to Gilbert Herbert, Peter Kohler, Paolo Piccione and Peter Quartermaine for their research and written contributions to this book, to John Peter for scanning and preparing the illustrations and to John Lee and David Salmo at Anova Books for overseeing the publication of the book.

Our thanks also to: Brian Beardsmore; Dora Ben Arzi; Anders Bergenek; Jonathan Boonzaier; Klas Brogren; Miri Bromand; David Buri; Carola Casson-Zogolovitch; Maurizio Cergol; Eric Chapuis; Andy Collier; Pamela Conover; Anthony Cooke; Brian Corner-Walker; James Cousins; Ron Cox; Shawn Dake; Moshe De Leon; Maurizio Eliseo; John Emery; Joseph Farcus; Susan Fino; Pier Luigi Foschi; Jean-Jacques Gatepaille; Andrea Ginnante; Dr. Ann Glen; Ambrose Greenway; Kevin Griffin; Klaus Guse; Robert Hochstadter; Alan Irvine; Ian Johnston; Ben Kaplan; Andrew Kilk; Peter Knego; Bård Kolltveit; Kay Kørbing; Peter Kørbing; John & Diana Lang; Kai Levander; Alex McFarlane; John McNeece; Al Mansfeld; Glenn Mattas; William Mayes; Catherine Moriarty; Ken Neil; Thomas Nøregaard Olesen; Stephen Payne; Dag Rogne; Don Ripley; Rickard Sahlsten; Avner Schatz; Burkhard Schütt; Ted Scull; David L. Smith; Myrna Spark; Stephen Spark; Les Streater; Søren Thørsoe; Robert Tillberg; David Trevor-Jones; Gordon Turner; Tage Wandborg; Lesley Whitworth; Mary Ward; Pauli Wulff; Alan Zamchick.

# INDEX